The Missionary Mind
and American East Asia Policy, 1911–1915

HARVARD EAST ASIAN MONOGRAPHS
104

THE MISSIONARY MIND
AND AMERICAN
EAST ASIA POLICY, 1911–1915

JAMES REED

Published by COUNCIL ON EAST ASIAN STUDIES, HARVARD UNIVERSITY, and distributed by HARVARD UNIVERSITY PRESS, Cambridge (Massachusetts) and London   1983

The Council on East Asian Studies at Harvard University publishes a monograph series and, through the Fairbank Center for East Asian Research and the Japan Institute, administers research projects designed to further scholarly understanding of China, Japan, Korea, Vietnam, Inner Asia, and adjacent areas.

Library of Congress Cataloging in Publication Data

Reed, James, 1945–
    The missionary mind and American East Asia policy, 1911–1915.

    (Harvard East Asian monographs; 104)
    Bibliography: p.
    Includes index.
    1. United States—Foreign relations—China.
2. China—Foreign relations—United States. 3. United
States—Foreign relations—1909–1913. 4. United
States—Foreign relations—1913–1921. 5. Missions—
China—History—20th century. 6. Missions—Japan—
History—20th century. 7. Missions, American—History—
20th century. 8. United States—Foreign relations—
Japan. 9. Japan—Foreign relations—United States.
I. Title. II. Series.
E183.8.C5R43 1983   327.73051   82-23616
ISBN 0-674-57657-8

To the memory of
Loa Kinney White, 1891–1979

Foreword

China has figured in the Western imagination from a very early time, but seldom in neutral terms. For reasons not thoroughly understood, the Chinese role in Western thinking has fluctuated between hope and menace. Europe's Middle Ages saw an alternation between the image of the supposedly benign Nestorian Christian rulers of Central Asia, who might come to the aid of Christendom against Islam, and the Yellow Peril of Chinggis Khan, whose horsemen might overrun Europe. Later came the idealization of the Confucian emperor during the eighteenth-century Enlightenment, followed by the denigration of China's backward heathenism in the nineteenth-century era of imperialism. Plainly Western images of China have been more changeable than the conditions of Chinese life.

Perhaps one reason for this hope/meance, love/hate attitude lies in the fact that Chinese civilization has been the other great alternative to Christendom, the society farthest removed, most independent and separate from the Atlantic community, a cultural *terra incognita.* Being so vast and distant, China could play many roles in our thinking, and indeed still does so today. Witness our successive attitudes toward Mao Tse-tung and the nature of his regime. Our view of China is at least as changeable as the situation there.

The new field of American-East Asian Relations has grown up to meet this specific problem: how to understand our changeable understanding of East Asia. The problem is not simple. East Asian studies have their own dynamics—languages, cultures, bibliographies to study, regions to explore—and so do American studies. Left to themselves, the two fields will seldom meet. China will figure in American folklore. America will figure in imperialism in China. But who will look at both sides? Who will scrutinize the Chinese as they get their impressions of the United States and the Americans as they act out their fantasies about Cathay? Students of American-East Asian relations have to see them from new angles, in a new perspective.

James Reed's study of the Missionary Mind is obviously not by someone devoted to Christian missionary work. Yet its view of the role of "Christian China," as a concept affecting American policy during the Wilson administration, is set forth with enthusiasm for a new vision of the truth. This bespeaks a member of the 1960s generation, but Dr. Reed is by no means typical of that time, as a brief look at his biography will indicate.

He was born in 1945 in Walla Walla, Washington. As he says, "Anyone growing up in Walla Walla knew all about missionaries. . . . the early history of the town was largely missionary." Moving to Seattle at age fifteen he became an outstanding high school debater, and when he went back East to Ripon College in Wisconsin he became a campus leader, editing the student newspaper. He came to Harvard and completed his MA in British history in 1968, right in the midst of the American student rebellion over the Vietnam War. Jim Reed says he "took part in no demonstrations and denounced no professors," but the message of that time nevertheless sank in—"that the Vietnam War was immoral, even criminal, and that the university, while not a major culprit, had allowed itself to become part of the problem."

He entered the Harvard Divinity School in 1969, took an MA in theological studies in 1971, and went on to complete his PhD in History in 1976, just in time for the onset of the current depression in the History field. Jim Reed met this situation by continuing as a teaching assistant at Harvard in Expository Writing (until 1979) and mainly by going into the communications field as a private enterprise. Originally called Boston Writing Associates, his firm has now grown into Commonwealth Communications,

Inc. Its business is expanding. Besides the usual aspects of public relations and management consulting for nonprofit organizations, the firm now offers "a product line called corporate historical services." Perhaps the above is enough to indicate that the author of this study of American policy formation writes from a considerable background of appropriate experience. He knows the language of Christian missions and undoubtedly shares some of their spirit of endeavor.

The role of missionaries in American policy formation reached its apogee, both for the Near East and for China, during the presidency of Woodrow Wilson in the second decade of the twentieth century. Statesmen of this era were often motivated less by concepts of national interest and hopes of business profit than by missionary claims of moral duty and benevolence. This was because, as Arthur Schlesinger, Jr., concluded after surveying the role of Christian missions in cultural imperialism, "The missionary impact on the American mind may have been more profound than its impact on the non-Western mind."* Dr. Reed pursues this theme in case studies of the influence of the organized missionary movement and its ideas on American diplomacy.

These studies are concerned with the American end of China missions, where it can be argued that those who made the effort to invade an alien culture received the major impact from the encounter. Similarly any traveler in earlier times (before air travel put us in cultural cocoons) usually experienced more culture shock in foreign parts than did the natives he came upon. In the strategic search for American-East Asian understanding, this volume contributes in a comparatively neglected area, at home. William R. Hutchinson has pointed out that "a subsequent comparative analysis, fashioned from *non*-Western perspectives . . . should be chapter two in any further development in this field."**

---

*Arthur Schlesinger, Jr., "The Missionary Enterprise and Theories of Imperialism," in J. K. Fairbank, ed., *The Missionary Enterprise in China and America* (Cambridge, Harvard University Press, 1974), p. 372.

**William R. Hutchinson, "Evangelization and Civilization: Protestant Missionary Motivation in the Imperialist Era," *International Bulletin of Missionary Research* 6.2 (April 1982), p. 50.

But in the immediate future Dr. Reed's analysis, building on a considerable body of work by Americanists, may be of special interest to Chinese scholars who are beginning a serious reappraisal of the Sino-American relationship. He shows that it rests on deeply engrained American proclivities.

John King Fairbank
December 8, 1982

Acknowledgments

This book was, in an earlier and more exuberant redaction, my doctoral dissertation at Harvard. The thesis was directed by Ernest R. May and John K. Fairbank.

The following friends also have helped: John English of the University of Waterloo, William R. Hutchison of the Harvard Divinity School, and James C. Thomson Jr. of Harvard's Nieman Foundation.

My thanks as well to Robert Hannaford, Cheryl Reed Hurwitz, Dena W. Reed, Jack Rice, Ellen Schrecker, and Florence Trefethen.

Among those who should be remembered are my teacher John Glaser of Ripon College, my friend Hugh MacKinnon of the University of Waterloo, and my maternal grandmother, Loa Kinney White.

Special thanks are due Deborah Addis of Salem, James Walters of Marblehead, John Wright of Salem and the Essex Institute, and sundry friends, relatives, neighbors, curators, librarians, money managers, historians, scribblers, old salts, young turks, and so forth, in the County of Essex and elsewhere.

Salem, Massachusetts
September 1982

Contents

Tables

Introduction

Considered historically, American East Asia policy may be distinguished by its lack of clear-sightedness. For much of the period the United States has pursued independent national policies toward East Asia—from the Open Door episode through the Vietnam War era—the lack of clear-sightedness has shaped the course of events. The absence of clear-sightedness, the inability to see situations for what they were and to deal with them accordingly, resulted in policies whose wisdom is much disputed.

During the first four decades of this century, the United States attempted to cope with the expansion of the Japanese Empire, which took place largely at China's expense, by a rhetorical defense of the Open Door policy. Because the American government at that time had few interests in the area to safeguard, the Open Door was based upon good intentions of a kind, but little else. As a result, the United States became bitterly estranged from Japan without accomplishing much on behalf of China. Four decades of the Open Door policy, in sum, helped provoke the unjustifiable Japanese attack on Pearl Harbor in 1941 and left the United States ill-equipped to deal creatively with the rising force of Chinese nationalism.

Postwar American policy toward Asia also has had peculiarly unhappy results. From 1946 to 1949, the United States supported the losing side in the Chinese Civil War. Following the Communist victory in 1949, the American government for more than two decades attempted to isolate the new regime diplomatically, making it an international outlaw. This moderated neither the domestic policies of the Peking regime nor its international behavior. Moreover, the policy of isolating China led to strains in America's relations with Britain, Canada, France, and other allies.

Much of postwar American policy toward other countries of East Asia can be traced to the trauma of Communist victory on the mainland in 1949. The "loss of China," as it was then called, led to a convulsion in American public opinion which, when exploited by politicians, produced some of the worst excesses of McCarthyism. This, in turn, effectively decimated the available expertise on East Asia in the State Department and encouraged successive administrations to regard as axiomatic the proposition that the American public would not tolerate the "loss" of another Asian country. The Korean War and the Vietnam War become understandable in this context.

Postwar American policy toward Japan, too, has had its vicissitudes. Yet, the history of American East Asia policy is by no means a history of failure only. Among its relative successes one may point to the Portsmouth Peace Conference ending the Russo-Japanese War, the Washington Conference of 1921-1922, the regeneration of the Japanese Empire after 1945, and other, less dramatic accomplishments in some of the smaller states of the region. But, taken as a whole, American policy toward the East Asia and Pacific region may be less remarkable for what it has achieved than for what it has failed to achieve; and this, again, may be explained largely by its lack of clear-sightedness—its seeming inability to grasp the essential nature of the larger aspects of the region, first Japanese expansionism, then Chinese nationalism, then revolutionary Asian nationalism generally; and its inability or unwillingness to fashion policies to deal with these forces in a way that would preserve American interests and contribute to the stability of the area.

This would seem to be more than a defect in policy. Because the foreign policies pursued by a democratic republic may be said to rest upon the virtue of the people, or at least upon that section of the public which is interested in foreign affairs, one also may suggest some deeper flaw in the society. Down to the late 1960s, the American public characteristically failed to see East Asia clearly, refused to recognize or countenance certain developments the United States nevertheless was powerless to change, and indicated an unwillingness to accept policies that would have been more in keeping with the national interest. Those who would seek some tragedy in our foreign relations need look no farther.

This lack of clear-sightedness, this selective perception and selective recognition of East Asia, can be attributed in large degree to the Protestant missionary movement. Over the course of a generation, the missionary enterprise, with its focus on China, produced a certain collective mentality that may be called the Missionary Mind. This collective mentality, consisting of a generalized sense of moral obligation toward Asia and toward China in particular, colored the attitudes of the foreign-policy public and shaped the policies pursued by government officials. Long after the missionary movement itself was on the wane, the Missionary Mind continued to exercise a profound effect on policy.

This book explores the connection between the Missionary Mind and American East Asia policy during the years 1911 to 1915. The choice of period is key, for these were the years when the intriguing concept of recognition, as applied to Asia, first received diplomatic attention and indeed formal diplomatic definition. Between 1911 and 1913, the Department of State addressed itself to the problem of recognizing the new Republic of China; with that government and its successor the United States maintained diplomatic relations until 1979. Moreover, in 1915, the American government fashioned the so-called nonrecognition doctrine, according to which the United States formally refused to recognize or countenance certain developments in Asia; this formed the legal basis for American policy toward Japan during the decade preceding Pearl Harbor, and its legacy was the policy of isolating Communist China diplomatically between 1949 and 1972, the date of the Shanghai Communiqué. Not until 1979 did the United States, "recognizing simple reality" at long last, break free completely (or so it may seem) from the attitudes and policies of 1911–1915. This, then, is an essay in recognition.

Part One

Mind

ONE

The Missionary Mind

The Missionary Mind was emotional. True with a vengeance during the late 1940s and early 1950s, this statement seems even truer for the years 1911 to 1915.

Comments from *Outlook,* a journal known for its sophisticated coverage of foreign affairs, provide an illustration. During the Twenty-one Demands episode, *Outlook* reported that it was experiencing a flood of mail, most of it highly emotional. "None of the letters it has received," the editor noted, "have thrown any light on the demands." The letters represented "expressions of feeling rather than contributions to the discussion." Though Americans, even at the highest level, seem to have done little critical thinking about East Asia, their emotional commitment obviously ran deep.[1]

This the historian might more readily understand if large numbers of American citizens had been of East Asian ancestry, which they were not. That Irish-Americans expressed concern regarding Ireland, Italian-Americans cared about Italy, and educated native-born Anglo-Saxons identified with Great Britain scarcely surprises us. Nor is it peculiar that Americans who spent their lives in East Asia, then called "the Far East"—businessmen, journalists, missionaries and the like—often developed a kind of affection for their adopted country. Lafcadio Hearn's enchantment with Japan and Pearl Buck's sentiments about China make a certain amount of sense. That millions of Americans not of Asian descent should articulate deep feelings about East Asia does not. Nor is it self-evident why Americans overwhelmingly preferred China to Japan. The answer seems to lie in the cultural history of the period, particularly its religious life.[2]

Perhaps the most important thing to appreciate about the Missionary Mind is also, in our present condition, the most difficult: that it was primarily religious. At that time, churches played an important role in people's lives. Most people seem to have attended church every Sunday, and many participated in church-related activities at other times. In rural areas and small towns, where most Americans then lived, churches were the dominant social and cultural institutions. They functioned as places to make friends, develop leadership abilities, maintain reputations and, not least, worship God. Here most Americans knowing anything at all about the subject first learned about East Asia. Asia was part of their religion.[3]

When Americans thought about East Asia, two ideas picked up in church ordinarily came to mind: "Christian Civilization" and "Christian China." These notions functioned as major social myths during the years just before World War I. The first—what we may call the myth of Christian Civilization—was the broader concept, conveying the general sense that the world was turning—or ought to turn—toward Christianity and democracy. What we may term the idea of Christian China was a particular national incarnation of the universal vision. Christian China was Christian Civilization in one country—an idea of considerable symbolic import for the future of the American way.

THE MYTH OF CHRISTIAN CIVILIZATION

To understand the workings of the Missionary Mind, we obviously need to know something about the meaning people attached to Christian Civilization, some of the mechanisms by which the myth gained currency, and we require at least a rough sense of its hold upon society.

The Meaning of the Myth. The missionaries and their supporters were in important ways rather different from us. Perhaps we understand them best if we picture them as inhabiting a world of their own imaginative construction. Inside that world, they spoke their own language, celebrated their own myths, and made obeisance to their own special symbols. Behind that universe of meaning lay a vision of what the phenomenal world through their efforts might become. They articulated their moral prospect sometimes in the rarefied language of theology, sometimes in the common coin of everyday speech. Those with a theological turn of mind made bold to announce the Kingdom of God; others spoke simply of making the world a better place. Whatever their idiom, almost all might agree with the mission-board secretary who defined the goal of the missionary movement as "a rounded, enlightened, prosperous, progressive Christian Civilization."[4]

Understanding missionary thought appears at first glance to be transparently easy. For the missionaries specialized in explaining exactly what they believed and why, spreading the word to everyone, literally begging people to listen. Because they took special delight in talking to one another, the historian should require little more than a brief listen in at one of their representative gatherings.

The largest such assembly of our period met early in 1914 at Convention Hall in Kansas City—the quadrennial convention of the Student Volunteer Movement for Foreign Missions. At a time when their more worldly contemporaries were beginning to trickle into Greenwich Village and Chicago's Near North Side, the missionary-minded young descended upon that Kansas capital for five days of discussion about Christian Civilization. Their watchword evinced the characteristic understatement of student movements: "The Evangelization of the World in This Generation." On the floor were 5,000 students representing 700 colleges, most of them hailing from the small denominational schools of the Middle West—Oberlin, Beloit, Grinnell, Carleton, and the like. In the press gallery, 50 newsmen were present to report the most important student movement of the day. On the dais sat the non-student elders of the missionary movement, including James L. Barton of the American Board, Robert E. Speer of the Presbyterian Board, Sherwood Eddy of the Y.M.C.A., William Jennings Bryan of the Department of State, and John R. Mott, the Student Volunteer chairman and dominant figure of the missionary enterprise.[5]

The speeches were true to form: the world, it was said, stands on the threshold of Christian Civilization. Mott himself, just back from a year-long trip around the world, described "the unprecedented world situation":

> There have been times when the opportunity in some one part of the world was as wonderful as now; but there has never been a time when, in the Far East, in the Near East, in Southern Asia, in all parts of Africa, in the East Indian island world, in many parts of Latin America, as well as Latin Europe, and Greek Europe, doors were simultaneously as wide open as they are before the forces of the Christian religion today.

Going on to depict the golden opportunities in each mission field, Mott ended his address with a word on China. Sherwood Eddy, fresh from an evangelistic campaign in China that won wide acclaim in the United States, followed Mott to the podium and declared, "We have long since ceased to doubt that we will win Asia for Christ."[6]

The apparent obtuseness of missionary rhetoric suggests that our understanding the myth of Christian Civilization may well involve greater difficulties than anticipated. Perhaps we should treat Mott's remarks primarily as an imaginative construction, for from this vantage point the myth of Christian Civilization would seem meaningful.[7]

Mott intended at least two levels of meaning. On the first he aimed to say that an "unprecedented world situation" existed as a matter of fact. "Let me give you a glimpse of some of the remarkable things I have seen with my own eyes," Mott continued, "that reveal these Christward world tendencies and movements."[8]

Now John R. Mott was not a stupid man. Honors graduate of Cornell, author of many books, most widely traveled member of his generation, Mott knew the world extremely well in his way. And his audience at Kansas City abounded with bright college students. The historian who has worked in missionary archives will readily attest to the mental aptitude and verbal ability of missionary persons generally. Since persons of this kind require facts, or something like facts, to sustain intellectual conviction, the propaganda arm of the missionary enterprise churned out masses of statistical data. At Kansas City, Mott recounted the details, country by country, illustrating the "unprecedented world situation." On one level, at least, the Missionary Mind regarded the dawn of Christian Civilization as a reality observable to the senses.[9]

At the same time, Mott's oratory obviously moves along a second plane of meaning. On this level, we encounter not the data of the senses but the articulation of feeling. In the rhetoric of John R. Mott, the emotions practically run riot; and the historian does not easily limn the religious affections. While the heroic sense is striking, most post-modern persons cannot begin to appreciate the full range of subjective meanings in traditional Christianity, for there are many things that do not meet the eye. The philosopher (William James) must remind us "how infinitely passionate a thing religion at its highest flights can be."[10]

Sincere religious feelings clearly dominate the plane of subjective meaning. Yet close analysis of the language of John R. Mott, quoted above, lays bare additional strands of passion woven into a fabric of highly specific cultural understandings. If we pull at the loose ends, the myth of Christian Civilization begins to unravel.

Observe that the "Christian" part really means evangelical Protestant. Mott's remarks imply that "Latin America," "Latin Europe," and "Greek Europe"—like the "Near East" and "Southern Asia"—lie outside Christendom. By innuendo Roman Catholics and Eastern Orthodox communicants are not genuine Christians.

And observe that the "Civilization" part really means Anglo-Saxon Civilization. Racial consciousness may be divined behind a mental map of Europe which parcels the continent into "Latin Europe," "Greek Europe," and—what is implied—Anglo-Saxon Europe. Cultural chauvinism, again by innuendo, denies the name of civilization to France and Italy. The passions of race and culture apparently inform the John R. Mott vision of the divine economy. Looked at closely, the myth of Christian Civilization— for all its universal pretensions—dissolves easily into the cultural values of a particular group in American society, the native-born white Protestants.[11]

The Making of the Myth. The myth of Christian Civilization took a century to make. From the founding of the American Board in 1810 until the 1880s and 1890s, foreign missions remained a minor concern of American churches. Till then, most missionary activity aimed at evangelizing the American West. Josiah Strong's best-selling work, *Our Country* (1886), while sometimes viewed by historians as a plea for overseas expansion, basically represented an appeal for more missionary effort at home. Not until the frontier closed did large numbers of Protestants direct their attention overseas. Able at last to take up the white man's burden, Americans by the end of that century were making large contributions to that transnational religious movement, previously dominated by missionaries from the British Empire, which James A. Field has characterized so precisely as "this Anglo-Saxon Islam." The torch was passed to the Americans during the World Missionary Conference at Edinburgh in 1910. Welcomed by the King, sponsored by Lord Balfour, attended by an array of notables from all over the Anglo-Saxon world, the Edinburgh Conference selected for its chairman the farm boy from Iowa, John R. Mott.[12]

Expanding the overseas effort required elaborate organizational structures to raise money and recruit missionaries. Alongside the bureaucratic, denominational mission boards run by ministers there grew up new organizations, dominated by laymen like Mott and Eddy, catering to specific groups—businessmen, women, college students, adolescents, Sunday School children, and the like. These institutions forged links with other Protestant bodies—the Y.M.C.A., Y.W.C.A., and the many denominational colleges—to consolidate their popular base. They built a communications network reaching into most Protestant congregations on this continent. Sedulously cultivating ministers and missionary committees in local churches, they arranged for missionaries on furlough to visit as many congregations as possible during their year off, and encouraged churches to support specific missionaries. They made sure that religious newspapers, which reached most church members, contained ample news about missions, and they flooded the local churches with printed matter—missionary magazines, missionary pamphlets, missionary biographies, histories of particular mission stations, accounts of specific mission fields, missionary memoirs, books by domestic leaders of the missions movement—an immense middlebrow literature. They even used the modern science of advertising to promote their message, which was always the same: The world is turning to Christ, and, if you cannot see your way clear to go to the mission field yourself, then surely you will help support by your prayers and by your offerings those who have responded to Christ's command.[13]

The campaign for Christian Civilization became a kind of crusade between the years 1905 and 1915. During that decade when a million immigrants a year from "Latin Europe" and "Greek Europe" swarmed onto Ellis Island, thousands of bright, young, well-scrubbed Protestant Student Volunteers sailed from San Francisco to build a Christian Civilization in Asia. Between 1905 and 1915, the number of missionaries doubled, and the budgets of the mission boards doubled too. By 1915, there were nearly 10,000 foreign missionaries. Mission-board budgets totaled $17 million per year, and the value of mission property abroad exceeded $50 million. The statistics are impressive. One in every 1,500 adult Protestants was a foreign missionary. Each year's mission revenues would have been adequate to underwrite a sizeable issue of foreign bonds on Wall Street. The dollar value of mission property abroad surpassed American financial investment in China.[14]

A great many people, not all of them professionally religious, pitched in. For example, businessmen played a leading role. Previously, as the *Literary Digest* noted, it was "chiefly the devoted women of the church who concerned themselves much about missions," but the Laymen's Missionary Movement, founded in 1907, changed all that. Headed by Samuel B. Capen, the wealthy Boston rug merchant prominent in urban reform and other civic affairs, the Laymen's Movement conducted massive fund drives among businessmen in every large and medium-size city, and this organization's success accounted for the bulk of the increased mission revenues. A single campaign in 1910 generated over $400,000 in New York, $166,000 in Philadelphia, $33,000 in Syracuse, $36,000 in Richmond, and similarly estimable sums elsewhere. The academic community also helped. Not to be undone by the likes of Grinnell and Beloit, the elite eastern universities made important contributions, Old Blue establishing the College of Yale-in-China, Old Nassau under Woodrow Wilson taking on the Peking Y.M.C.A., and even Harvard chipping in with a Shanghai branch of the Medical School. The myth of Christian Civilization, in brief, commanded the allegiance of many.[15]

The Myth and American Society. However widespread the myth of Christian Civilization, in the sense here employed, it did not gain universal acceptance. One large group, numbering about one-third of the population, had virtually no interest in foreign missions, Roman Catholics. A Catholic journal in Chicago wrote, "*Catholics simply have not thought about missions. . . .* They are *parishmen* entirely," and the leading Catholic periodical in the country, the *Catholic World,* failed to publish a single article on the subject. Perhaps this was because there were, at that time, no— that is, zero—American Catholic foreign missionaries. Though European Catholics carried on mission efforts far surpassing those of the upstart Anglo-Saxon sectarians, American Catholics had as yet no time, energy, or money. Made up primarily of impoverished immigrants, the Roman Catholic Church in America directed its resources toward building parish churches, supporting parochial schools, promoting group solidarity in an often hostile social environment, and otherwise making Boston, New York, Chicago, and other cities fit places for good Catholics to live. Catholics tended to worry more about the bigots at home than the heathen beyond the sea.[16]

And so, to Irish-Americans and Italian-Americans and other "hyphenated Americans," as they often were called by the dominant group, the slogans of Christian Civilization rang somewhat hollow. Recognizing a narrowly sectarian cause, American Catholics realized that Protestants regarded Roman Catholics in Latin America and "Latin Europe" as fair game. There may be something to learn from the Catholic perspective. That Catholics bothered to comment at all suggests considerable public awareness of the missionary enterprise. Catholics require serious attention, moreover, when the historian discovers them arguing that publications intended for general circulation—mass periodicals, specialized journals, even daily newspapers—bought the Protestant myth of Christian Civilization lock, stock, and barrel. For example, in the *Pilot,* official newspaper of the one-million-member Archdiocese of Boston, may be found harsh comments on the Protestant-controlled dailies. "In vain," commented a bitter *Pilot* editorial, "does one look in the press articles for an account of what is being accomplished by the Catholic missionaries. And so the impression given is that Christianity in these mission lands is eminently Protestant and that Catholicity there is a negligible quantity."[17]

Articulate Catholics also avoided the idea of Christian China. Noting that the latter derived from the Protestant imagination, the *Pilot* patiently explained that China in fact contained many more Catholics than Protestants, yet it pointedly refrained from evoking a myth of Catholic China. One article was entitled "China Is Not Likely to Trouble Itself About Religion." "Whether the people will content themselves with no religion or seek a new one remains to be seen," said the *Pilot*. Here, as elsewhere in Catholic literature, one gets the impression that these were slender years for Christianity in East Asia. Writing off the intellectuals, discounting mass conversion, the *Pilot* concluded by quoting a European missionary to the effect that perhaps some of the "'good, simple country people will look to the Catholic Church.'"[18]

Catholics had a point when they argued that the nation's newspapers and magazines often made themselves tools of the Protestant myth. The *Reader's Guide to Periodical Literature* indexed hundreds of articles on Protestant missions, many of them in mass-circulation magazines like the *Literary Digest,* and in other general publications such as the *Review of Reviews, World's Work,* and the *Atlantic Monthly.* The *Independent* and *Outlook* seemed to compete for the most extensive coverage. That not a single article indexed in the *Reader's Guide* bears a critical or even a skeptical title suggests that the doubters and unbelievers, of whom there were quite a few, particularly among young intellectuals, maintained—or were forced to maintain—a discreet silence regarding the sacred cow. In those days editors did not encourage attacks on missions and other "noble ideas."[19]

On the contrary, editors gave the enterprise wide coverage, and, to illustrate the point, the historian might display a nearly endless series of examples from newspapers, magazines, and journals of opinion. During April and May 1913, the *Chicago Tribune* published lengthy accounts of something called "The World in Chicago," a kind of missionary carnival drawing huge crowds to the Chicago Coliseum every day for slide shows, lectures, plays, the Chinese pagoda, the Japanese teahouse, the thatched huts of the dusky savages, church ladies dressed up as natives, even some live natives in their genuine native costumes, and the spectacular "Pageant of Light and Darkness," featuring a cast of one thousand. Involving over 20,000 volunteers from 600 Chicago churches, this event sometimes rated a full page in the "World's Greatest Newspaper."[20]

National magazines also called attention to missions. During the Twenty-one Demands crisis, the *Literary Digest* published a piece called "Christianity Reaching China's Leaders" with pictures of Sherwood Eddy leading a revival in the Forbidden City. Even *Outlook,* that relentless partisan of realism in foreign affairs, reported that "China shows a general readiness to give serious consideration to Christianity." Describing the progress of missions there, and in Africa, India, Turkey, and Latin America, a typical *Outlook* editorial concluded: "The development of Christian democracy and civilization which Americans are effecting in the non-Christian world, exhibiting world-power in its noblest form, is a fact of National interest, entitled to National attention and sympathy." *Outlook* believed in the missionary cause, as did the *Independent.* Though many other periodicals must have covered the missionary movement in depth just because it made good copy, the mass media did effectively broadcast the Protestant myth of Christian Civilization. One might easily multiply examples.[21]

The myth of Christian Civilization, thus, was a complex representation, involving several levels of intention, wherein close analysis reveals thought intertwining with emotion, religious belief with cultural predilection, cosmopolitan vision with tribal narrowness. It acquired currency through the propaganda apparatus of the missionary enterprise. As the cause gained momentum, becoming a major force after 1905, the myth took on a life of its own, spreading far beyond the mission crusade and the churches. By the years 1911–1915, it appeared to have seeped into nearly every corner of Protestant society and culture. Though Catholics, unbelievers, and certain others remained untouched, the Missionary Mind enjoyed a secure position on the American scene.

THE IDEA OF CHRISTIAN CHINA

Like most things public, the missionary movement remained the work of a relative few. Americans committed to what we have called the idea of Christian China probably totaled about five million adults—a large group, yet still a minority.

Mission-Board Policy. Between 1911 and 1915, mission-board secretaries gave more attention to China than to any other country. Quite practical in their way, these mission-board bureaucrats tended to invest their men and money where they foresaw the highest return; at that time, they sank around one-third of their resources in China. They had not always done so: during the 1870s and 1880s, for example, they had concentrated on Japan. Throughout the nineteenth century, they usually regarded China as a relatively poor market for Christian Civilization. Restrictions on missionary residence and travel, the hostility of the gentry, the tenacity of Confucian culture, the frequency and virulence of antiforeign rioting, the general unpopularity of the Christian message—all these made China seem less than ideal. Not until the 1890s did China surpass India in missionary personnel; not until about 1905 did China become the most promising of fields. When the Chinese abolished the traditional Confucian examination system in 1906, optimism increased at the mission boards, for China seemed plastic and Christianity appeared to have a chance. The contrast between the China of Boxer days and the "New China" of the late Ch'ing reforms became a staple of mission-board thinking, so that, from 1906 on, China missions grew rapidly, absorbing the largest share of the expanding mission revenues discussed above. Missions to Japan, meanwhile, developed at a modest rate. Over one thousand new missionaries went out to China—yet less than one hundred to Japan—during the period 1911-1916. The mission boards were committing themselves heavily to Christian China, as Table 1 shows:[22]

TABLE 1 American Missionaries to China and Japan, 1906-1916

Year	China	Japan
1906	1037	594
1911	1812	771
1916	2862	858

Sources: Harlan P. Beach, ed., *Geography and Atlas of Protestant Missions* (New York, 1906), II, 22-23; James S. Dennis et al., eds., *World Atlas of Christian Missions* (New York, 1911), pp. 86-87; Harlan P. Beach and Burton St. John, eds., *World Statistics of Christian Missions* (New York, 1916), pp. 62-63.

The China-Missions Constituency. By paying the bill for this expanding effort, millions of Americans acquired a personal stake in Christian China. Among the approximately 100 million Americans then alive, around 42 million belonged to churches. (These figures may seem low, but church membership was restricted to adults, and half the population was under twenty-five, the under-fourteen cohort numbering 30 million.) Sixteen million of the 42 million adult church members were Roman Catholic. Of the 25 million Protestants, over 5 million belonged to the Negro denominations, separated from the mainstream, occupying an anomalous position vis-à-vis Christian Civilization. And of the 20 million whites, around 5 million belonged to small denominations, mostly poor, which did not support China missions. This leaves a group numbering around 15 million. Mission officials, of whom Tyler Dennett was at that time one, estimated that one-third of these people made regular financial contributions. Around 5 million adult white Protestant church members, that is, gave money to advance the missions cause.[23]

The foreign-missions public had a definite denominational shape, as Table 2 indicates:

TABLE 2 Denominational Bases of the Missionary Movement, 1916

Denomination	Members (millions)	Mission Budget ($ millions)	Missionaries (total)
Methodist, North	3.7	2.9	1428
Presbyterian, North	1.6	2.3	1353
Baptist, North	1.2	1.3	688
Congregational	0.8	1.1	661
Methodist, South	2.1	1.0	382
Presbyterian, South	0.4	0.6	377
Episcopal	1.1	0.8	346
Baptist, South	2.7	0.5	307
Disciples of Christ	1.2	0.6	278

Source: U.S. Department of Commerce, Bureau of the Census, *Religious Bodies, 1916* (Washington, D.C., 1919), I, 30, 39, 96–97.

We are dealing here overwhelmingly with native-born whites. Black Protestants, and the largely immigrant Lutherans of German and

Scandinavian descent, carried on few overseas mission activities. Notice also that Southern white Protestants, though numerous, made much less impressive contributions than their co-religionists in the North. Southern Baptists comprised over twice as many members as the Northern Baptists but supported an overseas effort only half as large, and Southern Methodists performed weakly compared with Northern. Only the Southern Presbyterians could subscribe on the scale usual in the North. The Southern figures probably reflected the region's relative poverty. Yet money did not automatically convert into missions, for the Episcopal Church, that traditional haven of the wealthy and socially prominent, made only a moderate effort. Four churches of the North, the "main-line" evangelical denominations, predominated: Baptists, Presbyterians, Methodists, and Congregationalists. Here one would expect to find the real troops and cadres of Christian China.[24]

There was also a sex difference: the foreign-missions public contained more women than men. Table 3 demonstrates how the church membership figures on the four big missionary denominations break down:

TABLE 3 Distribution of Church Members by Sex, 1916

(%)

Denomination	Male	Female
Methodist, North	38	62
Presbyterian, North	36	64
Baptist, North	39	61
Congregational	39	61

Source: *Religious Bodies, 1916,* I, 40–41.

Through the Laymen's Missionary Movement the men of the churches assumed their share of the missions enterprise, but women remained numerically dominant.

Moreover, the constituency had a distinctly provincial character. The missionary-minded lived on farms, in villages, and in small towns more often than in cities, as Table 4 illustrates:

TABLE 4 Distribution of Church Members by Size of Community, 1916
(%)

Denomination	Under 25,000	25,000 and Over
Methodist, North	77	23
Presbyterian, North	63	37
Baptist, North	63	37
Congregational	64	36

Source: *Religious Bodies, 1916*, I, 121

Small towns, especially small towns in the Middle West, appeared to play a special role in the missionary enterprise. Though the point awaits quantitative confirmation, preliminary evidence suggests that provincial Midwesterners generally evinced greater interest than Protestants elsewhere. Their churches and denominational colleges formed the very center of missionary gravity. In the Middle West, the Methodist, Presbyterian, Baptist, and Congregational churches— where most self-consciously decent middle class citizens habitually worshiped—fairly buzzed with missionary activity. There a missionary on furlough could always find an audience. The region's many church colleges, which drew their students from the local elites, made every effort to advance the cause. Through official encouragement, the Student Volunteer Movement became the most prestigious campus activity. The church colleges even offered mission courses for academic credit; small wonder they regularly sent their Phi Beta Kappas off to China. In the Asian mission fields, the majority of the missionary body retained memories of a small town and a church college, not to mention tall sweet corn and new-mown hay. The Christian missionary, in this view, was provincial Midwestern society's greatest gift to the world.[25]

At the very least, a certain provincial mentality did seem to characterize the missions constituency. Henry May has shown how native-born Protestants of the period were undergoing considerable social and cultural strain. Though it is perhaps easy to overestimate the degree of their fears—this was an age given to hyperbole—a certain apprehensiveness did appear to exist about the survival of their traditional way of life. Protestants worried about their churches, now bitterly divided between defenders of the old-time religion and the liberal-Social Gospel types who made a separate peace with the modern world. Provincial Protestants also worried about cities and everything thought to go with cities: Roman Catholics and even East European Jews, labor violence, socialism and materialism, unbelief, the liquor trade, the white-slave traffic, the tango and other sensual popular dances, birth control and divorce, to name but a few. In his Kansas City speech, Mott alluded darkly to the "cancerous and leperous growths of the non-Christian civilizations that are eating into the very vitals of Christendom." Many Protestants shared his anxiety regarding the future of "Christian America." There was the sense that the old America based on the church and simple republican virtue might be slipping away. This was connected with concern over the fate of Christian Civilization, for Americans scarcely could feel secure in the possession of Christianity and democracy so long as the wide world itself remained hostile. Eventually, the worriers became crusaders, those most worried about Christian America crusading for temperance, those most worried about Christian Civilization crusading for missions; many joined both movements. Prohibition and Christian China took root and flourished in the same social soil. Aspects of a common provincial mentality, both causes may be viewed as symbols of cultural identity or reflections of cultural strain.[26]

With these facts and some imagination, one may begin to picture Christian China's American constituency. In the wide sense, it included most native-born white Protestants, from the highest Anglo-Catholic to the humblest Southern Baptist. The mission propaganda network must have exposed nearly all such persons to China missions, leading them at least to link the ideas "China" and "missions." This group comprised around 15 million adults. Because families in those days averaged more than two children, the total community may have been twice that size. Despite enormous internal variation in income level and life circumstance, this was the dominant group in American society.[27]

The China-missions public (properly speaking) comprised a more select group. No doubt these people varied in the amount of time they could spare, some serving on missionary committees, most too busy to do much besides read missionary literature and listen to visiting missionaries. But they all made regular financial contributions, and we have estimated that they numbered around 5 million. If Sunday School children and adolescents are added, the total would probably reach 10 million. Again, the constituency included more women than men, more Northerners than Southerners, more rural and small-town folk than city people. The main-line evangelical denominations centered in the North and Middle West gave the most money and supported the most missionaries. Small towns in the Middle West seemed to generate the most enthusiasm and supply the ablest personnel. And this public appeared somewhat anxious about the survival of Christianity and democracy at home and abroad. The Protestant community, all in all, had a substantial investment in Christian China.

China Missionaries and Their System of Communications. The missionaries gave the most—themselves. When a missionary spoke of Christian China, he was talking about his life work. It was tangible: a Foochow congregation, a Canton hospital, a Chinese merchant involved in the Tientsin Y.M.C.A., a bright senior at St. Johns's University in Shanghai considering government service. Christian China, in this sense, had flesh and blood. But it was also a dream, and the Missionary Mind often failed to distinguish the two levels of reality. Moving effortlessly from the budget of the Shanghai Y.M.C.A. to a vision of China redeemed, this mentality blended facts with sky-high hopes, the present melting into the future. James W. Bashford, sometime President of Ohio Wesleyan and then Methodist Bishop of Peking, told the 1910 Edinburgh Conference that, in China, "more than one-fourth of the human race stands at the parting of the ways. Not since the days of the Reformation, not indeed since Pentecost has so great an opportunity confronted the Christian Church." Though Christian China in fact numbered fewer souls than Methodist Ohio, the habit of optimism ran deep (it was part of the job). What the missionaries actually did in China has received treatment elsewhere and need not be repeated here, except to note that they contributed to Chinese development through their hospitals, Y.M.C.A.s, and denominational colleges. If the missionaries habitually overstated their achievements, this is perhaps to be expected.[28]

As propagandists for Christian China the missionaries seldom missed a trick. The ability to write well, even at interminable length, was an advantage, and even the garden variety of missionary seemed comfortable with the written word. A certain number wrote books that people appeared to read. Arthur Smith's *Uplift of China,* for example, sold over 75,000 copies in 1907 and went through numerous editions. The best-known missionary authors— Smith, Gilbert Reid, W.A.P. Martin, and others enjoyed a comparatively large following. Other missionaries, their names largely forgotten now, from their mission compounds out among the Chinese penned thousands of articles for mission journals, church newspapers, and national magazines. Virtually all missionaries corresponded regularly with their mission boards in New York or Boston and their families, friends, and home churches in small-town America. One can imagine the stir coming over a small community in Illinois, say, when the postman came around with a letter all the way from Peking, China; or the excitement during Sunday service at the First Presbyterian Church of Watertown, New York (where Robert Lansing served as Elder before moving on) when the minister read aloud a letter from Ernest J. Weekes, their man in Canton.[29]

Prolific writers, missionaries were also excellent public speakers. During their sabbatical year, they ordinarily went on speaking tour around the country, preaching the guest sermon on Mission Sunday, speaking before the young people's group, the Sunday School children, and the ladies' mission circle, showing slides of

China on Sunday night. During a week in Lincoln, Nebraska, in 1912, James Bashford gave 6 addresses on China, speaking at the three largest churches, at Nebraska Wesleyan, and at the State University. All kinds of people thereby learned about East Asia from someone with first-hand knowledge. This scenario repeated itself thousands of times each year in small communities across the United States. Because missionaries (like academics) took every seventh year off, at any given time hundreds were stumping the churches. Now, if we assume there were 300 such missionaries (this is roughly correct) and we further assume that each missionary spoke only twice a week (this may be low), then there were more than 30,000 missionary addresses on China every year. The ramifications are incalculable. But it is fair to surmise that, from time to time, Protestants everywhere enjoyed personal access to someone who lived in China. Missionary visitations usually made an indelible impression on public opinion in provincial communities otherwise starved for information. Thus did the missionaries achieve one of their main objectives—to bring light to those dwelling in darkness.[30]

Small-town Protestants thereby came to love China, after their fashion. While seeming to remain largely indifferent to European nations, their imaginations fired at the prospect of Christian Civilization in Asia. Collective representations are rarely built in a day; the creation of a China constituency therefore required patient labor.[31]

Observe the conceit of Christian China in a small American community, Madison, New Jersey—a tidy, prosperous, rather quiet college town where, in 1913, the New York mission boards arranged for the churches to sponsor a community program on China during Lent. Over three hundred people paid 80 cents to sign up. Meeting in small groups to discuss the text, *China's New Day* by Isaac T. Headland, they assembled every Tuesday to hear authorities—mission-board secretaries, China missionaries, Chinese Christians. Robert E. Speer of the Presbyterian Board discussed China's "Break with the Past"; the head of the Episcopal Board talked on "The Church in China and the Church at Home"; and the group also heard John E. Williams, Vice President of the University of Nanking, describe the "Educational Revolution," and Helen B. Montgomery, author of *Western Women in Eastern Lands,* depict "The Chinese Woman." The Chinese discussed "Medical Missions in China" and "The Chinese Republic from the Chinese Point of View." Rarely, if ever, had Madison seen so many authorities on things Chinese, and it is not difficult to visualize the effect.[32]

Madison citizens felt so strongly that nineteen wrote letters to President Wilson, letters that would seem to us quite innocent of policy. The writers basically just wanted America to help. One called for a new China policy "for the sake of Christianity, and for the uplift of the Chinese people." Another wrote that Washington should "help her in establishing the Christian Religion, and a system of Finance and Education." All radiated warmth towards "our youngest sister republic." A typical Madison townsperson foresaw "the rapid forwarding of the cause of Christ in the world." In small-town New Jersey, as elsewhere, Christian China did indeed seem to mean something.[33]

Japan in the Missionary Mind. Christian Japan, meanwhile, had largely disappeared from the Protestant moral imagination. Naturally, this caused concern at the mission boards. In 1912, the influential *Missionary Review of the World* reported that "the attitude of the people of the churches at home is not encouraging. Japan, once the most popular of subjects for a home audience, no longer, it is said, arouses any enthusiasm." College students planning missionary careers also had lost interest in Japan. "For some years," noted the *Missionary Review,* "there has been a difficulty in obtaining candidates for missionary service in the Japanese Empire. Volunteers have discriminated against the country. They have been ready for India, China, Africa, Arabia, in fact almost anywhere, but many have actually declined to consider a call to Japan."[34]

Japan missionaries often seemed troubled by these attitudes at home base. While knowing that mission-board budgets would never be tailored to the vagaries of public sentiment (mission-board secretaries believed that Japan needed Christ just as badly as China did), and knowing that they had powerful friends on the liberal-Social Gospel wing, notably the Federal Council of Churches (among the urban-oriented minority were those who found social service in the Tokyo slums as exhilarating as Hull House), nevertheless Japan missionaries expressed alarm at the erosion of their once-flourishing base. They voiced special concern about the dearth of enthusiasm on college campuses, for that ultimately would threaten the survival of their enterprise. As Sidney Gulick, Christian Japan's answer to Bishop Bashford, wrote to the American Board in 1913: "Evidently young people are not volunteering for Japan, so if we are to get them, they must be *sought out* and definite propositions laid before them." Christian Japan, it would seem, was an idea whose time had come and gone.[35]

China and the Protestant Imagination: Some Speculations. The student of culture may well ask why the 5 to 10 million members of the foreign-missions public were investing so much in China while largely neglecting Japan. The question is worth asking even if it cannot admit of a final or even tidy answer.

The rigorous may wish to avoid the somewhat shopworn notion that Americans have always been fascinated by China. This explanation tends to confuse the China-minded few—on Chestnut Street or the water side of Beacon, or elsewhere—with the many. Among American Protestants, the China missionaries usually regarded China as fascinating, but this did not mean that churchgoers at home necessarily shared their view. Is China inherently more interesting than Japan? Again, Japan was all the rage in the 1870s and 1880s. Even Bishop Bashford recalled at the Edinburgh Conference that "Japan a quarter of a century ago constituted the most important and hopeful mission field on earth."[36]

So it is not entirely obvious why Protestants now viewed China as the most promising East Asian repository for Christian Civilization. Actual conditions in the Asian mission fields did not seem to dictate a clear-cut choice. Neither country was Christian, neither was really democratic. In retrospect, the case for Japan appears equally good, if only because Christians formed a higher percentage of the population there, Christianity influenced intellectual life more deeply, and because, whatever the progress toward popular sovereignty in China brought about by the late Ch'ing reforms, the 1911 Revolution, and the early Republican experiment with representative institutions, these cannot compare with evolutionary Japanese developments. While China was experimenting with modern politics, Japan enjoyed a relatively stable political system, with a written constitution, a functioning Diet, articulate public opinion, organized political parties, and the like. Moreover, the Taishō Political Crisis of 1912-1913 produced a constitutional arrangement not unlike the kind the British once called "responsible government." American perceptions of China and Japan seem curious in this context.[37]

One cannot attribute this solely to missionaries and mission propaganda, for Japan as well as China enjoyed missionary services. The same mission journals opening their pages to Christian China also published articles on Christian Japan; the national periodicals carrying missionary accounts of American leadership in Chinese affairs printed stories of similar purport regarding Japan; the transpacific mails bringing descriptions of the late Ch'ing reforms did not embargo letters from Japan. "There has been seen in Japan," wrote an American Board missionary in 1910, "a development along lines of material progress more rapid that the world has ever before witnessed." While China missionaries were portraying the Republican Revolution as a landmark in popular government, Japan missionaries reported the "Tide of Rising Democracy" discerned in the Taishō Political Crisis. "I am impressed at the rapidity with which events have moved during this second year of Taisho," wrote the Kyoto Y.M.C.A. secretary in 1914. The most recent democratic tide, he wrote, "reached its crest during the late winter months when there were over-thrown in succession two strong Cabinets, resulting in the unexpected and most significant calling to the Premiership of Count Okuma, who has stood for two decades as the embodiment of what the Bureaucrats have most hated and dreaded. Count Okuma has enlisted a strong ministry which stands for democratic and progressive policies." It would be difficult to prove that Japan missionaries home on furlough exuded any less enthusiasm than their Chinese counterparts. Bishop Bashford may have spoken almost every day, but Sidney Gulick usually outdid him. "I am carrying a pretty heavy schedule of addresses," he wrote in 1914, "generally speaking two, sometimes three, occasionally even four times a day." Since China missionaries outnumbered Japan missionaries, one might reasonably expect rather more American interest in China, but missionary propaganda alone clearly fails to explain the lopsided shape of Protestant opinion.[38]

Perhaps an answer—however speculative—lies somewhere in the interaction between the East Asian missionary and his American constituents. Remember that a missionary was not a foreign service officer. Writing an article or giving a speech, his primary goal was not to report but to advocate or persuade. This was sometimes difficult. "The difficulty between the missionary and the man in the pew," observed the American Board's *Missionary Herald,* "is that they rarely see eye to eye." The missionary ordinarily addressed an audience knowing very little about East Asia, and he wanted to convince them in an hour. One may appreciate his frustration on finding "a large part of that time expended in a rather vague lesson on missionary geography." What to do with the remainder? It seems reasonable to assume that the Christian missionary, like all successful communicators, developed a sense for his audience— and played to it. The missionary would have known what people wanted to hear and what they were tired of hearing. On the assumption that audiences generally were looking for an overseas realization of the Christian America of their imaginings, one may infer that, when the missionary made out a reasonable case for his own mission field, the audience warmed up—and, when he could not, the audience lost interest. If this is true, then it is worth going on to inquire why the China missionary did the best job of telling people what they wanted to hear. The evidence, though necessarily impressionistic, may not lack the power of suggestion, even if an answer, at best tentative, contains but the color of truth.[39]

It may be suggested that American Protestants became excited when they heard a China missionary because his message was calculated to make their world seem more secure. Those afraid of Roman Catholics could relax a little upon hearing that China would soon convert to evangelical Protestantism. Mission propaganda often cultivated this notion. For example, in 1911, the *Missionary Review* reported that "the blood of the martyrs in China has become the seed of the Church. . . . Doors are opening, China is changing, an empire is being reborn." Another typical piece, this one in 1913, commented on "the unprecedented ripeness of the field for Christian harvest." The good news extended to the Chinese political scene. In 1912, an American Board missionary back from a tour of the Peking countryside remarked that the peasantry expressed "the greatest eagerness to learn what a republican form of government involves and the desire to have a share in it." Note the political prospect suggested in the *Missionary Review*'s article on the opening of the Chinese Parliament in 1913: "The world's youngest republic inaugurated its congress on April 8, amid great joy and rejoicing. Five hundred representatives . . . were present. They were all clothed in European fashion, with frock coats. The old queues and robes have disappeared. Bands played, and there was great joy and rejoicing among the people. So China has passed another mile-stone on her way toward liberty and light." According to non-missionary observers, the Chinese Parliament opened amid scenes of chaos. Be that as it may, China missionaries saw what they wanted to see and told their constituents what *they* wanted to *hear*. They created an image of China that was basically innocent.[40]

The Japan missionary, by contrast, appeared to have little opportunity (or inclination) to traffic in visions of innocence. His work took place in a relatively modern country. As a report to the Edinburgh Conference stated, "Japan is one of the great Powers of the world. . . . It has a constitution, an Imperial Diet, and a most efficient army and navy. In industry and commerce it competes with the industrial nations of the West. For these and other reasons the problems of Christian work in Japan much more closely resemble those in Great Britain or in the United States of America than do those in any other country to which missionaries have gone." Japan had grown up, and the missionary had trouble explaining this to provincial Americans. Ordinarily the Japan missionary's message emphasized the challenge of Christian work in an urban industrial society. Prostitution, noted the *Missionary Review*, "flourishes in Japan as in no other country in the world." Another *Missionary Review* piece conceded that nonreligious institutions now dominated Japanese education: "The Christian schools used to be the best in the country; now they have become relatively less efficient with the improvement of the national school system." Generally, Japan missionaries seemed to refrain from promising instant evangelization. Christianization, wrote Sidney Gulick, "is not a program to be completed in one generation; it will need rather five generations and perhaps ten." Though this vision of a Christianized modern social order had appeal to advanced members of the Protestant community, it naturally failed to generate enthusiasm in the hinterlands.[41]

One item in the Japan missionary's message proved especially hard to sell—racial equality. Race cut to the quick.

The racial attitudes of missionaries varied enormously. Wholesale bigots were unusual—such persons having little motivation to leave home—and missionaries married to native Christians were also rare, but there were many of the Social Gospel wing whose views were quite enlightened. Even so, it is fair to generalize that most missionaries held views at variance with the idea of human equality. Even these may be said to have loved their native charges, in their way. One may observe this habit of mind in Donald MacGillivray, one of the best-known China missionaries, as expressed in a letter regarding property suitable for a new mission building in the International Settlement at Shanghai: "The difficulty," he wrote, "is that if you buy a small piece in a vacant field, within a short time you will be surrounded by Chinese and Japanese neighbours, and how ever so much we may love these nations—a Mission House, such as ours, occupied by those engaged in literary work, should not be closed in by Orientals for health reasons." Love at a distance—the idea somehow made sense in the Missionary Mind. In 1914, a Los Angeles missionary wrote the State Department a letter characterizing the dominant California sentiment toward Asians as "unChristian," citing scripture on human brotherhood, and ending: "P.S. I omitted to say, I do not think we should admit Orientals & *low* Europeans as equals, for they are not. And I am adverse to intermarriage with Orientals. (I have taught Chinese in Mission Schools.)" China missionaries, nevertheless, seemed generally more advanced than their constituents. Yet, they tended to avoid the issue, both in public and in private, because it was dynamite.[42]

Japan missionaries confronted the issue directly. They had little choice. Their Japanese friends seemed to ask, with some regularity, why Christian America's Congress and Christian California's Legislature considered anti-Japanese legislation every year. As the American Ambassador to Tokyo, George W. Guthrie, wrote in 1913 to Secretary Bryan, the Japanese "assert that when we talk of the 'fatherhood of God' and the 'brotherhood of man,' we mean only 'white men,' and that the 'yellow men' and the 'black men' are excluded from that brotherhood." Japan missionaries, severely embarrassed, made an appropriate response. American-Board missionaries led the way, advocating federal legislation to naturalize resident Asians and admit future immigrants on the same basis as Europeans. The American Board even pointed to Hawaii as the model for future race relations. Methodist, Baptist, and other Japan missionaries embraced the cause, which enjoyed the support of Lyman Abbott and most of the *Outlook* staff, the Dean of the University of Chicago Divinity School, and the Federal Council of Churches. The last of these established a Commission on Relations with Japan and conducted nationwide campaigns to eradicate race prejudice.[43]

China missionaries, meanwhile, despite their record during the 1905 anti-American boycott, seemed largely to avoid the immigration issue now. During 1911-1915, other matters loomed larger in China than did immigration. Yet, by neglecting to promote the movement, the China missionaries disappointed, even enraged, their Japan counterparts. Their eagerness to touch virtually every major question in American East Asia policy except race drew a bitter rebuke from Sidney Gulick. "If China missionaries would only join in this campaign and help get the American Chinese Exclusion law repealed," he wrote in 1915, "their agitation would be most welcome." China missionaries must have believed the issue was best left till the future, when China would be strong.[44]

We may now speculate why American audiences embraced the message of the China missionary. In his hour with them, the missionary appears likely to have skipped over the race issue, answered the usual queries about where the mission field actually was on the map, described his own work, and projected an image of China in most respects consistent with Christian America. He seems likely, in fine, to have spoken not of prostitution and slums but of simple republican virtue, not of modern industrial civilization but of an ancient empire reborn.

Naturally, there were exceptions, some notable. A number of China missionaries, mostly Social Gospel workers based in the treaty ports, consistently addressed the problems of modern society. Y.M.C.A. secretaries and missionary educators, among others, positioned themselves on the cutting edge of change. Through contact with merchants and students, liberal missionaries became sensitive to nationalism and other modernizing impulses of urban Chinese. But most missionaries, like most Chinese, missed out on these adventures because they lived in the countryside. (In Japan, by contrast, missionaries usually resided in cities.) In any event, the great majority of China missionaries, when they wrote magazine articles or gave speeches in rural or small-town America, concentrated on their religious work in their own Chinese villages. If this seemed innocent enough, what the missionaries said of Chinese affairs in general must also have come across as basically innocent. Even liberal missionaries could play to a small-town audience by depicting an essentially adolescent Asian land, eager to learn from the United States, where the young people attended church colleges just like Oberlin and the small businessmen supported the Y.M.C.A. One way or another, the China missionary, unlike the Japan missionary, seems effectively to have escaped some of the burdens of the modern world.[45]

Native-born white Protestants, generally, may have preferred China to Japan precisely for this reason. "Christian China," in this sense, may be viewed as one of the ways provincial America represented its own existence to itself—a symbol, that is, of American innocence reborn in East Asia.

THE MISSIONARY MIND IN ACTION

Whatever their achievements in East Asia, the China missionaries were clearly successful at home. Letter after letter, article after article, speech after speech accumulated. Day by day, the idea of Christian China insinuated itself in the minds of Protestant churchgoers. It entered their emotional structure. After 1905, Christian China formed the centerpiece of the myth of Christian Civilization. By 1911, the Missionary Mind cared about China as nowhere else in the world.[46]

The Missionary Mind and the Protestant Community. Without pretention to psycho-history and without embarrassment, the historian may inquire further into the meaning—that is, the subjective meaning—that American Protestants attached to China. For their sentiments, if saccharine to our taste, were not trivial to them. One finds evidence of this in Minneapolis where, in May 1912, over 800 delegates assembled for the Twenty-sixth General Conference of the Northern Methodist Church, the largest Protestant denomination, numbering nearly 4 million adult members. No missionary meeting nor congress of clerics, the Methodist conference drew 33 attorneys and judges, 25 college presidents, 23 bankers, and numerous merchants, manufacturers, teachers, farmers, real estate men, doctors, and insurance men—a representative slice of the churchgoing Protestant elites. Following days of routine business, the convention suddenly caught fire when Christian China seemed to materialize before its eyes. Here was the scene, reported by a church newspaper, as two Chinese Christians stepped to the dais:

> It was a thrilling moment when these leaders from far-off China stood before their brethren. . . . Patriotism and Christianity met and flowed on together, gathering power until the entire conference was upon its feet, cheering, shouting, and waving handkerchiefs. Hearts swelled and eyes grew dim as, in the midst of Dr. Wang's speech, someone started "My Country 'Tis of Thee." How the great anthem bellowed and surged throughout the auditorium. The first republic and the last joined hearts and voices in a mighty burst of patriotic fervor as the audience rose to its feet and sang, as only Methodists can sing, "Sweet Land of Liberty."

For all its hokum, the incident tells us something about the inner meaning of Christian China. Note the fusion of religion and national identity: "Patriotism and Christianity met and flowed on together." Note also the vision of transpacific innocence: "The first republic and the last joined hearts and voices." In the Methodist universe, Christian China occupied a central place.[47]

The Missionary Mind and Social Action. The idea of Christian China can be seen to have enjoyed a national following. At every level of society, and in virtually every community, there were people who cared about China. Now the Missionary Mind, though often quite intelligent, following Chinese affairs closely, in its way, was also characteristically gullible; and grasping at straws was not unknown. Large numbers of Protestant Americans wanted very badly to believe. During 1913, for example, many people seemed ready to believe just about anything that might take their minds off the white-slave traffic thought to be sweeping the big cities. Whatever the psychological foundations, the Missionary Mind of Protestant America in April of that year allowed itself to be swept away by an unwarranted euphoria regarding Chinese developments. The episode affords the opportunity to observe the Missionary Mind in action on a national and international scale.[48]

On April 17, Chinese President Yuan Shih-k'ai issued an appeal to the small body of Chinese Protestants to pray for him and his regime on Sunday, April 27. Yuan Shih-k'ai, who was not a Christian man, was nevertheless familiar with political calculus, so that seasoned interpreters naturally viewed his move as a means to manipulate American public opinion. Old China hands, those habitually jaundiced observers, expressed grudging appreciation. Dismissing Yuan's action as "arrant humbug" and "a piece of perfectly gratuitous hypocrisy," the leading British resident of Tientsin saw reason to worry about his American friends. "How the wily Chinaman must be laughing up his sleeve," wrote William McLeish to former Harvard President Charles W. Eliot, "at the easy gullibility of pious America."[49]

Still, the appeal for prayer caused considerable excitement in the United States. On April 17, the Associated Press bureau chief in Peking cabled the news home, where editors, presumably recognizing good copy, placed it on page one. When newspaper readers opened their papers on April 18, they saw headlines reading "China Asks for Prayers," and, reading on, they learned that Yuan's message represented "striking evidence of the extraordinary changes which have taken place in the nation since the revolution." Even the uninnocent *New York Times* carried the story on the front page. Perhaps ironically, the good news from China arrived at a time of acute tension in American-Japanese relations. As the Japanese were threatening to lodge formal protest over a bill in the California Legislature expropriating the lands of Japanese farmers, the Chinese were readying themselves for prayer.[50]

The matter of prayer came up first thing at the President's Cabinet meeting that morning. As described by Josephus Daniels, the meeting began with Secretary of State Bryan reading aloud the AP despatch in the *Washington Post* and remarking (even though the Department had yet to receive word of the matter) that Yuan's appeal represented "the most remarkable official document that had been issued in a generation." President Wilson, a regular correspondent of several China missionaries, emphasized that "he did not know when he had been so stirred and cheered as when he read that message in the paper." Wilson said he had considered asking the American churches to join the Chinese churches in prayer but had decided that the separation of church and state rendered this course unwise. Only Secretary Redfield of the Commerce Department, of those present at the Cabinet meeting, appeared to express a measure of skepticism. But the President considered that "we ought to accept the official appeal of wishing the prayers of Christians as honest and earnest and join with the Christian people in China in praying for the peaceful organization of the republic of China." Daniels himself, who as Secretary of the Navy forbade liquor in the officers' mess, reminded his colleagues that "faith without works is dead."[51]

Later, Bryan cabled the Chargé in Peking requesting details. The following morning, E.T. Williams, former China missionary, cabled back the text of Yuan's appeal but did not otherwise comment. The Secretary then relayed Williams's cable to the Protestant mission boards (the Catholic hierarchy was not informed). Next day, the Federal Council of Churches sent out the message to the 150,000 Protestant churches, asking them to hold religious services for China on Sunday, April 27.[52]

For a week, the news received wide notice, especially in religious newspapers. The Chicago *Advance* (Congregational), the Cleveland *Evangelical Messenger* (Evangelical), the Philadelphia *Christian Instructor* (Presbyterian), the Boston *Watchman Examiner* (Baptist), and other church papers gave the story full play. The influential *Christian Herald,* a nondenominational paper edited in New York, interpreted Yuan's move as a world-historical event: "It reminds one of the act of Constantine that made Christianity the religion of the great Roman Empire and the sign of the Cross the banner of its imperial legions, or of the zeal of Charlemagne in subjecting pagan nations to the yoke of Christ." The matter also received continuing coverage and editorial comment in major metropolitan dailies such as the *New York Evening Mail* and the *New York Tribune.* "In fact," the *Literary Digest* reported, "the incident seems to hold scarcely less interest for the lay press than for the religious press."[53]

On Sunday, April 27, Americans prayed. As reported in the *New York Times,* special services for China took place at churches all over the city and throughout the United States. Even though, as the *Times* reported, there was no sign of Christian prayer along Mott Street in Chinatown, other Americans did indeed seem to be praying. From Salem, Oregon, a woman wrote: "We held a little prayer meeting after the regular morning service in the Presbyterian church and asked that China would have guidance, direction, and discernment given her at this critical time of her existence as a nation." At the First Congregational Church in Berkeley, California, the minister intoned:

> Almighty God, Ruler of Nations, who has made of one blood every nation of men, and who hast promised to draw all men unto thyself, we thank thee to-day that thou hast drawn to thee the hearts of men across the sea. . . . We remember, O Lord, the noble army of martyrs who gave their full measure of devotion that the people of China might be emancipated from superstition. . . . We pray thee, O Lord, to give to China a new freedom, with which the political freedom so recently attained is not to be compared, even the freedom with which Christ shall make her free. Grant to the citizens of this sister republic a unity of spirit previously unknown amid her provincial isolations and sectional jealousies. Give to her lawmakers a vision of the kingdom as a pattern for the temple they are building.[54]

Yet Secretary Bryan, of all people, missed church, for he was traveling that Sunday on the Overland Limited, going to the Coast to confer with California Governor Hiram Johnson on the anti-Japanese legislation mentioned above. In his address to the California Legislature that Monday, Bryan reminded his listeners that the bill also affected Chinese, for whose eternal salvation they had prayed the day before.[55]

Elsewhere in America, Catholics also prayed that Sunday for a foreign prince—Pope Pius X. At Sunday Mass, Roman Catholics listened to the most recent Apostolic Letter issuing from the Holy See. The day of prayer for Christian China seemed to pass unnoticed and unobserved in Catholic America. Roman Catholics made no novena for the Chinese Republic and celebrated no solemn Te Deum for Yuan Shih-k'ai. Like other outsiders, they inhabited a different moral universe.[56]

Presumably, Protestants said millions of prayers for China on April 27, 1913. Yet what happened that day was unusual only in one respect, that it was a national happening; as a local occurrence praying for China took place all the time. John R. Mott prayed; Bishop Bashford and other China missionaries did a great deal of praying, as did the people in the American churches; they prayed when the missionary came around, prayed when the mission committee made its report, prayed on Mission Sunday; the Methodists prayed at Minneapolis, the Student Volunteers prayed at Kansas City; 5 million adults making financial contributions must have remembered China in their prayers; in Madison, New Jersey, people prayed, and one may suppose they even prayed at "The World in Chicago." The fact seems to be that, during the years 1911 to 1915 at least, Christian prayer was the principal American activity regarding East Asia. Understanding this, the historian can begin to appreciate why Americans characteristically responded to problems in East Asia policy with "expressions of feeling rather than contributions to the discussion."

Yet there were also interests in Asia of another kind.

TWO

The Business Mind

Men doing business with Asia did not, as a rule, have missionary minds. Concerned with the markets of Asia rather than the soul of Asia, businessmen measured the meaning of the East in bales of raw cotton, barrels of kerosene, bolts of unbleached cotton cloth, and the daily quotations for East Asian government securities on the New York bond market. Though a few businessmen were also religious activists whose interest in East Asia transcended the material, most traders, investment bankers, and corporation executives confined themselves to business affairs. They were in it for the money: thus the business mind held attitudes toward China and Japan markedly different from the perspectives common in the Protestant religious community.

Unlike the missionary-minded, businessmen regarded Japan as the most promising part of the East Asia and Pacific region, and the difference is illuminating.

AMERICAN INTERESTS: THE MATERIAL VIEW

In every area of economic activity—trade, direct investment, and indirect (or portfolio) investment—Japan was more important than China to most American businessmen. No doubt a major reason was that Japan was well on its way to becoming a major industrial nation, with modernization multiplying business link-ages to America.

Trade. Between 1911 and 1915, the Japan trade boomed while the China trade remained relatively flat and generally two or three times smaller, as Table 5 illustrates:

TABLE 5 United States Trade with China and Japan, 1911-1915
(millions of dollars)

Year	China		Japan	
	Exports	*Imports*	*Exports*	*Imports*
1911	19	34	37	79
1912	24	29	53	81
1913	21	39	58	92
1914	25	39	51	107
1915	16	40	42	99

Source: U.S. Department of Commerce, Bureau of Foreign and Domestic Commerce, *Statistical Abstract of the United States, 1915* (Washington, D.C., 1916), pp. 254, 352.

Though both trades tended to expand until 1914, when World War I created unsettled business conditions, expansion was most marked in the case of Japan. American exports to Japan increased by more than 50 percent between 1911 and 1913. The curve of exports to China rose more modestly, the dollar value of the peak year, 1914, standing only $6 million higher than in 1911. It may be notable that American exports to Africa were more valuable than those to China for every year of the period.[1]

The characteristics of American trade with East Asia remained much as they had been for some years: merchandise traveling mostly in foreign bottoms, principally Japanese; commerce being asymmetrical, the United States purchasing much more, generally two times more, than it sold; items of exchange remaining largely agricultural, the United States taking Japanese silk and Chinese teas in return for the traditional, rather basic, commodities. Principal articles of export to China were cotton cloth, illuminating oil, tobacco, and wheat flour; those to Japan were raw cotton, wheat flour, illuminating oil, and machinery.[2]

Yet certain features of the East Asia trades may be worthy of comment. For example, it may be noted that Japan relied much more heavily on trade with the United States than China did. In 1914, the United States accounted for 16 percent of Japan's imports and 34 percent of her exports, but only 7 percent of China's imports and 12 percent of exports. Japanese exports to America reached $107 million in the peak year, 1914. Beginning in 1912, the United States ranked as Japan's principal trading partner, a condition that did not go unnoticed among American businessmen, diplomats, and Commerce Department officials.[3]

Moreover, Japan provided a market, small but growing, for industrial goods. Japan's drive to become the industrial equal of the modern West continued apace and with it an expanding demand for industrial products. American exports to Asia generally consisted of consumer goods and raw materials: in 1914, consumer goods accounted for 54 percent of American exports, raw materials for 27 percent, foodstuffs for 13 percent. Capital goods, amounting to 6 percent, went mostly to Japan. In 1913, Japan purchased $3.5 million of engines and machinery—a 300 percent increase in two years. Among those expecting the trend to continue were Thomas Sammons, then American Consul-General in Yokohama.[4]

Finally, it may be instructive to note a development in the fabled China market: the effective decimation of the once-flourishing trade in American cotton cloth and cotton piece goods to Manchuria. Though the other segments of the China market tended to be fairly stable—the trade in kerosene fluctuated between $4 million and $6 million, and the tobacco trade was reasonably reliable—the market for cotton cloth, almost all of the latter destined for Manchuria, was different (see Table 6). Now the cotton-cloth market had been in trouble for some years, the decline beginning soon after the Russo-Japanese War. Unbleached cotton cloth, in particular, had grown heavily dependent

TABLE 6 Total American Sales of Cotton Cloth to China,
1911–1915

(millions of dollars)

Year	
1911	7.6
1912	4.6
1913	8.0
1914	2.8
1915	1.4

Source: *Journal of the American Asiatic Association,* XIII (March 1913), 35; ibid., XIV (March 1914), 35; ibid., XVI (March 1916), 35.

on Manchurian markets. In 1911, Manchuria absorbed nearly one-half the total American exports of that commodity, generating over $7 million in sales—more than one-third the total value of American exports to China. In 1912, revolutionary disturbances contributed to an overall decline in sales, which dipped to $4.6 million, and, though the return of order led to temporary recovery in 1913, the following year sales came to only $2.8 million and in 1915 to a mere $1.4 million. Americans had lost the Manchurian market forever, to the Japanese.[5]

The causes were basically economic. While it is true that the Japanese were the preponderant power in southern Manchuria and that the South Manchuria Railway gave preferential rates to Japanese goods, a combination of circumstances perhaps naturally productive of bitterness among certain mill-owners in New England and the South, prominent import-export men in New York and Shanghai gave credit where it was due—Japanese business acumen. An editorial in the *Journal of the American Asiatic Association,* the principal business periodical specializing in East Asia, correctly blamed the "apathy of American mill owners in failing to adapt their goods to the new demands of the Chinese markets." One might add that the American trade tended to be inefficient. Americans milled cloth in South Carolina and elsewhere; shipped it to Shanghai, where it was consigned to foreign agents; the latter transshipped the goods to Manchuria, where they were sold to yet another set of merchants; and so on. The Japanese, often using American cotton, milled in Manchuria and sold direct. Yet, though unable to compete with the Japanese in Manchuria, American textile manufacturers recouped their China losses in the Philippines and other markets, so that their overall export picture remained healthy.[6]

The Manchurian disaster seemed to deepen the conviction of American businessmen that, just as the future of American trade lay with Japan more than with China, any dramatic expansion of China's foreign trade would, in the first instance, likely benefit the Japanese. "It is not to be expected," observed William C. Redfield, a New York businessman and future Secretary of Commerce, in 1912, "that they [the Japanese] will fail to supply the great China market with cotton goods and with everything else they are able to take to a market which they understand better than anybody else and which is just across the road from their own mills."[7]

Direct Investment. Japan was acquiring significance in this financial area. In 1914, the only year for which reliable American estimates are available, direct capital investment in Japan seems to have totaled about $58 million (as compared with $42 million in China). Unlike American investments in China, which were largely mercantile and seemingly contained limited growth potential, investments in Japan promised a future as bright as that of the Japanese industrial economy.[8]

If China held out few investment prospects for Americans, these limitations presumably derived largely from the underdeveloped nature of the Chinese economy. The steps taken by China in the direction of economic modernization during these years, however dramatic by comparison with the traditional Chinese economy, obviously did not suffice to make China a modern country. Continuing economic backwardness functioned as a drag on investment opportunity.[9]

Such investment opportunities as China offered, moreover, seemingly had been snapped up already by other foreign nations. Compared with those of the major Treaty Powers, American investments in China were quite modest. In fact, American investment in mission property accounted for almost one-quarter of the total figure of $42 million, in comparison with German investments six times that size and British capital investments well in excess of £100 million sterling. In 1914, American capital represented only 3 percent of foreign investment in China. Since nearly three-quarters of American investments were located in the International Settlement at Shanghai, where British interests, financial and otherwise, enjoyed dominion, the American stake in China may be regarded as essentially a protectorate or subsidiary of the British presence.[10]

The character of American enterprise in China also seemed to limit its growth potential. American capital investments largely took the form of trading houses and sales organizations. Though some few of these were efficient organizations, particularly Standard Oil, which used up-to-date marketing techniques to supply oil for the lamps of China, and British-American Tobacco, which distributed cigarettes to Chinese villagers, most of the 130 or so firms appeared to suffer from lack of modern managerial expertise. Moreover, American businessmen generally lacked the credit and banking facilities necessary for expansion into economic sectors beyond foreign commerce. Though the International Banking Corporation maintained branches at Shanghai and other treaty ports, its capabilities were restricted to currency exchange and commercial paper, so that any sophisticated transaction had to go through one of the great foreign banking houses in Shanghai—the Deutsche-Asiatische Bank, the Yokohama Specie Bank, or the Hong Kong and Shanghai Banking Corporation. The absence of a full-service American financial institution inhibited growth of American investments, which remained primarily mercantile.[11]

American investments in Japan were of a somewhat different order. Though the total of $58 million was not yet astronomical, much investment was industrial or in sectors directly related to the industrial economy.[12]

Already a number of American multinational corporations

maintained important subsidiaries in Japan. American capital and technology were particularly prominent in the electric utility industry. Of the multinationals, General Electric appears to have invested most heavily in Japan. After 1905, G.E. enjoyed effective control of Tokyo Electric and in 1910 acquired comparable power over Shibaura Electric; the company also had substantial interest in Nihon Electric. Westinghouse also participated in joint ventures with Japanese, as did Western Electric, whose controlling interest in Nippon Electric led to close relations with Mitsui and Company.[13]

Though perhaps less romantic than oil for the lamps of China, electric power for the homes, streets, subways, and factories of modern Japan illuminated vistas of future business opportunity for Americans. G.E. President Charles Coffin, a frequent traveler to Japan, often made the case for U.S. investment in the Japanese industrial economy. The manager of the Yokohama Specie Bank's New York branch also solicited American investment capital. In a 1911 speech, R. Ichinomiya called for additional joint ventures based upon "cooperation of the Western manufacturers and Japanese merchants, the Western manufacturers attending to the productive end and the Japanese to the selling end of the business."[14]

Japan, in sum, appeared to offer American businessmen a favorable investment climate. The rapid modernization of the economy, the favorable political environment, the record of business success—these augured well for the future of Japanese markets.[15]

Portfolio Investment. Japan's primary economic importance to the United States lay in the area of portfolio investments. Between 1905 and 1915, American investment bankers lent a total of $197 million to East Asian governments. For all the vigorous efforts of the Taft Administration to promote loans to China, almost all this capital was invested in Japan.[16]

Left to their own devices, American bankers were reluctant to lend money to the Chinese. It made little business sense. In a country that remained an international debtor (the United States, that is) down to the Anglo-French loan in late 1915, the investing public was generally unused to purchasing foreign securities, and banking houses therefore proceeded with due caution. Under normal circumstances, China was among the last places on earth a prudent American investor wanted to place his capital. He usually could get a higher interest yield elsewhere, and at much lower risk. As Willard Straight of J.P. Morgan and Company expressed the matter to Paul Reinsch, American Minister to Peking, in 1914: "As you will appreciate, the man in the street regards China as a heathen land, full of revolutions and capable of defaulting on its bonds." Ordinarily, investors would not purchase such obligations unless secured by Chinese government revenues, preferably collected by foreigners backed by the diplomatic muscle of the Treaty Powers. But, in other ways, these complications made Chinese finance seem even less attractive to American bankers, for they entailed lengthy negotiations in Peking and Europe, and in the end the deal could easily fall through for reasons of international politics. Signed, sealed, and delivered, such an arrangement still was unlikely to be very profitable, owing to the cost of financial representation in Europe and Peking and the heavy cable traffic. It was a messy business, all and all, which American bankers generally preferred to avoid.[17]

Nevertheless, in 1909, at the request of the Department of State, J.P. Morgan and Company, Kuhn, Loeb, and Company, the First National Bank, and the National City Bank, all of New York, pooled their resources to form the so-called American Group, and Willard Straight left State's Far East Division to become the Group's chief negotiator in Peking. In 1910, the Department secured the admission of the Group to the consortium controlling Chinese finance. Henry P. Davison of Morgan, responsible for the Group's affairs in Europe, studied up on China in preparation for his first serious international negotiating. The American Group was from first to last an artificial financial instrument, called into being by the State Department because it would not have materialized on its own, which served the Republican Administration out of motives that Secretary Knox never tired of describing as basically "patriotic." Its relations with the Department were never wholly smooth, there was considerable friction among its members, and, perhaps not least, it was a business failure. In 1912, the *New York Times* reported that the American Group had so far failed to turn a penny of profit.[18]

The various projects advanced by the Department of State for American Group participation—the Hukuang loan, the loan relating to the proposed railway from Chinchow to Aigun in Manchuria, the currency-reform loan, and the reorganization loan requested by the Chinese Republican regime in 1912—generated much paper and consumed no little time and energy, but produced very little. "Up to the present time the results have been largely confined to literature and oratory," wrote Willard Straight in a Christmas greeting to President Taft in 1912. "I trust that some day we shall have something to show besides 'hot air' and hope." At that time the Chin-Ai loan, together with the Knox neutralization scheme of which it formed the financial centerpiece, had long since been abandoned, and the currency-reform loan had been consolidated with the reorganization loan (the so-called Six-Power loan for £60 million sterling), the negotiations for which were still in progress. The only tangible achievement was the American Group's share of the Hukuang loan, a mere $7 million, issued in New York in 1911. President Wilson's decision, in March 1913, to withdraw diplomatic support from the American Group terminated American participation in the Six-Power loan.[19]

Wall Street then resumed its instinctive attitude toward China. "It is doubtful," observed the *Journal of the American Asiatic Association* in the summer of 1913, "if a Chinese loan could be issued successfully in New York." In the following years, the financial climate remained unfavorable.[20]

This brought considerable vexation to Paul Reinsch who, as Minister from 1913 to 1919, tried hard to stimulate American investment in China.[21] The year 1914 provided Reinsch with several frustrating illustrations of how very little Wall Street cared about China. Early that year, through Reinsch's good offices, the American Red Cross obtained a one-year option on a river-conservation project, the Huai River Conservancy. Having spent hundreds of thousands of dollars on China famine relief, the Red Cross proceeded with some enthusiasm, hiring a reputable New York engineering firm, J.G. White and Company, and moving to raise a $20 million loan for the construction work. But the investment bankers refused to underwrite, and, when Reinsch approached the House of Morgan for an explanation, Willard Straight replied that "the willingness of bankers to undertake commitments of this sort is very largely dependent upon confidence in their ability to dispose of bonds when purchased." And so, he concluded, "much as I should like to see some of our great banking houses take a chance and enter the Chinese field, this appeals to my sense of adventure rather than to my business judgment."[22]

Another of Reinsch's projects, this one involving Standard Oil, also languished. Through the skilled negotiating of W. E. Bemis, company Vice President responsible for marketing kerosene in China, Standard entered into a joint venture whereby it acquired petroleum drilling rights in Chili and Shansi. However, the arrangement was contingent upon the successful multimillion-dollar issue in New York of unsecured long-term Chinese government obligations. "If the Standard Oil Company has had the confidence to go into China," Bemis asked, "why do not our bankers put their money into the country?" In the end the deal fell through for various reasons, high among them Wall Street's continued unwillingness to fish in the troubled waters of Chinese finance. In a personal letter to President Wilson, Reinsch remarked on the American financial community's "indifference and hostility." The banking houses of the old American Group," he wrote, "cultivate a general pessimism with respect to American interests in China."[23]

By that time, when the $7 million Hukuang loan was the only Chinese obligation to which the investing public had ever subscribed, Americans had purchased $190 million in Japanese bonds. Because of investor confidence in the soundness of the Japanese economy and in the willingness of Japanese governments to satisfy their bondholders, new issues floated in New York found underwriters quickly, went fast in public offering, and were subscribed many times over. The forging of strong financial links between New York and Tokyo resulted primarily from natural economic forces. Requiring no prodding from the Department of State, no humiliating hypothecation of Japanese revenues, and no threat of force on the part of Treaty Powers, and therefore perhaps lacking the high drama of dollar diplomacy, this was a business development of first importance.[24]

American financial interest in Japan began during the Russo-Japanese War when, through the efforts of Jacob Schiff of Kuhn, Loeb and Company, Wall Street undertook to finance a sizeable portion of the Japanese military effort. Following the conflict, Japan entered on a period of rapid industrialization, necessitating continued heavy borrowing overseas. The outstanding war debt of £82 million sterling, along with additional debt issues to finance the burgeoning industrial sector, made Japan a major player in Western credit markets. New York, though not yet fully come of age as a financial center, was already sharing in the profits of Japanese modernization.[25]

These portfolio investments consisted primarily of four series of Japanese government obligations issued originally in New York in 1904–1905 (and later refunded), and an issue of Tokyo municipal bonds offered during 1912. Kuhn, Loeb, the National City Bank, and the First National Bank did most of the underwriting and ranked as the leading institutional investors. Individual investors also found these securities attractive. In 1912, for example, though money was tight, the investing public snapped up $10 million in Tokyo bonds within a few days. Maturing forty years after date of issue, Japanese obligations had attractive coupons: two series worth a total of $55 million yielded 6 percent, one series totaling $10 million carried a 5 percent yield, and two series valued at $125 million altogether bore interest at 4 percent. The total interest payments exceeded $9 million per year, a considerable sum. To appreciate its magnitude, compare $9 million in profit on Japanese government obligations with the total value of American exports to China, which fluctuated between $16 million and $25 million. Assuming the China trade operated on a modest

profit margin, as its highly competitive nature would suggest—say
10 percent—one is led to conclude that interest on Japanese bonds
probably was several times more valuable.[26]

In finance, as in direct investment and trade, the material relations between the United States and East Asia remained at
bottom the story of Japanese preponderance.

THE SIGNIFICANCE OF AMERICAN INTERESTS

In overseas trade and investment, Canada, Europe, and Latin
America were more important to the American economy than was
East Asia. From this fact, at least one writer on American East
Asia policy has concluded that East Asia was a region of "insignificant value."[27] Close examination, however, reveals that such
a view is misleading, for American interests were effectively more
important than they may appear.

The Economic Significance. The movement of goods across the
Pacific accounted for only a fraction of America's foreign trade
(see Table 7):

TABLE 7 American Exports by Geographical Destination, 1911–
1915

(% of total dollar value of exports)

Region	Year				
	1911	*1912*	*1913*	*1914*	*1915*
Europe	64	61	60	63	71
North America	22	23	25	22	17
Latin America	13	13	13	12	9
Asia	4	5	5	5	4

Source: U.S. Department of Commerce, Bureau of Foreign and Domestic Commerce,
Statistical Abstract of the United States, 1915 (Washington, D.C., 1916), p. 365.

The value of American exports rose from $2 billion in 1911
to $2.8 billion in 1915, of which Asian customers purchased
between 4 and 5 percent, China usually buying approximately
1 percent and Japan about 2 percent. The peak year, 1913,

saw combined sales to China and Japan totaling $79 million—slightly more than 3 percent of all exports, which that year reached $2.5 billion. So, from the grossest perspective, Asian commerce made little contribution.[28]

Yet it was of no small importance to the great port cities of the Pacific Coast, for San Francisco, Portland, and the Puget Sound cities, especially Seattle and Tacoma, depended heavily on foreign trade. In 1915, $23 million in trade passed through the port of Portland, $136 million through the Puget Sound ports, and $158 million through the port of San Francisco. The bulk of American commerce with China and Japan went through these ports.[29]

East Asia being vital to their commercial prosperity, it is not surprising that trade associations and other business-oriented groups on the Coast accorded China and Japan their sustained attention. This was particularly true in the Bay area, where, in its weekly business luncheons at the Palace, the Commonwealth Club often heard from experts on Asia, and where the Chamber of Commerce, most important commercial body on the Pacific Coast, maintained a Committee on Foreign Trade specializing in the Orient. The President of this Committee, Captain Robert Dollar, the most prominent local merchant trading to Asia, could, from his office on the fourteenth floor of the Merchants' Exchange, of which he was also head, look out, after the fog burned off, on a harbor fairly bustling with Oriental commerce. In 1912, for example, Japan accounted for $24 million in imports, a figure three times larger than that for any Western country; and exports to Japan stood at $12 million, several times more valuable than those to any other nation (exports to China being worth around $1 million).[30]

Intercourse with Asia mattered significantly to Portland, center of the flourishing trade in wheat and wheat flour, and to the Puget Sound ports, which together handled an even larger volume of such trade than San Francisco. Of all American cities, Seattle enjoyed the closest commercial relations with Japan. Japanese businessmen were there on the spot, in force, to facilitate business transactions (Seattle had the largest Japanese community in the country). In 1909, a party of prominent Japanese businessmen, headed by the financier Shibusawa Eiichi, conducted a trade mission to Seattle, and a group of Seattle businessmen later paid a return visit. The Seattle Chamber of Commerce, which maintained ties with the Chamber in San Francisco, followed Asian developments closely. With Japanese merchant vessels dominating the sea lanes of the Sound, and cargoes for Japan piling high on the docks along Alaskan Way, Seattle businessmen naturally regarded Japan as possessing considerable economic promise. "The large trade that is being built up between the Orient and Puget Sound ports," observed a Seattle despatch to the *New York Times* in 1911, "has inclined merchants here to favor closer relations with Japan." There, as elsewhere on the Coast, trade with Asia, though relatively inconsequential to the nation at large, was of great local significance.[31]

Moreover, a number of commodities of some importance to the American economy depended on East Asian trade. Unbleached cotton cloth, kerosene, and raw cotton, products heavily reliant on export, had important markets in the East. With respect to unbleached cloth, in 1911, China absorbed more than one-half the total exports and, by 1915, still accounted for over 10 percent. Standard Oil of New York sold nearly one-third of its total exports of kerosene to Asian customers. Under the direction of W.E. Bemis (China), and of R.H. McNall, who performed the same marketing function for Japan, millions of barrels went out every year. In 1912, Standard sold $4.5 million to Japan and $4 million to China, and, though the figures fluctuated from year to year, Oriental sales of kerosene usually generated about 30 percent of the company's export earnings.[32]

Approximately one-half the total American exports to Japan consisted of cotton, so essential to the economic well-being of the South. In 1912, raw cotton sales produced $32 million of the $53 million in exports to Japan, nearly 10 percent of total foreign sales. The cotton trade was booming, as was the trade in silk. Though an import rather than an export, it is notable that Japanese silk supplied around three-quarters of the American market. Generally accounting for about two-thirds of American imports from Japan—$68 million out of $107 million in 1914—raw silk was destined for the garment district in New York. Silk, cotton, unbleached cloth, illuminating oil—such were the ties that bind.[33]

And, just as trading relations were of greater concrete significance than might be supposed, so capital investments, whether of the direct or portfolio kind, were not without value (see Table 8):

TABLE 8 Total American Direct Capital Investments by
Geographical Areas, 1914
(millions of dollars)

Area	
Canada	$618
Mexico	587
Europe	573
South America	323
Asia	120
Africa	13

Source: Mira Wilkins, *The Emergence of Multinational Enterprise: American Business Abroad from the Colonial Era to 1914* (Cambridge, Mass., 1970), p. 110.

China and Japan together accounted for $100 million of the Asian sum, or a modest 2.7 percent of the world total. Yet it is noteworthy that this sum amounted to one-sixth the figure for Canada and nearly one-third that for South America. And it may be instructive to recall certain of the corporate players: Standard Oil, British-American Tobacco, the International Banking Corporation, General Electric, and Westinghouse—leading multinationals.[34]

Yet, Asia's principal value to America was probably in the area of portfolio investments. The New York Stock Exchange in 1914 listed around a dozen foreign government obligations, of which five were East Asian. Their face value, as noted earlier, was $197 million. Mira Wilkins has estimated that Americans held $900 million of foreign bonds in 1914. Simple arithmetic, therefore, tells us that Asia accounted for around 22 percent of the total overseas portfolio, China about 1 percent and Japan approximately

21 percent. Kuhn, Loeb, and Company possessed greater holdings of Japanese government obligations than of all other foreign securities combined.[35]

Nearly one-quarter of Wall Street's overseas portfolio; the interests of major multinational corporations; trade that was vital to the Pacific Coast—these material relations were not altogether insignificant.

The Political Significance. As their economic importance might suggest, these business interests enjoyed a certain access to the levers of power. It is possible to estimate the size of this interest group. Most businessmen occupied primarily with Asian trade or investment seemed to be located in the following cities: Boston, New York, the Puget Sound ports, Portland, San Francisco, Yokohama, or Shanghai. In the American community at Shanghai, numbering 1,200, around 120 were businessmen. So, if the same proportion, one in ten, obtained at other treaty ports where there were sizeable concentrations of Americans, the total American business community in China probably numbered about 200. A roughly comparable situation existed in Japan, with around 100 businessmen in the Yokohama area and smaller groups at Kobe and elsewhere. So perhaps 200 would be a reasonable figure for Japan as well. Though lacking figures on Pacific Coast merchants, the historian may safely surmise that the number of merchants required to handle the trade at the Coast would not have been less than the number so occupied in East Asia. This assumption yields a minimum of approximately 400, and, if the numbers for each city reflected the dollar value of trade, one would expect the largest concentration in the Puget Sound ports, a somewhat smaller group in San Francisco, and a much smaller group in Portland. Perhaps it would be safe to estimate 200 for Seattle, 50 for Portland, and 150 for San Francisco. Fixing the size for Boston and New York also involves a measure of guesswork. Though no Boston statistics are readily available, it would appear certain that the number trading to Asia could not have exceeded the 50 in Portland, and two dozen may be more likely for this declining mercantile community. And for New York, the membership rolls of the American Asiatic Association list around 200 names. All in all, our survey yields a total census somewhat in excess of 1,000, and though this probably is slightly conservative— the actual figures for the West Coast may well have been larger, and there doubtless were a certain number outside the major centers—it probably would strain credulity to imagine that the group was more than twice this size. One may, therefore, reasonably conclude that the business community vitally interested in Asia numbered between 1,000 and 2,000 persons.[36]

These persons, though obviously a tiny minority, apparently alerted the wider business community to the significance of American interests in East Asia. Perhaps their success derived in part from their strategic location. No thin layer spread across the continent, men doing business with Asia were concentrated in a handful of cities which thereby acquired, or seemed to acquire, a certain regard for Asia. It is notable that newspapers and journals thought to be read by businessmen in those cities paid attention to American interests in China and Japan. One would expect to find this at the Coast, where newspapers attuned to the needs of local businessmen, notably the *San Francisco Chronicle* and the *Seattle Times,* in fact expressed no little concern. Yet, one also discovers this in Boston and New York. The *Boston Transcript,* a newspaper known for its sophisticated coverage of business and finance, was sensible of the New England textile industry's interest in Oriental markets, a subject discussed from time to time on the editorial page, as in a 1915 account of America's "very substantial interests in China's trade." In New York, the influential *Journal of Commerce,* object of a careful study by Paul Varg, gave substantial news coverage and made editorial comment on East Asian topics. The editor of *Bankers' Magazine,* Charles Conant, concerned himself with East Asia, as did the business section of the *New York Times.* Important developments in Asian finance, moreover, might be found on that paper's front pages, and editorials were not unknown. A 1915 editorial, for example, argued that "our Far Eastern trade must be protected, as it is too important to the whole country, including California, to be given up." Whether in

New York, Boston, or on the Coast, such sentiments appeared to reflect the local presence of prominent businessmen materially involved with East Asia.[37]

For such businessmen did not lack prominence in their local communities. They were well organized. Those in the Pacific Coast ports looked to the local Chambers of Commerce for protection and advancement of their interests. Those in New York, Boston, and elsewhere on the East Coast joined the American Asiatic Association, reputedly one of the most powerful commercial organizations anywhere, enjoying close relations with the Merchants' Association, the American Manufacturers' Export Association, the New York Chamber of Commerce, and other influential groups within the elite world of New York business. To facilitate the flow of useful information, the Association published its authoritative monthly *Journal.* It sponsored sumptuous banquets at Delmonico's and a luncheon club called India House in Hanover Square, halfway between the trading houses along the East River and the counting houses of Wall Street. It also maintained continuous communication with the leading American commercial bodies in East Asia, the American Association of China (at Shanghai) and the American Association of Japan (Yokohama).[38]

As is perhaps instinctive with such groups, the Pacific Coast Chambers and the Asiatic Association discovered the road to Washington. But their roads were different and, owing to their immense geographical distance from the nation's capital, four days by train, the West Coast Chambers seemed somewhat less skilled at the game of political influence. So, to compensate for their relative lack of Washington connections, they hired a lobbyist. It requires little imagination to visualize how a visit from him or a letter from the Chamber at Seattle, Portland, or San Francisco could work a certain effect on a West Coast Senator or Representative. Back East, the Asiatic Association moved even more comfortably through the corridors of power. Knowing the ways of Washington, as befitted a group including James R. Morse of the American Trading Company, Silas Webb of the China and Japan Trading Company, Frank Vanderlip of the National City Bank,

Jacob Schiff of Kuhn, Loeb, and J.P. Morgan, Jr., the Asiatic Association routinely despatched men of substance when circumstances seemed to warrant. During the Taft Administration, however, this was not necessary, for policy-makers came to them: among State Department officials maintaining regular membership were Willard Straight, William Phillips, and Francis M. Huntington Wilson. And, though relations with the Wilson Administration were rather less cozy, even Secretary Bryan felt obliged to address one of those richly liquored dinners at Delmonico's.[39]

Groups with this kind of political savvy, and interests of the importance described, deserve better from the historian than to be dismissed as of "insignificant value." A look into the deep structure of American interests in East Asia suggests that they were vitally important to certain cities, certain industries, certain corporations. And, just because they involved powerful groups and prominent individuals, they acquired political significance. Though doubtless less important than American interests in Europe, Canada, or Latin America, they were too important in themselves to be ignored.

ASIA AND THE BUSINESS COMMUNITY

The mind of the business community differed markedly from the Missionary Mind. Though one can perhaps too easily underestimate its reserves of sentiment, the business mind was generally straightforward and realistic. Though perhaps not exactly subtle, the commercial mentality deserves brief treatment here, if only to suggest a contrast with the views of hinterland Protestants.

Business Attitudes toward China. Certain business views may be surprising. For example, it appears that businessmen, at least in their sober moments, expressed a certain amount of skepticism about the legendary China market. "It is a common expression used of China in speaking of it commercially that that country is the world's greatest market," observed a leading import-export man in the *New York Times*'s Annual Review of Business in 1910.

"That is quite true in prospect. Meanwhile, something is the matter with trade there."[40]

It is true that what Paul Varg has called "the Myth of the China Market" enjoyed a certain currency in some sections of the business community. No doubt some persons did continue to dream about those 400 million customers. In 1913, the American Manufacturers' Export Association invited Paul Reinsch to address their annual convention "on the topic of commercial interests and possibilities in China," just as, in 1915, a prominent Richmond businessman wrote his Virginia Congressman that China represented "the most valuable field in the world which we now have the opportunity of developing." But talk of this kind, whatever it had been earlier, now seemed relatively unusual: periodical literature featured only a handful of articles on the China market, most of them modest. And men actually doing business with China appeared to cultivate a pronounced restraint. In 1914, the *Journal of the American Asiatic Association* called attention to a statement appearing in some business publication to the effect that China offered "many wonderful opportunities . . . for increased American trade." Noting that such rhetoric was "calculated to bring a smile to the countenance of the Old China Hand," if only because the trade itself "shows no sign of boom," the *Journal* remarked those "'many wonderful opportunities' which seem to be most apparent to those who know least about them."[41]

This calculated pessimism seemed to color the business view of Chinese affairs generally. The attitude of old China hands, in particular, toward China and the Chinese usually reflected the semicolonial cast of mind of their British counterparts. Parroting their jaundiced judgments, aping their treaty-port manners, striving for social acceptance, American traders in Shanghai affected a certain British disdain, which they transmitted to associates in America. So, from the *Journal of the American Asiatic Association,* for example, one receives the impression that China was really rather dreadful, and the news was usually bad, not least because it derived in the first instance from the *North-China Herald,* annual reports of the British China Association, and other habitually reactionary sources. China is contemptibly weak; China will not put her house in order; China does not pay her bills: these and other staples of the so-called Shanghai Mind abound.[42]

Perhaps it was to be expected that American businessmen would express hostility toward Chinese nationalism. In addition to reasons of cultural style, their economic interests may have dictated this position, for the latter depended, at least in some measure, upon a structure of semi-colonial arrangements involving the Imperial Maritime Customs, the foreign concessions, and other features of the Unequal Treaties; and the Chinese nationalist movement at least implicitly threatened this regime.[43]

Examples of anti-nationalist business sentiment are not far to seek. A lengthy analysis of Chinese politics appearing in the *Journal of the American Asiatic Association* in 1910 maintained that the late Ch'ing reforms were virtually worthless, mere window dressing for a decaying regime, because, while reform edict after reform edict had flowed from the Vermillion Pencil, "such effort has so far had but little practical result." While, in one sense, this was all to the good, for the anti-opium drive, if effective, doubtless would generate increased addiction to "morphia pills and whiskey," the "rights recovery movement" obviously "has its foundations in the desire of its promoters to retain for themselves the opportunities for illicit gain which attach to native-managed enterprises," and the slogan "China for the Chinese" was "merely the cry of the 'Young China' party, who, with minds half opened by a smattering of Western education (an educational condition which has been described as 'pestilential'), are simply endeavoring to upset the ancient conditions of their country for their own material advantage." Further in this vein, the American Association of China in its 1911 annual report discussed a number of "disquieting signs," including the "spirit of insubordination so common among the student class," and a 1912 editorial in the *Journal of the American Asiatic Association* characterized Chinese objections to the Six-Power loan as deriving from an "exaggerated sense of national dignity."[44]

Yet it would be indiscriminate to conclude that old China hands despised all things Chinese. Expressions of contempt, though often real enough, could sometimes be a pose; Anglophilia, while pronounced among New Yorkers or Bostonians, was perhaps less common among those of the Pacific Coast; there were the usual exceptions; and perhaps it is fair to say that most businessmen, like most missionaries, loved China after their fashion. Mah-jongg at the Palace, gin and tonic at Astor House, good fellowship at the Shanghai Club, and even thirteen-year-old girls—China provided pleasures great and small. The plentiful supply of cheap servants made a special contribution. "I should advise engaging a 'boy' on arrival at Shanghai," wrote E.B. Drew, a Harvard man with the Maritime Customs, "to look after personal comfort, buy tickets, attend to luggage, find carriages, sedans, rickshaws, etc.—& accompany you in shopping. Such a 'boy' would save wear and tear in a thousand ways. He could be found, I think, for $15—Gold— (or less) a month. . . . such a fellow (a sort of valet) would expect to attend on you day and evening, wherever you go and whatever you do." Whatever the sweetness of life in old Shanghai, such affection as businessmen evinced for China and the Chinese seemed rarely to extend beyond the gates of the foreign concessions.[45]

Business Attitudes toward Japan. Regarding Japan, the situation was rather different. In the business mind, the Japanese, though obviously different from white men, seemed to have themselves an organized country with which it was possible, even quite profitable, to do business.

Japanese businessmen made it easy for Americans by coming to the United States: in Seattle, San Francisco, and New York there were sizeable concentrations. Japanese businessmen at the Coast were typically importers and exporters. Those in New York represented a more elaborate presence. Japanese cotton-buyers opened offices, as did Mitsui and other zaibatsu, and the Yokohama Specie Bank maintained an establishment. All told, over a hundred Japanese businessmen worked in New York, keeping themselves current on business opportunities with the *Japanese American*

Commercial Weekly and relaxing with their associates at the elegant Nippon Club.[46]

Then as now, Japanese businessmen enjoyed a reputation for combining shrewd bargaining with warm personal relationships, which was much appreciated. Shibusawa Eiichi became the friend of Robert Dollar, who called at his house whenever in Tokyo. In 1910, Shibusawa hosted a banquet in honor of Dollar and his traveling companions from the Pacific Coast. Takahashi Korekiyo, another gnome of Tokyo, developed a friendship with Jacob Schiff, who took care of Takahashi's daughter for three years at the Schiff residence in New Jersey. Schiff was personally acquainted with many leading Japanese businessmen, as was Charles Coffin of General Electric.[47]

These friendships, of undoubted authenticity, formed part of a larger picture. If American business attitudes toward China seemed effectively semi-colonial, those regarding Japan appeared to treat that country as a kind of equal, to which was due a certain dignity and consideration.[48]

The Asiatic Association's annual dinner in 1911 provides an illustration. The program was given over to celebration of the new Treaty of Commerce and Navigation with Japan. Signed February 21, ratified by the Senate two days later over objections from Pacific Coast members, and proclaimed on April 5, it drew quite a crowd to Delmonico's: the big import-export men—Silas Webb, James R. Morse, Albert Cordes, I. Osgood Carleton, Lowell Lincoln, Thomas Phelan; the Wall Street contingent—Jacob Schiff, Frank Vanderlip, H.P. Davison, and sundry lesser fry; and numerous Japanese—machinery buyers, cotton men, silk importers, traders in porcelain, the Mitsui man, and the manager of the Specie Bank, among others. From Washington President Taft sent his regrets and Secretary Knox, who was accompanied by other senior officials. The guest of honor was the Japanese Ambassador, Baron Uchida; and the master of ceremonies the Honorable Seth Low, scion of a family long interested in Oriental trade, President of the Association, and sometime Mayor of New York.[49]

The after-dinner speeches singled out peace, prosperity, and friendship as the enduring themes in Japanese-American relations. Baron Uchida set the tone by emphasizing the contribution growing commercial and financial linkages would make to the stability of the Pacific basin, and Seth Low's remarks reinforced this view. War was ridiculed: "Surely there is ample room on the broad Pacific and abundant opportunities in the regions that border its shores," observed the Secretary of State, "for the peaceful enterprise of all nations for all time to come"; and Representative William Sulzer, Chairman of the House Foreign Affairs Committee, expressed the conviction that the United States and Japan would "work together to solve the problems of the Pacific for the lasting benefit of civilization and the material good of the civilized world." The high point came during the speech by Charles Coffin, who recounted twenty years of G.E. activity in Japan: "In that whole period we have never had an acrimonious discussion. In that whole period we have not only never lost a dollar of money, but we have never seen a moment when we felt that our money in Japan was in jeopardy." Following sustained applause, Coffin concluded: "And the lessons we have learned from our Japanese friends—of high ideals, patience, kindness, thoughtfulness, generosity, abounding hospitality—are more and more abiding, and I can say for myself, of greater interest and value than all the lessons I have learned in all my life in my commercial relations with other people." Later, one of those present at Delmonico's recalled a "mood of exalted sentiment, somewhat rare at such celebrations in New York."[50]

Yet, businessmen's ability to understand Japan and the Japanese may be said to have operated within certain limits. Liking the Japanese basically because they were good customers, businessmen did not seem overly sensitive to non-material dimensions. One might easily overstress the point: "While we of this association are concerned primarily with Oriental trade," insisted an officer of the Asiatic Association, "we are not wholly sordid," and it is true that some businessmen were deeply interested in Japanese civilization. In New York, a number of prominent businessmen, many of them financiers, patronized the Japan Society, the premier organization promoting understanding of Japanese culture. Jacob Schiff and August Belmont served as officers, while the membership rolls included nearly every name of Wall Street distinction: H.P Davison, Thomas W. Lamont, Frank Vanderlip, James Stillman, Benjamin Strong, Isaac Seligman, Paul Warburg, Otto Kahn. Moreover, certain New York businessmen amassed admirable collections of Japanese color prints and other art objects. Boston also had an active Japan Society, as did San Francisco (Robert Dollar was an officer).[51]

Additionally, it may be notable that businessmen turned out in numbers to hear missionaries home on furlough from Japan. While finding it difficult to generate excitement in country churches or from small-town audiences, Japan missionaries were known to encounter warm receptions from urban businessmen. In 1914, for example, Sidney Gulick reported to the American Board that he had discovered considerable interest in Japan when addressing the New York Chamber of Commerce, the Merchants' Association of the City of New York, and business audiences in Chicago, Minneapolis, and elsewhere.[52]

Yet, as a group, American businessmen gave little evidence of comprehensive interest in Japanese affairs and displayed limited understanding of Japan's national aspirations. With rare exceptions, they did not seem to follow Japanese politics closely. Thus, informed comments on the Taishō Political Crisis were unusual: even the *Journal of the American Asiatic Association* published only a single brief article. And businessmen did not appear to share Japanese opinions on racial equality. Though businessmen voiced opposition to immigration legislation in Sacramento or Washington whose passage threatened to disrupt U.S.-Japanese relations—the Asiatic Association roundly condemning the bigotry of labor unions, California demagogues, and the San Francisco mob—they were not racial liberals. Businessmen were prepared to speak out against legislation the Japanese might regard as more outrageous than usual, but they were seemingly unable, or unwilling, to recognize how race as such had poisoned the international relationship. It is notable that none of the trade associations espoused the idea, so common among missionaries to Japan, that Japanese immigrants should be admitted freely. The native mind adhered to certain distinctions. In 1915, R.J. Caldwell, New York cotton goods manufacturer, wrote the State Department to criticize anti-Japanese agitation in California as harmful to American trade: "Japanese," he observed, "are preferable to Italians anyway." Willard Straight, as private businessman, referred habitually to the Japanese as "the Banderlog," Rudyard Kipling's "Monkey People." The historian, in sum, has no reason to suppose that businessmen's racial attitudes differed markedly from those of Americans generally.[53]

Coming Full Circle: Willard Straight as Businessman. A semi-colonial view of China, an emphasis on economic cooperation with Japan—such attitudes were common among American businessmen. Even Willard Straight eventually fell victim to this relentless commercial logic.

Among diplomatic historians, Straight has acquired a reputation as arch-enemy of Japan. The hardening of his views while war correspondent, Consul at Mukden, head of the Far East Division, and negotiator for the American Group, is familiar material. Straight is best known for vigorous advocacy of policies calculated to check Japanese continentalism, particularly in Manchuria. Interest in him usually peters out, however, in 1913 when the Wilson Administration abruptly terminated his services. In one way this is unfortunate because a study of his later career, such as it was, suggests that his attitudes turned around when he became a private businessman.[54]

In fact, his attitudes toward Japan seemed to be mellowing during his final year with the American Group. A visit to Japanese-occupied Korea in February 1912 may have precipitated the change. Writing to a British friend, Straight heaped praise on Japanese public administration of Korea: "It may all be advertisement, but it's a damned effective one, for the little devils are efficient and you can't get away from what they are doing, or do aught but admire it." Straight concluded: "Perish the thought, but one could not help thinking that we might all be better off if these little devils had charge of China's destiny, after all."[55]

During the remainder of 1912 and early 1913, Straight seemed increasingly open to economic cooperation with Japan. A month after the Korea visit, he told a British diplomat in Peking that, if the United States "can work in partnership with Japanese interests, no one will be more pleased than I myself." While involved in negotiations for the Six-Power loan to China, he seemed to be drifting toward rapprochement with Japan. In an early 1913 letter to Frank McKnight, House of Morgan representative in Peking, Straight wrote: "I quite agree with you that the time may not be very distant when our best chance of successful and profitable business in China will be to work more or less along the lines of combining our financial strength with the political influence of Japan." And on March 14, four days before President Wilson withdrew diplomatic support, Straight informed McKnight that he harbored no personal objection to "a hard and fast financial alliance between the American Group and Japan." That such an arrangement might militate against the aspirations of patriotic Chinese did not in itself appear to bother him. "It is impossible not to recognize that . . . a definite understanding with us would sooner or later be utilized by Japan for the exploitation of China," he noted. "Mind you, I am not criticizing the Japanese for this. On the contrary, I admire their intelligence and foresight, and should think that co-operation with them might very well be profitable for us."[56]

Following the collapse of the American Group, Straight's attitudes appear to have evolved into something like conventional business views. Settling into a position at J.P. Morgan, he would not have failed to note the quotations on Japanese bonds. Within a month after Wilson came to power, Straight joined the Japan Society, soon rising to be an officer; within the year, he replaced the aging Seth Low as President of the Asiatic Association.[57]

Regarding China, his views gradually became less than romantic. More and more, Straight saw China as a bad risk. Recall his remark to Paul Reinsch, in 1914, that a Chinese loan "appeals to my sense of adventure rather than to my business judgment."[58]

The newly positive assessment of Japanese expansion in China seemed to deepen in 1914 and 1915 as the World War destroyed the old power balance in East Asia. During the Twenty-one Demands episode, Straight argued that the United States should take no action whatever in opposition to Japanese continentalism. In a March 1915 cable to the staff of the *New Republic* (founded with his wife's money a few months earlier), Straight said that a diplomatic protest would carry the moral weight of a "snowball in hades." In April, he wrote J. A. Thomas, Shanghai manager of the British-American Tobacco Company: "In a way I am sorry for China, and in another way I feel the probabilities are that it will be better in the long run for all concerned." Straight continued: "A good many of our friends in New York are very much exercised and it seems they think they are going to help the situation with a lot of bombastic conversation. This, as you know, will get us nothing, and will only tend to antagonize the Japanese, who seem to have the matter well in hand."[59]

By degrees shedding the habit of mind of the dollar diplomat, Willard Straight now favored economic cooperation with Japan and did not care much about China. Such were the seductions of the private sector.

Taken together, this chapter and the preceding may suggest that the religious and material interests cut in rather different directions. Where the Missionary Mind was concerned with China, the business mentality would focus on Japan. If Protestants living on farms and in small towns regarded China as compelling because it represented the rebirth in East Asia of an essentially innocent way of life, urban businessmen found Japan the most important part of Asia precisely because it had lost its premodern innocence. How these divergent mentalities figured in the mind of the foreign-policy elites remains to be seen.

THREE

The Mind of the Foreign-Policy Public

The Missionary Mind was, of course, deeply moral, even moral-istic, and, because this moral sense directed itself overseas, one would expect some influence, however diffuse, upon American public opinion regarding foreign affairs.

To the extent that American East Asia policy centered on a kind of rhetorical defense of China against Japan, one might sur-mise that the seeming public consensus undergirding such an approach reflected the Missionary Mind more than the business mentality. American trade and investment in China, however frequently invoked as rationale for policy by persons who did not have to do business there, represented the least attractive segment of the East Asia market. While the China market was not without value, the American business mind generally favored a low-key attitude toward the entire region based on good relations with Japan.

The resultant victory of the religious over the commercial men-tality is explained by certain peculiar features of the community concerned with foreign affairs. If this community—the foreign-policy public surveyed brilliantly by Ernest R. May[1]—could be described as serving the national interest at least tolerably well in regard to Europe, one would hesitate to say the same about East Asia, for a number of policy essentials were missing. Though our evidence for this is fragmentary and our argument must proceed obliquely, we shall see that American public opinion toward East Asia policy evinced certain weaknesses, intellectual and structural, which opened the way for the Missionary Mind.

ASIA IN THE MINDS OF THE CRITICAL AND ARTICULATE

It is said that one characteristic of a healthy public opinion is general agreement on the goals of American diplomacy. In the absence of such common purpose, the nation, in this view, might not always be able to pursue coherent and consistent policies to advance its interests. In order to avoid the possibility of divisiveness, which can lead to politicization, at least a rough agreement would seem necessary among the more articulate voices. This was the theory.

Yet, such a consensus appeared to be absent, at the very highest levels, regarding East Asia policy. Though the Open Door idea remained popular among a subgroup of the general population, a number of authorities on foreign relations publicly criticized the concepts and methods of American diplomacy in East Asia. Thus, the foreign-policy elites lacked cohesiveness. Critical, articulate opinion ranged over a wide field of policy options. One can distinguish several schools.

The Open Door Realists. One line of thought, while generally accepting the Open Door as the framework of policy, argued for substantive change in the goals or tactics of diplomacy. Persons holding this view tended to be critical, sometimes severely critical, of the seemingly moralistic point of current American policy. Yet, critics of moralism might have very different ideas of what a more realistic Open Door would look like.

Thomas F. Millard, for one, gave vigorous exposition to the view that the Open Door should be backed by military force. Author of *America and the Far Eastern Question* (1909) and other books, editor of the *China Press* at Shanghai, Millard was a strident foe of Japanese policy in China. In his view, America ought to play a more active role in East Asia because of China's potential strategic and economic importance. Positing a basic incompatibility between Japanese and American interests, Millard professed to see "a genuine community of interests with China and the United States." "On a day not far distant," he told an American audience in 1910, "I hope that an American statesman will define our attitude toward China in words something like these: 'The United States of America considers the territorial integrity of China and her political autonomy within the entire limits of the Empire as now constituted to be important to its (the United States') interests and to the preservation of the existing *status quo* in the Pacific Ocean, and would regard any encroachment or aggression upon either, by any nation whatsoever, as inimical to the interests of this nation.'" Millard warned that "our Eastern policy will not be respected until the world is convinced that failure to consider and meet our reasonable wishes carries a probability of war." This policy idea, which perhaps flowed logically from the assumption that Chinese and American interests were identical, always enjoyed a certain following among the more radical partisans of China.[2]

A different sort of realist critique was found in the *New Republic*. Deriving partly from owner Willard Straight's Asian experiences and from the editors' own animus against moralism in the conduct of foreign relations, this viewpoint tended to see the Open Door Policy as irresponsible. It is notable that, while focusing on power relations, the liberal journal was not unaware of American business interests in East Asia. During the Twenty-one Demands episode, the *New Republic* argued editorially: "From a purely commercial standpoint, it will in many ways be easier for us to cooperate than to compete with the Japanese in China. Certain lines of business may suffer, but in general the result should be advantageous."[3]

But the *New Republic* concentrated its fire on the Open Door's lack of political realism. The editors—Herbert Croly, Walter Weyl, and Walter Lippmann—maintained that officials from John Hay to Secretary Bryan generally had pursued East Asia policies bearing little relation to the American national interest. They inveighed against the moralism and legalism of these policies for having produced a potentially dangerous overcommitment: dangerous to the United States because it might lead unwittingly to greater political involvement than the national interest would warrant; dangerous because the country lacked the military resources to avoid diplomatic humiliation; even immoral because the policies led Chinese patriots to expect concrete support which never would be forthcoming. A 1915 *New Republic* editorial argued that the Chinese ultimately would not regard as true friends a people "who, when they cried for the bread of intervention, have given them repeated assurances of our distinguished consideration." Observing the Twenty-one Demands crisis, the editors were led to a devastating judgment on the pattern of American diplomacy since the Open Door:

> We have posed as the guardians of the "open door" and the "integrity of China." These pledges ... have never been galvanized into more than stenographic action. . . . In reality our chief claim to an influence in China arises from the fact that Secretary Hay once coined a phrase which answered a riddle that perplexed the chancellories of Europe. This we deified as a Doctrine and called it the "open door." It was consecrated in official correspondence, editorial comment and after-dinner speeches. But though its head was of diplomatic brass, its feet were of rhetoric and nothing more, and the idol has fallen. Mr. Wilson and Mr. Bryan cannot be blamed for what has happened, nor Mr. Taft and Mr. Knox, nor Mr. Roosevelt and Mr. Root. They have been but the high priests of our national and irresponsible good intentions.

The *New Republic* concluded that "those who turn over the pages of our diplomatic history, if they be honest, will feel ashamed."[4]

Yet, whatever their sense of shame, the *New Republic* editors seemed to propose no constructive policy alternative. Relations with Japan received little attention, the race issue was largely neglected, and no breakthrough was made in conceptualizing the problems of the region.

Another realist critic was Lewis Einstein, an experienced diplomat, author of a book on foreign relations and frequent commentator. First Secretary of the Peking Legation during the

Taft-Knox period, Einstein was instrumental in enabling the dollar diplomats to fashion a "cooperative policy" following the collapse of their independent approach to Manchuria in 1910.[5]

Out of office after 1913, Einstein went public with a devastating critique of Open Door moralism. Writing in the *Journal of the American Asiatic Association* following the outbreak of world war in East Asia, Einstein questioned whether successive administrations had not erred in their various attempts to check Japanese continentalism. Perhaps the Open Door policy, by acquiring its anti-Japanese point, had developed "a rigidity and absence of suppleness which deprived it in great measure of utility as a free instrument in sustaining oversea interests." Perhaps, also, the United States thereby had maneuvered itself "into positions involving considerable risk without substantial cause of hope of commensurate benefit." Noting that Japanese continentalism in China posed little danger to Western economic interests ("Restraints of trade by her agents there have more often been alleged than proved"), Einstein doubted that American policy-makers had any business "badgering Japan because of her action in Manchuria."[6]

In general, the diplomat suggested it might prove wiser to restructure American East Asia policy along "more modest lines." Such a policy would recognize the boundaries of public tolerance: it would continue to center on China, if only because "a strong American moral influence exercised through educational, philanthropic and religious institutions has acted as a sentimental tie"; and it would be complicated by race legislation, which "cannot avoid giving legitimate offense to a proud nation."[7]

A more targeted or finely calibrated policy might benefit China as well as the United States. American diplomacy could fulfill a useful function as mediator between China and the Treaty Powers, and there doubtless would be appropriate occasions to comment on "the conditions of Japanese stewardship of her Chinese possessions." But Einstein considered that it was "the height of folly" to "seek gratuitous grievances in what are after all regions of secondary importance." Einstein continued:

> In considering the permanent aspects of our Far Eastern policy we must definitely admit that Japan has there great and legitimate interests exceeding our own. If we place ourselves in a permanent attitude of blocking her oversea development, we envenom a situation already difficult and run the risk of bringing about a conflict from which the main benefits we shall derive, will have been the consciousness of the faultiness of our diplomacy and absence of our military preparation.[8]

Beyond the Open Door. Other men of affairs argued that the United States needed a fresh approach to the problems of the East Asia and Pacific region. Some would retain a role for the Open Door; others would see the policy abandoned. These root-and-branch critics might rely on economic, political, or even moral arguments. Or they might combine these considerations, sometimes in ingenious ways.

Lindsay Russell, a prominent New York lawyer, was among those arguing that the Open Door should be scrapped. A leading member of the foreign-policy establishment, Russell served as President of the Japan Society from 1907 on and, in 1918, was named first Chairman of the Council on Foreign Relations. Well-connected and articulate, he possessed a tidy and almost ruthlessly logical mind.[9]

Russell maintained that, the Open Door having been proven a dismal failure, the United States should adopt a totally new East Asia policy designed to further its real interests. These he considered to be primarily economic. Distressed over the seemingly erratic, not to say quixotic, course of American diplomacy, he urged a "constructive and consistent policy" toward the entire region, centering on close relations with Japan. Perhaps reflecting his ties to the business community, Russell welcomed Japanese hegemony over East Asia because the latter would hasten economic modernization everywhere, including China, thereby expanding the volume of trade with the United States as well as creating fresh opportunities for American capital investment. The path of economic wisdom lay in "using Japan as an entrepot and a middleman through whom to sell goods and finance Oriental enterprises" rather than in competing with Japan for the China market. Dismissing the Philippines as "utterly useless" when measured against their original purpose as a commercial base to capture the China trade, Russell noted that, after fifteen years of effort, the China market still absorbed "scarcely the output of a single modern industrial plant." Writing in 1915, he suggested that the State Department would be wiser to replace the Open Door doctrine with a policy of pan-Asian provenance: "I believe that on the whole 'Asia for the Asiatics' is the best doctrine for the United States as well as for China and Japan."[10]

Though perhaps not entirely free of his own illusions, Russell did not participate in the commoner habits of mind. He seemed to understand enough world history to know that the United States was not entirely blameless in the matter of China's territorial integrity. That there were such things as treaty ports, wrested from Chinese sovereignty by dint of arms, with the United States "boldly following in the wake of war and aggression applied by other nations," did not escape him. In fact, Russell argued that, from China's standpoint, it happened as a result of the treaty with the United States of 1844 that China's "integrity was given its first, and perhaps most vital blow." Not wholly unsympathetic to China, Russell speculated that, after a certain period of Japanese domination, China would modernize its economy, put its house in order, build up its army, and achieve independence, just as Japan had. But he failed to see how an Open Door policy could contribute materially to China's salvation, and besides, it occurred to him, "with the Monroe Doctrine to uphold on this hemisphere, the troubles in the Caribbean countries and revolutions in Mexico, with 10,000,000 blacks in the South whose relations to our own people [sic] are still to be properly adjusted, and with the Philippines and their serious problems, to which are to be added the many complications with European countries arising out of the present war, the United States has its full share of the white man's burden."[11]

Yet there were other opinion leaders who, while eschewing the

cold-roast realism of the Wall Street lawyer, also favored good relations with Japan. The impulse to move beyond the Open Door
might derive as easily from moral considerations. The white man's
burden, moreover, might appear different to different people.
Certain Americans, no less virtuous, perhaps, than their Sinophile
neighbors, believed America's duty consisted of cooperating with
Japan. Others subordinated all aspects of East Asia policy to the
general issue of world peace. Such critics usually regarded im-
proved Japanese-American relations as a key.[12]

The latter perspective was perhaps best exemplified in the *Independent,* an influential weekly edited by Hamilton Holt, a
leader of the American peace movement. The peace movement
commanded great intellectual prestige among citizens interested
in foreign affairs, and Holt's pacifism was of the kind—common in
those days—that was informed by an understanding of world
politics. A keen student of Pacific affairs, Holt visited East Asia,
enlisted Asians, including Count Okuma, as contributors to his
journal, and took active part in the Japan Society and other such
organizations.[13]

Criticizing American East Asia policy for containing the seeds
of war, the *Independent* maintained that its anti-Japanese thrust
derived ultimately from race prejudice. The magazine viewed the
American public's apparent opposition to Japanese immigration,
and American diplomacy's intermittent resistance to Japanese
continentalism, as aspects of the same problem. And just because
the main goal of Japanese policy from the Meiji Restoration on
had been "to make herself the equal of any civilized nation in existence," war with Japan would remain a distinct possibility so long
as white refused to accept yellow as equal. The *Independent's*
policy alternatives usually focused on the immigration issue. In
November 1913, following a period of strain in American-Japanese
relations arising from discriminatory land legislation in California,
the journal suggested that the two nations negotiate a new treaty
explicitly granting Japanese the right to own land, and it urged
Congress to repeal the law forbidding American citizenship to
Asians. Because Chinese no less than the Japanese were affected,

Chinese immigrants having been excluded since 1882, the *Independent* found it difficult to take altogether seriously the much discussed traditional friendship for China. "China will side with Japan in any vital issue between the white and yellow races," declared a 1914 editorial: "When will our statesmen and leaders of public opinion learn that such disgraceful disregard of the consequences of our actions as now characterizes our Oriental policy will in time involve us in serious international complications?"[14]

The *Independent* therefore implored policy-makers to go as far as they possibly could toward treating Japan, in particular, as an equal. Seeing no legitimate objection to Japanese power as such, the journal endorsed the Japanese idea of a "Monroe Doctrine for Asia," which seemed to promise stable conditions throughout the region. Upon the outbreak of world war, the *Independent* argued that the United States could best promote the peace of the Pacific basin by "assiduous cultivation" of Japan based upon explicit recognition of Japanese paramountcy in East Asia. During the Twenty-one Demands crisis, the *Independent* reasoned that, inasmuch as the white Treaty Powers had no evident moral claim to leadership in that part of the world, and that China, by reason of its weakness, necessarily would remain passive in its international relations for many years,

> Japan has the same rights in Asia that we have in America under the Monroe Doctrine—that is, the right to maintain Asia for the Asiatics as we do America for the Americans. Not only has Japan this right to assume the political primacy of the Far East, but it is her duty to do so. Otherwise China may be dismembered and Japan may be compelled to wage further wars against encroaching rivals. When China becomes Japan's equal in power . . . she can share with Japan the responsibility of maintaining Asia against the White Peril.

Yet, for all its sensitivity to certain East Asian aspirations, and for all its moral depth, the pacifist journal never evinced comparable sympathy for Chinese nationalism, which sometimes resisted the ambitions of the Japanese Empire.[15]

Meanwhile, the need for a new East Asia policy received robust advocacy in the tough-minded pages of *Outlook*. This popular weekly, a kind of house organ of the Progressive movement, reflecting the thinking of former President Theodore Roosevelt, its Contributing Editor, stoutly opposed sentimentalism in American diplomacy and beat the drum for a bigger navy. Its views on East Asia policy hinged on the frank recognition that Japan possessed the plenitude of power. During his second Administration, Roosevelt had based his policies on this fact, and little had changed in the interim. *Outlook's* strenuous espousal of good relations with the Japanese, drew upon Roosevelt's sense for diplomatic realism, Editor Lyman Abbott's moral sense regarding the race issue, and the aesthetic sense of Managing Editor Hamilton Wright Mabie, the literary critic, whose fascination with Japan resembled that of Lafcadio Hearn.[16]

For all these reasons, *Outlook* noted that Japan was the most important part of East Asia and therefore should serve as the focal point of American policy. Though expressing no particular objection to the notion of an Open Door in China, a noble idea so long as the Great Powers that ran the place could agree on exactly what it meant and where it applied, *Outlook* held that American diplomacy must be conceived in a wider frame. It should concern itself primarily, not with some condominium of the Treaty Powers bearing obscure relation to the American national interest, but rather with "the only organized country in the Orient," Japan. This meant that American policy should seek accommodation with Tokyo, if possible by assuaging at least some of the immigration grievances, certainly by accepting Japanese leadership in East Asia: "The Japanese are Orientals," *Outlook* explained:

> To them Asia is precisely what the Americas are to the Americans. The Japanese has also a Monroe Doctrine. He believes that Asia should be primarily for the Asiatics. Both England and America have shut the door in the face of his working people and have told him they must stay in Asia. It is natural, therefore, that he should be anxious to preserve Asia for the Asiatics.

Another *Outlook* editorial observed:

When the educated Japanese looks at Asia, he finds it largely under Western rule. He finds England in India; England and Russia in Persia; England, Russia, France, and Germany exercising practical control over what are known euphemistically as "spheres of influence in China. . . ." Under the circumstances he naturally asks himself how the integrity of Japan, the only well-organized and independent country in the Far East, can be maintained.[17]

Like the *Independent, Outlook* isolated race as the root cause of tensions across the Pacific. A December 1914 editorial noted that

many American newspapers, and some American public men, have apparently taken the attitude that Japan has no rights in the Far East, and that any Japanese activity beyond the boundaries of the islands is an insolent interference with Occidental interests. At the bottom of this spirit lies the deep-rooted feeling among many Western people of the inherent superiority of the Western races over the Eastern. Until that assumption is abandoned by the leaders of the Western races, the West will never understand the East and will never do it justice; and the peace of the world will never be secure.[18]

Like other pro-Japanese sources, *Outlook* assumed a rather hard-nosed posture toward China. Though perhaps reflecting Colonel Roosevelt's well-known contempt for weakness, this attitude seemed to come primarily from unwillingness to wish away the facts of power: the prerogatives of the Treaty Powers, the strength of the Anglo-Japanese Alliance, and, during the World War, the Japanese paramountcy. *Outlook* reasoned that, in order for China to realize its potential, it would require foreign assistance, and that Japan was best equipped for the job. "China is incapable of self-development without very substantial aid during the next two or three decades, and must be for a number of years under tutelage," the editors concluded in 1915. "It is the ambition of Japan, which has learned so rapidly and so successfully in the school of Western commercialism and industrialism, to be the teacher and director of China in these matters." However, once China had modernized, there would, of course, ensue a massive adjustment in its international relations, and at that point the West, having learned to treat the Oriental as an equal through its dealings with Japan, could the more easily grant China its destined eminence in world affairs. "The modern world stands at the parting of the ways," the journal opined: "It must choose whether East and West are to be friendly rivals for power and trade in the future, or whether they are to waste the most precious possessions of civilization—time, resources, opportunities, men, prosperity—in repeating the ancient blunders of antagonism, injustice, race hatred." In this way, *Outlook,* while no partisan of Chinese nationalism, did not neglect the larger aspects of the region, and, while concerned with political expediency, was not insensible of change.[19]

This journal, along with the other authorities discussed, is of interest chiefly because of implications for our understanding of public opinion. One does not mean to urge the importance of any single source, for the list is highly selective; the historian might easily make substitutions or additions. Nor does one mean to imply that the sample is representative, for it deals only with critics of American policy. Nor does one need to consider here whether these articulate sources created public opinion or merely reflected it (this whole matter is controversial).

What this survey should suggest, rather, is the absence of consensus, among the articulate, regarding the proper goals and tactics of American East Asia policy. Instead of a coherent dominant vision, which responsible citizens might have refined this way or that, one finds the full spectrum of opinion on every key issue: basic perceptions of the East Asian situation, the relative importance of China and Japan, the significance of the region, the nature and value of American interests, the framework of policy, the definition of power. Though all very interesting in one way, in another this indicates a certain disarray or intellectual confusion, or perhaps worse, or perhaps something else, among the body of citizens specially concerned with foreign affairs.

THE MIND OF THE OPINION LEADERSHIP

Perhaps an historical sociologist will one day reconstruct the upper reaches of American society on the eve of World War I; perhaps some social historian will conduct a census of persons owning formal attire—until then, one is left with impressions. And one has the impression that small numbers of men, usually wealthy, influenced the opinions of larger numbers, drawn primarily from the bureaucratic and professional classes, thereby effectively creating a public consensus to undergird American foreign policy. Yet, one also gets the distinct impression that the usual leaders of public opinion generally knew little about East Asia policy.

Men of affairs were preoccupied with Europe. These educated, well-traveled, urban professional men generally believed that Europe and America belonged to a common culture area; the sense of kinship with Great Britain was especially meaningful. This, combined with economic ties and the undoubted importance of European politics, made Europe still the center of the world in American eyes. Europe was accessible: those seeming to lead American opinion on foreign-policy matters ordinarily would have learned about Europe in school; could read books about Europe, sometimes by European authors in languages other than English; and sometimes could keep themselves current on European politics by reading European newspapers or periodicals. Many appeared to have European friends, relatives living in Europe, or European business associates, and at this level of society there was a good deal of transatlantic correspondence and travel. These European connections, in sum, gave the foreign-policy elite its reputation for expertise, its mystique of special knowledge, by reason of which other citizens interested in foreign affairs (the rank and file of the foreign-policy public) looked to them for guidance.[20]

When asked to comment on an issue in American relations with European countries, the foreign-policy elite would have been able, in most cases, to offer plausibly informed opinions. Approving of administration policy, they could marshal intelligent arguments on its behalf; disapproving, they would have possessed the background to suggest a better one. Yet, when confronted with an issue in American East Asia policy, the foreign-policy elite seemed beyond its depth. Neither knowing much nor caring much about Asia, they would have lacked the ability to explain or defend government policy in other than superficial terms. Likewise, the elite would have been unprepared to take the initiative in forging a new public consensus behind some alternative policy. If this assessment is correct, the usual foreign-policy opinion leaders (most of whom, it would seem, were lawyers or businessmen, or urban patricians of uncertain occupation),[21] would have been essentially incapacitated when East Asian matters appeared suddenly on the public-policy agenda. They would have been unable, that is, to play the leadership role with anything like their customary intelligence and insight.

The main reason for this seeming failure, ignorance, deserves examination. (By ignorance one means not dullness of mind but lack of information.) In order to command respect or deference from other citizens interested in foreign affairs, an opinion leader clearly would have needed to demonstrate that his conclusions were based upon unimpeachable sources of information. Such a person, attempting to guide opinion on East Asia policy matters, might have established his claim to expertise by saying one of the following: 1) that he had visited East Asia and had observed the situation at close range; 2) that some reliable observer had provided him with firsthand knowledge; or 3) that his opinions reflected authoritative printed materials—a well-respected book, a reputable newspaper, or the like. One must doubt that the numerous lawyers among the foreign-policy public, given the legal mind's contempt for hearsay, would have settled for anything less. Yet this evidentiary rigor must have made it difficult for the foreign-policy elites to speak authoritatively on East Asia, because reliable sources of information were in very short supply.

Firsthand Knowledge. Very few members of the foreign-policy opinion leadership seem to have lived or traveled in Asia. For most men of affairs, there was little reason to go. Only a handful, mostly from Seattle or San Francisco, went regularly to Asia on business, for it was ordinarily more convenient to deal with East Asian businessmen living in the United States (especially Japanese) or with American agents permanently resident in East Asia. Robert Dollar, the San Francisco businessman, made the trip about once a year, but this was unusual, for the voyage was long and expensive, necessitating extended absence from one's home and business base. From New York or Boston, the quickest route to Shanghai, via Montreal and Vancouver, required three full weeks and something like $500 (at a time when $3000 was a high yearly salary). The time and expense also inhibited tourism.[22]

Wealthy Americans, it is true, had by this time acquired a certain taste for European travel. Every year, there were ladies and gentlemen, attracted by the museums and spas or perhaps simply bored by the prospect of yet another summer at Newport, Lenox, or Bar Harbor, who evacuated the Eastern cities in late spring and sailed for Europe. Yet members of this social stratum, for whom time and money posed no obstacle, rarely visited China and Japan. "The trend of American travel and interest outside the boundaries of the United States has been toward Europe," complained the *Journal of the American Asiatic Association,* "thus leaving graver interests than those in the Atlantic to the merely curious attention of our people."[23]

Former Harvard President Charles W. Eliot, for example, who would rank on any list of foreign-policy opinion leaders, did not visit East Asia until late in life, when he did so under the auspices of the Carnegie Endowment for International Peace. Prior to his 1912 trip, Eliot knew very little. The friend and confidante of many European leaders, Eliot had no regular East Asian correspondent. Before leaving, he asked E.B. Drew, a retired old China hand living in Cambridge, to send him information on the places to visit, things to do, people to see. What Drew produced was a combination Chinese Baedeker and list of tips, to drink bottled water, use the Hongkong and Shanghai Bank, stay at the Palace, buy books at Kelly and Walsh—the sort of advice Charles Eliot would never have needed when planning one of his many trips to Europe. Like other privileged persons of his generation, Eliot seemed to know the fashionable districts of London and Paris nearly as well as the Back Bay and the Upper East Side: but Peking and Tokyo drew a blank.[24]

The sequel is instructive. Upon returning home, Eliot lectured on East Asia, wrote letters to the *New York Times* and published a book called *Some Roads Towards Peace*. Intelligent, abounding in good will, and rather superficial, one of its principal policy recommendations was establishment of a free American public library in Peking. Yet Eliot was lionized by the national opinion elite, his publishers brought out an edition of 100,000 copies, and other leaders sought him out for his considered views. In March 1913, Professor Goodnow of Columbia, the political scientist and would-be man of affairs hired recently by Yuan Shih-k'ai as constitutional advisor, wrote Eliot a letter confessing "my ignorance of Chinese conditions" and asking for sage advice. Equipped with the firsthand knowledge of a few months' travel, Eliot now qualified as an East Asia expert.[25]

President Eliot's assumption of this particular mantle, though dependent upon a pre-established authority, supports the general absence of real East Asian expertise in American society and indicates the credibility conferred by travel in China and Japan.

Because few members of the foreign-policy establishment seem to have visited Peking and Tokyo, as a group they lacked firsthand knowledge of East Asian affairs. Logically, this should have induced a certain reticence, and probably a certain conservatism, regarding East Asia policy matters. Lacking the mystique of special knowledge, moreover, the opinions of the establishment might yield to the authority of others.[26]

Connections with Experts. Lacking firsthand information, a person accustomed to lead public opinion on foreign affairs might cite the judgment of someone equipped with this knowledge. Such an authority presumably would be a recognized expert on East Asia with wide experience there, or perhaps some local business or professional man with Asian connections. Yet, even such second-hand expertise seemed difficult to acquire (or rarely was acquired) in most areas of the United States.[27]

Though the historian cannot know the exact figure, it is certain that the number of Americans possessing authoritative opinions on East Asia was quite small. Contemporary estimates ranged between 50 and 100 persons. In June 1913, the *Journal of the American Asiatic Association* published a list of 50 names, mostly businessmen and related men of affairs, specially qualified to lead American opinion on Asia. A few years later, George Bronson Rhea, editor of the *Far Eastern Review,* the leading American business journal in East Asia, told then Secretary of State Robert Lansing that he had written a book he intended to publish privately: "It is not for general circulation," he wrote, "being limited to an edition of 500 copies, of which I hope that no more than a hundred will be necessary to place this question before those whose opinion is worthwhile." Whatever its exact size, this small group of East Asian experts, most of whom seemingly knew one another, many of them regular correspondents, gave every sign of general isolation from the national opinion elite. In May 1913, the Asiatic Association complained that "many intelligent men versed in the affairs of the East and well acquainted with conditions there, had no outlet for expression of opinion or dissemination of the facts that they had gathered which was at all adequate to the importance of the subject."[28]

If the usual shapers of national opinion had little exposure to the views of the tiny network of East Asia authorities, there may have been greater possibilities of local contact with such experts in the cities having commercial ties with East Asia. Even so, the extent and significance of this must not be overstated.

For example, one might suppose that elite opinion at the Pacific Coast would be well acquainted with East Asia. But trade was one thing and the intricacies of foreign affairs something else again. Thus, despite the presence in Seattle of 200 import-export men, and another 50 in Portland, and what one knows to have been a certain public awareness of East Asian trade, the historian remains skeptical that those distant provincial cities, in that un-selfconscious region, carved so recently from the forest, contained full-fledged foreign-policy elites. San Francisco, it is true, may have had such a group, owing to its self-conscious cosmopolitanism, the aspirations of its Nob Hill families, the availability of a forum at the Commonwealth Club, the proximity of academic expertise at two fine universities, the activities of the Chamber of Commerce and the Japan Society, and the undeniable interests of 150 merchants trading to East Asia. Yet, a San Francisco foreign-policy elite, if such it was, operating without benefit of a quality newspaper, geographically (and psychologically) isolated from major American population centers, could not have possessed more than local— or at best regional—influence. In any event, there is ample reason to doubt that elite opinion on foreign-policy at the Pacific Coast reflected much sophistication about Asia. "People who are well informed otherwise," wrote Robert Dollar in his private diary, "are ignorant of conditions and even of the geography of China." The San Francisco businessman went on to recount the time he addressed a Seattle audience only to discover, halfway through his speech, that nobody present had ever heard of a city named Wuchang.[29]

Much the same might be said of elite opinion in centers such as Boston and New York, which had commercial ties to the Orient and a certain number of resident East Asia experts. Upper-class Boston—a tight, clubby little place with a sense of history, peopled by graduates of the same university (Harvard), dominated by families grown rich on the old China trade—here one might expect considerable interest in East Asia.[30]

Yet, if this had been true it would almost certainly be reflected in the letters of Senator Henry Cabot Lodge, who carried on a huge correspondence with his many Boston friends interested in foreign affairs; and it is not. Only three of Lodge's correspondents had traveled in Asia—William Cameron Forbes, Governor-General of the Philippines under President Taft; Harvard Professor Barrett Wendell, the historian of literature, who had visited Japan; and William Sturgis Bigelow, physician to Henry Adams, lecturer on Zen Buddhism, and patron of the Museum of Fine Arts, to which he donated 26,000 Japanese pieces—and it is notable that even these three ordinarily wrote about European affairs. A careful search will not turn up more than two letters, in a collection numbering many hundreds, which can be said to deal primarily with East Asia. Lodge's other correspondents almost never commented on Asian affairs. In Boston, as in nearby Salem, Asia remained primarily a romantic memory.[31]

If Boston was small, New York was just the opposite: already one of the world's great cities, vast, forbidding to all but the very rich, capable of erasing almost anyone, principal winter address of the national elite. Here, too, East Asia was largely neglected. Despite the presence of the Asiatic Association and the Japan Society, there is little evidence that the body of New Yorkers leading opinion on foreign-policy matters regarded China and Japan with utmost seriousness. Though the possibility of contact with experts may have been considerable, such connections seemed rarely to be made. Willard Straight, for one, often complained about this. In May 1913, Straight told a friend how disappointed he had been at the reception accorded William J. Calhoun, American Minister to China during the Taft Administration, when Calhoun addressed a group of prominent New Yorkers at the Whitehall Club: "Old Calhoun is back and has been handing out a good line of dope," Straight wrote. "It really makes no difference, however, for no one seems to know anything and everybody seems to care less." New Yorkers were too busy to bother with East Asia, as Straight explained the following year to George Bronson Rhea: "Everybody in this country has so many troubles of their own that they haven't much 'pep' left to go out borrowing additional difficulties in order to protect their future markets in China."[32]

Yet, in New York, as in Boston and at the Pacific Coast, there was at least some opportunity, however rarely taken, for a foreign-policy opinion leader to hear authoritative worldly advice on East Asia. In most American communities there was no such possibility. In his speech at the Whitehall Club, William Calhoun admitted he had remained largely ignorant of East Asia throughout his career as lawyer and judge in Chicago. "I went to China," he said, "without knowing a single thing about the country. I had no impressions for or against it." No doubt he spoke for many.[33]

Reading. Lacking connection with an expert, a member of the foreign-policy elite might have attempted to compensate by reading. One may assume that these were relatively well-educated men, most of them the products of a college education (then restricted to approximately 5 percent of the population). Though bookish persons too easily overestimate the role of books in shaping the opinions of decision-makers—most of society's leaders seem to learn more from their peers or private networks than from books—the historian may surmise that most men of affairs did a certain amount of reading, consuming at least one newspaper a day, several magazines a week, and perhaps a book from time to time. However, if the books, magazines, and newspapers that such individuals were likely to read gave reasonable coverage of European news, their treatment of East Asian affairs was relatively poor.[34]

Now the ability to read critically in any field derives in most cases from formal educational training. Foreign affairs being a sometimes arcane subject, it may well prove inconvenient for a busy or professional person to interpret developments in exotic regions without the appropriate background. To form an intelligent opinion about East Asia would have required a measure of familiarity with the region's history, culture, and present conditions. Usually, this knowledge would have been acquired in some educational institution.

Yet such subjects rarely were taught. In elementary and secondary schools, textbooks on geography and world history devoted only 1 percent of their attention to China. At the university level, only a handful of research institutions offered regular academic courses on East Asia.[35]

This reflected the relative poverty of American scholarship on China and Japan. Though certain leading universities had one or two East Asian specialists—Frederick Wells Williams at Yale, Paul Reinsch and his successor Stanley Hornbeck at Wisconsin, and others at Columbia, Cornell, Chicago, Stanford, and the University of California—and despite the presence of Chinese students on many college campuses in consequence of the congressional "remission" of the Boxer Indemnity in 1909, the American academic community evinced relatively little sustained interest. The *American Historical Review* published only a single article on East Asia during the years 1911-1915. The trendier political scientists, too, made little enduring contribution. In January 1913, the *Annals of the American Academy of Political and Social Science,* seizing the moment to increase understanding of the Chinese Republican Revolution, published a special issue with sixteen articles, fourteen by amateurs (chiefly missionaries and Chinese undergraduates), bearing titles such as "A Wedding in South China" and "The Life of a Girl in China." Two obscure academics contributed, as did a professional explorer who, having accompanied the Duke of Bedford on a recent hunting trip, wrote a thoughtful piece on the mammals of Eastern Asia.[36]

If, owing to this scholarly lacuna, schools and universities generally neglected East Asia in their curricula, then one would expect the foreign-policy elites, who would have received their education years earlier, when the veil of ignorance was even more tightly drawn, to lack the necessary background in the subject. "There is no comprehensive education in this country on the subject," lamented the *Journal of the American Asiatic Association,* "and no systematic study of the history and affairs of Eastern Asia and the Pacific. There is a general belittling among even the most intelligent of the importance and dimensions of the subject." This must have limited the ability of men of affairs to reach judgments about current events in East Asia which they happened upon in their reading.[37]

In reading newspapers, for example, it must have been difficult for them to make sense of various key developments. Newspapers generally spared them this hardship, however, by giving rather limited coverage to East Asian affairs. The Hearst papers, it is true, did not hesitate to spread anti-Japanese war-scare stories across the front pages, the most notorious, in 1912, accusing

Japan of hatching plans to establish a naval base in Baja California. Yet, one may assume that the Hearst readership included relatively few opinion leaders. Even so, the metropolitan dailies patronized by the foreign-policy elites appear to have given East Asia equally shallow, if less scandalous, treatment.[38]

Not much hard news got through. The Associated Press bureau chief in Peking attributed this to the fact that "the telegraph tolls are so high, and I am required to cut the service down to barest necessity of the news." But the high cable costs (one dollar per word) do not explain why American editors routinely buried important news from East Asia in the inside pages. Certain dramatic events made the front pages—the 1911 Chinese Revolution, the 1913 crisis in U.S.-Japanese relations, Japan's entry into the World War, the Twenty-one Demands—but other significant developments received short shrift, and it was a rare day when East Asian news was featured more prominently than European.[39]

Even the best American newspapers usually gave poor coverage to domestic politics of China and Japan. The Taishō Political Crisis of 1912 and 1913, and the series of events in late 1913 and early 1914 by which Yuan Shih-k'ai terminated the brief Chinese experiment with free institutions, for example, did not reach the front pages, and some leading metropolitan dailies virtually ignored them. At least one sophisticated paper, the *Boston Transcript,* carried no news at all on the expulsion of the Kuomintang deputies in November 1913 and did not report the forcible closing of the Chinese Parliament two months later. In Chicago, the *Tribune* found space on page 8 for the first of these stories, but the second it neglected entirely, in favor of a local story, a happier story, about China: "China Awakening on Broad Scale," being some account of Sherwood Eddy's address the night before to a crowd of 4,000 at Orchestra Hall. The *Tribune* reported the Taishō Political Crisis in factually thin articles and did not comment editorially.[40]

Much the same pattern obtained in the *New York Times,* then as now the principal source of daily information for Americans serious about foreign affairs. Yuan's move against the Kuomintang rated a short article on page 8, the ending of the Parliament an even briefer note on page 3. Coverage of the Taishō crisis took the form of abbreviated stories on the inside pages, and during the entire episode the *Times* never saw fit to print a single "background" article or editorial comment. Over against this seeming indifference to the progress of democracy in East Asia may be set the *Times's* close attention to the struggle in Britain to break the power of the House of Lords, meriting numerous front-page stories and eight editorials, and, for what it is worth, massive coverage of the coronation of King George V. It is notable that the *Journal of the American Asiatic Association* expressed disgust with the news and comment, much of it "crudely erroneous," appearing in "a New York newspaper which takes itself and its readers with extreme seriousness." "If stuff like this can pass among educated people as intelligent comment on Chinese affairs," the editor queried, "what can be expected of the yellow, the reckless, the uninformed journalism that caters to the ignorance of the multitude?" In darkest Manhattan, as in other cities, what the man of affairs could learn about East Asia by reading his daily newspaper seemed distinctly limited.[41]

Nor could he garner much from most of the periodicals he was likely to read. The magazines followed the pattern set by the newspapers: considerable attention to military affairs and other dramatic events, little regard for domestic politics, no systematic concern, coverage that was uneven and generally unsophisticated. Only the *Outlook* and the *Independent*, both of them critics of American East Asia policy, can be said to have given sustained attention to China and Japan. The *New Republic*, while opposing sentimental diplomacy, did not really cover East Asia in depth, and its comments were sometimes inaccurate, as in its second issue, when the editors apparently forgot about the economic preeminence of Shanghai and referred to Tsingtao as "the most important commercial center in China." But the *New Republic* was better than most elite periodicals, such as the *North American Review*, the *Nation*, the *Review of Reviews*, and the *Atlantic Monthly*, which rarely carried articles on China or Japan.[42]

The international relations of East Asia also received limited coverage in American magazines. Many important subjects went virtually unnoticed. A citizen wishing to read up on topics such as the Anglo-Japanese Alliance (renewed in 1911), the U.S.-Japanese Commercial Treaty of 1911, or the Unequal Treaties, would have found little material. Of the 111 publications indexed in the *Reader's Guide,* only 4 carried stories on the Anglo-Japanese Alliance, 2 on the Commercial Treaty, and 2 on the Unequal Treaties. The only magazines covering all three subjects were the pacifist *Independent* and the progressive *Outlook.* Unless he subscribed to one of these, a member of the foreign-policy elite was unlikely to encounter discussion, or even basic factual information, on the power realities of the Pacific basin. It is notable that the *Journal of the American Asiatic Association,* always hungry for authoritative comment, usually deferred to British publications.[43]

Finally, there seemed to be no current authoritative books available on American East Asia policy as such. Only one appeared to command general respect among East Asian experts—*American Diplomacy in the Orient,* by John W. Foster, a former Secretary of State now an international lawyer in Washington. But Foster's book, published in 1903, concluded with the Open Door notes, and there was seemingly no judicious up-to-date treatment. Thomas Millard's books, along with the writings of Homer Lea, dealt with the first decade of the twentieth century, but these did not enjoy the confidence of the cognoscenti. The Asiatic Association, for example, made no secret of its disrespect for Mr. Millard, a man possessed of "a more or less acute form of Japophobia," and General Lea was thought to be unspeakable. Among other books in circulation, Paul Reinsch's *Intellectual and Political Currents in the Far East* (1911) neglected foreign-policy issues, Sidney Gulick's *American Japanese Problem* (1914) dealt only with immigration, and H.B. Morse's writings lacked an American focus. Recognizing the need for a timely study, the Carnegie Endowment in 1913 commissioned Professor Reinsch; and, when Reinsch went to Peking, Stanley Hornbeck assumed responsibility. But the new book did not appear until 1916.[44]

Precisely because the bookshelf seemed empty, the magazines unmindful, and the newspapers thin, the small section of elite opinion that really knew and cared about East Asia in a political way spared no effort to educate the others. In New York, the Japan Society sponsored foreign-policy discussions at the Hotel Astor, exhibitions of Japanese flower arrangement at fashionable places in the city, tea ceremonies, and lectures on Japanese painting at the Metropolitan. In Boston and San Francisco, the local Japan Societies also offered full public programs. In Worcester, Massachusetts, the pioneering diplomatic historian George H. Blakeslee persuaded the department of history at Clark University to host the first American academic conferences on Asia: three such meetings took place in Worcester between 1910 and 1912; a fourth at San Francisco in 1915. In Boston, certain citizens, having lived or traveled in the East, formed the East Asiatic Society, which met for dinner regularly at the new Harvard Club on Commonwealth Avenue: "The society is small," wrote chairman John Gardner Coolidge, "and the proceedings are perfectly informal." In New York, again, the Asiatic Association in 1913 took the initiative in founding a new organization for scholarly exchange and public information called the Asiatic Institute, observing, "It is certainly necessary that the progress of the islands and continents of the Pacific should be at all times clearly understood by an influential and powerful body of our people." But the goal of educating the foreign-policy opinion leadership would not be achieved for nearly two generations.[45]

If, as has been argued, the usual leaders of public opinion lacked firsthand knowledge of Asia, ready access to persons so equipped, and adequate exposure to authoritative printed material, what consequences might be likely? Though the study of vacuity has its limitations, certain inferences naturally suggest themselves.

First, the historian may infer that the accustomed opinion leaders, when faced with the necessity to say something meaningful about East Asia policy, would have experienced a certain intellectual paralysis. Exactly how they might have "toughed it out" (admissions of ignorance being undignified if not fatal) remains a subject for speculation. But one may surmise, intuitively, that the foreign-policy elites would cling instinctively to whatever American diplomatic traditions or precedents they might be able to remember. Regardless of vagueness, regardless of irrelevance to the objective situation, such a touchstone would be better than nothing. Insofar as the phrase "Open Door" may have been such a one, it may thus be considered not so much a policy construct as an implicit confession of ignorance, a substitute for thought. Certainly ignorance is a poor seedbed for change.

Second, the historian may deduce, from the fact of widespread ignorance among the elite, that the usual structures of foreign-policy opinion-formation did not altogether obtain in respect to East Asia. One may well question whether this pervasive, elite ignorance could have gone unnoticed among the larger body of citizens concerned with foreign affairs. Assuming it did not, as one may reasonably suppose of intelligent persons, the historian may then posit that such citizens would turn naturally to such authoritative sources as did in fact exist and were close at hand. The impulse to do so may logically have received an assist from the manifest confusion or lack of consensus on policy fundamentals characterizing the truly articulate (the various policy critics, discussed earlier).

In any event, it is fair to conclude that there was a certain emptiness about Asia in the mind of the foreign-policy public. And it may be that the mind, like nature, abhors a vacuum.

THE FOREIGN-POLICY PUBLIC AND THE MISSIONARY MIND

There is ample evidence, necessarily general and circumstantial, to suggest that the Missionary Mind rushed in to fill this vacuum. Cultural causes being, in the nature of things, diffuse in their effects, one must not expect to find in this causal chain the same mechanical simplicity or empirical directness one might have encountered in elementary physics. Prime movers are usually difficult to pin down. Yet there are considerable data which, in their cumulative weight, are persuasive and encourage us to go on.

There is evidence, that is, to render likely the hypothesis (as our scientists would call it) that the Missionary Mind exerted a considerable and perhaps decisive influence on the foreign-policy public.

For a point of departure, juxtapose the foreign-policy opinion elite to the religious opinion elite (represented by the China missionaries). On the one side, there was ignorance and indifference regarding East Asia, in effect an abdication of the leadership role; on the other, firsthand knowledge of East Asia, broadcast in person, orally, approximately 30,000 times per year. Recall, also, the highly articulated missionary communications network operative at times when the missionary could not be physically present. And assume, for the sake of argument, that, inasmuch as the foreign-policy public and the foreign-missions public were drawn from the dominant socio-religious group, there likely would be a certain overlap or interface. Would it, then, not be reasonable to surmise that the Missionary Mind, in the manner of lantern slides projecting on a blank screen, gave a definite shape and value to American thinking about East Asia?

Before any discussion of the evidence for this, it is necessary, for analytical purposes, to distinguish what the missionaries did not or could not do.

The Missionaries and International Politics. With certain notable exceptions, missionaries ordinarily maintained no pretensions to expertise in foreign relations. Indeed, they rarely addressed the subject. The historian reading through their letters home to mission boards, or one of the Protestant missionary magazines, receives only an occasional hint that American relations with East Asia involved considerations such as navies, treaties, trade, or even formal diplomatic intercourse.[46]

Missionaries saw themselves as doing the work of God; foreign policy belonged to the city of Man. "God does not look upon man as belonging to either nations or races," observed a Federal

Council of Churches official. They were good people, but they were not men of affairs. Missionaries, their minds given over to visions of a new international order where the usual bases of relations among states would give way to something infinitely finer, generally cultivated indifference to the daily realities of power. Missionaries tended to avoid explicitly political questions. While it was true that a certain number could always be counted upon to sign petitions, write the President, or even lobby in Washington, it took an extraordinary event to bring them out of the religious woodwork. They knew their Chinese, they knew their metaphysics, better than their international relations.[47]

Anti-Japanese Feeling. It seems clear that Protestant missionaries played a very minor role, at worst, in fostering that "sense of estrangement" from Japan charted with such insight by Akira Iriye. This wave of opinion, started during the years 1897–1911, continued to receive encouragement from certain American sources: Pacific Coast politicians; labor union leaders; Hearst chain journalists (whose idea of news embraced lovely white maidens found dead in the flea-bag hotel rooms of debauched Japanese); and, perhaps not least, the Navy officer corps, whose War Plan Orange was really a war plan yellow. "I have noticed," wrote President Eliot to Columbia's Nicholas Murray Butler, "that every time the proposition comes before Congress to increase our Navy the chief reliance is on the statement made by American Army and Navy men to the effect that war with Japan is inevitable, and that we must be prepared for it."[48]

Yet, though exacerbated by certain individuals and institutions, anti-Japanese feeling in America seemed to have its roots in the racial fears of the general population. Without intending an exhaustive explanation, the historian may suggest that these fears attached themselves to Japan more than to China because China was weak and Japan was strong. Anti-Japanese feeling seemed most pronounced in California. "Don't be afraid of Japan, or let them bulldoze you," wrote a San Francisco man in 1914 to the State Department: "We want, must have an Oriental Exclusion law—include the Japs with the Chinese—all the yellow or Asiatic races—they are a worse menace than the Chinese—and the sooner a firm stand is taken with Japan, the better—they are such impudent, conceited little fellows—breed like Rats—they would own the Pacific Coast in another generation." Another representative of vintage California racism urged the federal government, in the event of war, to "place every Jap in California under immediate arrest and transport them to some eastern point in Kansas or some Middle West state." But anti-Japanese sentiment was by no means restricted to the Pacific Coast. In Cincinnati, for example, a 1914 vaudeville show called "The Yellow Peril," dealing with a Japanese diplomat's plans to blow up the navy yards at Boston, Brooklyn, Newport News, and San Francisco, schemes foiled by the even greater cunning of an American female detective, played before packed houses.[49]

Yet, however widespread geographically, and whatever its manifestations, anti-Japanese opinion seemed rarely of missionary origin. Against any evidence of whispered anti-Japanese racism on the part of China missionaries, for example, must be weighed the overwhelming fact of nationwide campaigns for racial equality led by Japan missionaries. For this reason, the Protestant missionary movement as a whole would appear to have had little responsibility for bad feelings toward Japan or the political uses to which they were put.

The Politics of Race. The race issue abounded in political possibility, and, if missionaries as a group bore little relation to it, a look at the politics of race may be nonetheless interesting for what it may suggest regarding American thinking about East Asia.

Briefly, Japanese immigration and related questions ranked high each year on the political agenda at Sacramento and Washington. Inasmuch as the number of Japanese coming to the United States had diminished to a trickle as a result of the Gentleman's Agreement negotiated in President Roosevelt's day, the issue was essentially artificial. Yet, just because it seemed to elect people to public office on the Pacific Coast, and because it was connected with general race and immigration questions, Japanese Exclusion found its way onto the legislative calendar.[50]

Congressional debates on Asiatic Exclusion, though unedifying, make interesting reading, for they suggest that race prejudice ran very deep indeed; and, more to our purposes, that Americans generally may not have distinguished sharply between Chinese and Japanese. These attitudes the historian finds among proponents of Exclusion laws, principally West Coast Congressmen and their Southern allies, and equally among Members opposing such measures, always on pragmatic grounds. In 1914, for example, Representative Hayes of California moved a perfecting amendment to the Immigration Bill hoping, as he told the gentlemen of the House, "to give the world notice that it is our intention to maintain this country as a residence for members of the Caucasian race [applause] and for them only." The gentleman explained: "We upon the Pacific coast have this problem before us all the time. Many of our brethren in the South have this same problem before them, and, as I said before, I am offering this amendment not because I have any racial prejudice, but because I recognize that the Caucasian, the African, the Mongolian, and the Malay races are so totally dissimilar that it is desirable from every racial standpoint that they should be kept separate." No one objected to the principle. "The gentleman from California [Mr. Hayes] knows that he strikes a responsive chord in my bosom," said Congressman Slayden of Texas, a leading opponent of the measure, "and in that of every man on the floor of the House when he advocates the purity of the race. God Almighty Himself hates the hybrid."[51]

At no time during these debates did any Member of Congress rise to defend the idea of racial equality; at no time did the presumed strength of sentimental pro-Chinese opinion in the United States lead a Member to drop a bill in the hopper liberalizing Chinese immigration. "Will not some Congressman introduce a bill to repeal the Act forbidding the naturalization of Mongolians?" asked the *Independent* bitterly in 1913: "It might get enacted in the course of half a century."[52]

The Congress being, for better and worse, a highly representative place, the historian may well doubt that any set of attitudes toward Asia was quite so widespread and deeply held as this. In this sense, the public mind, though still a blank screen, was tinted with a rather menacing yellow. The whole character of American thinking about Asia tended to the abstract: as late as 1942, 60 percent of Americans, as revealed in a "scientific" opinion poll, could not locate China on an outline map of the world.[53]

Yet, race consciousness alone, however basic a factor in American East Asia policy, and however productive of venom, cannot make plain why the United States was prepared, after its fashion, to defend China against the perceived threat from Japan. Nor can any seeming strength of general anti-Japanese feeling explain why China in specific was chosen as the spot for symbolic, as distinct from physical, confrontation. (Events are basic, but the mind organizes reality.) For this the mind of the foreign-policy public would have required something additional to be flashed on that blank screen: a certain idea of the national interest. Here the role of the Missionary Mind (even though missionaries themselves seldom addressed the issue directly in technical terms) was important and apparently crucial.

The Symbol of the Open Door. The commonest conception of the American national interest seemed to involve the perceived necessity to maintain the Open Door policy in China. Of course, the Open Door, by virtue of its vagueness, was capable of meaning various things. To the commercial-minded, it usually meant most-favored-nation status; to those thinking in political terms, the maintenance of the status quo. Those few persons familiar with the terms of the Open Door notes and subsequent American documents and international agreements might well prefer even more restrictive definitions. East Asia experts and other realists probably would focus on specific situations, often muddy, in light of the Open Door clause in the Anglo-Japanese Alliance.

Yet, as Paul Varg and others have shown, and as one would perhaps expect from the general ignorance of East Asia detailed above, the Open Door usually assumed a form in the public mind that is not easily recognizable by the international lawyer or the close student of East Asian history and affairs. The Open Door seemed to evoke something like the following cluster of notions: that the United States, unlike the other Powers, had never asked for an inch of Chinese territory and had never sought special advantage; that Secretary of State John Hay had exercised bold and effective leadership in announcing the Open Door principle and by securing agreement from the other Powers; and that, because of this historic policy of friendship, the United States occupied a special place in the hearts and minds of Chinese.[54]

Now, without oversimplifying this collective representation, and without overlooking the occasional presence of other elements, the historian may observe that, insofar as the above notion detailed what the Open Door policy putatively had done to further Chinese interests as distinct from American, it was an essentially missionary idea. The presumption of innocence, friendliness, self-denial, moral leadership—these are redolent of the Missionary Mind more than the mind given over to great power politics. Indeed, the only international actor characteristically possessing such attributes was precisely the Christian missionary. One may therefore surmise that this symbol of the Open Door, though by no means narrowly doctrinal, belongs prima facie to the Missionary Mind by reason of elective affinity (to borrow a term from German sociology).

There is also the argument from exclusion. Of the three mentalities that theoretically were possible—the Missionary Mind, the mind of the foreign-policy elite, and the business mind—the last two seem rather unlikely. The mind of the foreign-policy elite, perhaps casting around in the darkness for some conception of the national interest, however crude, however ad hoc in nature, would not have been able, in its ignorance, to play other than a secondary or derivative role. For, though the Open Door might seem a convenient touchstone, it would have left ambiguous markings on any substantive policy; and though one may perhaps too easily underestimate a policy framework which, not wholly unlike the Monroe Doctrine, was capable of generous as well as self-interested construction, it is unreasonable to suppose that gentlemen accustomed to defining the American national interest would have operated in this case, in the absence of heavy Protestant missionary influence, largely as advocates of the interests of some other nation. Moreover, the business mind, as discussed in the preceding chapter, while not entirely indifferent to the China trade, and of course not opposed to some Open Door for commerce, conceived of America's East Asian interests in a wider frame. Even if, like good Victorians, businessmen may have believed that trade served certain, even transcendental, purposes of benefit to all, the interests they tended were clearly and frankly their own.

Just as the argument from exclusion points to the Missionary Mind, so do certain empirical items of indirect evidence. Perhaps the most important clue derives from the virtual certainty of overlap—very considerable overlap—between the foreign-policy public and the foreign-missions public. Inasmuch as the policy public tended to be drawn, as its relative wealth and education would suggest, from the dominant socio-religious group, it would have been exposed, ipso facto, to the Protestant missionary enterprise. In fact, it is reasonable to infer that the bulk of the foreign-policy group, like most Americans active in civic affairs, maintained membership in the Protestant churches supporting China missions. On the assumption that the percentage financing the missions cause was comparable to that of Protestants generally, one may surmise that a sizeable minority of the foreign-policy public, possibly as much as one-third, was not simply familiar with China missions but involved to some degree.

Though, in some households, missions may have concerned women more than men, the overall picture is clear; and it seems likely that what was true for the body of the foreign-policy public was also true of the opinion leadership. The occupational groups to which the foreign-policy elites were likely to belong, business and the law, had a distinctly Protestant ethos at the highest levels. As late as the mid-1950s, when Harold Isaacs made a careful study of opinion leadership, 137 out of 181 persons interviewed were Protestants. Isaacs also found that 123 of these Protestants, roughly 90 percent, first learned about China from missionaries and missionary propaganda in their churches, and that the attitude toward China most commonly uncovered was "a glowingly sentimental feeling."[55]

Such linkages between the policy elites and China missions seemed even commoner during the years when the missionary tide was at full flood. Though lacking data for a statistical profile, the historian notes certain fragmentary evidence sustaining this impression. For example, in Chicago, where one would be hard-pressed to find a man more socially prominent than Cyrus McCormick, President of International Harvester, one discovers him also to be a generous patron of the missionary cause. When Professor Paul Reinsch received the appointment to Peking, McCormick invited Reinsch to come down from Madison for a meeting with him, John R. Mott, and other missionary leaders. In Boston and New York, where most mission boards maintained headquarters, their executive committees were top-heavy with Christian gentlemen recruited from the national business and professional elites, as were the boards of trustees of the one dozen or so Christian colleges. Among the trustees of the New York-based Canton Christian College, for example, were John W. Foster, the international lawyer and sometime Secretary of State, and Seth Low, President of the Asiatic Association and former Mayor of New York. In San Francisco, the Missionary Mind was well represented by Captain Robert Dollar, President of the powerful Merchants' Exchange. Dollar gave money, gave speeches throughout the Bay area on behalf of missions, visited mission stations during business trips to East Asia, and, in 1911, in his home city, served as "Grand Marshal of twenty thousand Sunday School workers that paraded here, each man carrying a Bible in his hand."[56]

Again, this was a religious society, in some ways even a communal society, and, if such direct missionary connections were perhaps less usual among urban elites than small-town elites, that ancestral home of the Protestant missionary enterprise, their cumulative import will seem plain enough.

Briefly, supporters of China missions who were also members of the foreign-policy opinion elite were naturally disposed to the United States pursuing a "Christian" policy in East Asia. While statesmen must be realistic and responsible, it was essential that the character of American policy toward East Asia appear consistent with the goals of Protestant religious philanthropy. The United States being, in a special sense, a Christian country, it was vital that its foreign policies scrupulously avoid behavior tending to besmirch the name of Christian Civilization in the eyes of weaker peoples.[57]

The missionary-minded discussed this important matter during the 1910 Edinburgh Conference, where there was a special commission on "the Relations of Missions and Governments," chaired by an American Episcopal layman of whom the *New York Times* said editorially that on "any list of half a dozen leading citizens of New York his name would surely be included, and would be likely to stand at the head"—Seth Low. In an address entitled "The Duty of Christian Nations," delivered to an audience including William Jennings Bryan and the Reverend Henry Stimson, Sr., Low defined "some of the larger aspects of that relationship between Missions and Governments":

> It is of much less consequence to the missionary to enjoy the political support of his Government at home than it is that he should have the moral support of that Government. And by that moral support I mean that whenever the Government of a country whose public opinion is predominantly Christian illustrates in its dealings with non-Christian races . . . high ideals of justice, of fair dealing, and of respect for the rights of others, even when they are weak, the cause of the missionary is powerfully reinforced. On the other hand, when the Government of a country whose public opinion is predominantly Christian [*sic*] fails to illustrate such ideals, the work of a missionary is made infinitely more difficult. The missionary can face with equanimity risks to his own life, because he knows that the blood of the martyrs is the seed of the Church; but not the best missionary of them all can avert the disaster to his cause which comes when such a nation fails to live up to its own ideals.[58]

Correctly or not, the missionary-minded among the foreign-policy opinion leadership seemed to regard the Open Door policy as an embodiment of those Christian ideals. Viewed from this angle, and without denying that other angles might produce a more self-interested prospect, American China policy could be described as the government analog to missions. Certainly the language used to characterize our East Asia policy reverberated with missionary overtones.

Though the historian might well expect such language to issue in something like inverse proportion to knowledge of objective conditions in East Asia, this was not necessarily the case. The Missionary Mind seemed capable of sweeping everything before it. At the first of George Blakeslee's Asia conferences, Professor Frederick Wells Williams, a Yale historian equipped with the Chinese language, ended his thoughtful, nuanced paper on Sino-American relations with the following pieties:

> In the hundred years since that intercourse began we have refused to yield to the temptation presented by military weakness unexpectedly exposed. We have steadily refrained from coercing a helpless people .... We have never menaced the territorial integrity of China and have been among the foremost in upholding her sovereign rights to her own soil. ... We have endeavored to treat the Chinese Empire as honorably as other countries and have consistently desired to include men of every race and color in the great family of nations so soon as they could prove their birthright by the plain tests of morality and culture. In policy, if not always in performance, America in her relations with China has tried fairly to maintain the high ideals of a Christian nation.[59]

Further instances of this mentality, in public rhetoric, print, and private correspondence, are plentiful. Writing to John W. Foster in 1911, Professor Williams expressed the scholar's sense of "gratification" arising from "the reflection that we have at least refrained from bullying Asiatics." Christian nations, like Christian gentlemen, did not bully the weak. Foster himself, in *American Diplomacy in the Orient*, presumably was participating in the Missionary Mind when he wrote:

It is a matter of pride and of confidence for the future to be assured that the conduct and policy of the government, from the beginning of its history, in its relations with the Orient have been marked by a spirit of justice, forbearance, and magnanimity. Its early and its later intercourse with China, Japan, and Korea has been that of a friend interested for their welfare, ready to aid them in their efforts to attain an honorable place among the nations, and willing to recognize the embarrassments which attended those efforts.

The grandfather of John Foster Dulles opined: "This task will be well done if it shall aid in giving to the world a freer market, and to the inhabitants of the Orient the blessings of Christian civilization."[60]

Such sentiments, expressed here by several of the country's leading authorities on East Asia, appear to have been rather common among foreign-policy opinion leaders and the wider public concerned with foreign affairs. To the extent that these persons were drawn (as was ordinarily the case) from the major Protestant denominations, they would have been likely to evince the missionary habit of mind in their approach to foreign affairs generally. (The historian who appreciates the full dimensions of the missionary movement begins to view that generation's idealism and moralism, so despised by the realists of a later day, in a more favorable or more understanding light.)

Yet, only in East Asia policy, because of the relative weakness of American national interests, the general absence of worldly opinion and the unique strength of the China-missions constituency, did the Protestant missionary enterprise make a definitive contribution. The Open Door policy, as popularly conceived, rested upon a conception of America's proper role in East Asia that was missionary in character. The China missionary, for all his claims to nonpolitical status, seems to have been the pivotal figure in the education of the foreign-policy public. If this is true, then the Open Door policy itself, whatever its patina of realism, was in a certain sense the ghost of the Missionary Mind.

Certainly this hypothesis would be worth testing in concrete situations.

Part Two
Policy

FOUR

Recognition:
The American Public and the Chinese Republican Revolution

The Missionary Mind, in its approach to international politics, was essentially innocent. Often, even usually, there was lacking that somber vision of power realities which may be said to characterize the mind of the foreign-office professional. For, while the missionary may well have been able to see more clearly or more deeply into the nature of things than the diplomat or the policy-maker, nevertheless, the world of affairs, with its battleships and power relations and treaties, was more likely to manifest itself to the official than to the Missionary Mind. There was a basic difference between the two mentalities, a difference of perception and sensibility. Yet, both mentalities made their claims on the general public, and, insofar as those claims related to separate realms, there rarely was occasion for conflict; in fact convergence was probable. But, in the event the official mind and the Missionary Mind found themselves at cross purposes, then the body politic was subject to confusion. And the Republic was unlikely to emerge healthier (or wiser) from the experience.

This potential conflict, which had long been dormant, was raised to the level of national consciousness at the time of the Chinese Republican Revolution. At that time, the two divergent mentalities entered upon a fierce struggle for the allegiance of the foreign-policy public. At issue was the kind of Chinese government Americans could or could not recognize. This was to become a recurring theme in American East Asia policy, and so the episode possesses inherent interest.

Moreover, an inquiry into America's response to the Chinese Revolution, spanning the years 1911–1913, provides the ideal laboratory for the historical scientist to test the hypothesis that the Missionary Mind was the unelected governor of the foreign-policy public.

THE OFFICIAL REACTION

As modern revolutionary upheavals go, the Chinese Revolution of 1911 seems relatively innocent. Producing little bloodshed, no remaking of class relations, no world-historical individual, and no new ideology, it brought no massive adjustment to international relations. Yet it was a great revolution when it happened.

It contained elements of high drama which a world grown unaccustomed to war and revolution watched with amazement. The September rioting in Szechwan; the Wuchang Army mutiny on October 10; the devolution of power to provincial authorities; the eleventh-hour attempt of the Manchus to save themselves by recalling Yuan Shih-k'ai; the Yangtze Valley battles, such as they were; the emergence of a revolutionary government at Nanking, where Sun Yat-sen assumed power in late December; most wonderful of all, the Manchu abdication a few months later, the Chinese Imperial state of millennial foundation being swept away in favor of a Republic headed by Yuan Shih-k'ai, who was styled President. "Yes," wrote Sir John Jordan, the British Ambassador and dean of the Peking diplomatic corps, "who would have dreamt 15 years ago that the burning question here in 1911 would be Monarchy versus Republic!" [1]

In general few persons abroad knew enough about Chinese conditions to make sense of the Revolution, a difficulty shared by most foreigners in China and perhaps also by most politically conscious Chinese. Sun Yat-sen, for example, learned of the Wuchang mutiny while reading the *Denver Post*. Under the circumstances, people tended to see what they wanted to see: old China hands fearing the worst; missionaries hoping for the best; diplomats and other professional observers, when they were honest, admitting to considerable confusion. "It is difficult to form a satisfactory opinion of the situation, that is, one on which reliance can be placed or which approaches anything like a conviction," wrote American Minister William J. Calhoun in spring 1912. "The situation changes so rapidly," he continued,

> there are so many phases to it, and there is so much mystery about it, that one never knows what to believe or expect. There is no public press upon which to rely for information as to current events. There are no statesmen or publicists who formulate or publicly discuss principles or policies. Officials, however high in authority, cannot be relied upon to tell the truth, at least all the truth, upon any question of public interest. Until now political agitation has had little or no place in the life of China; therefore, there are no political parties, no organized public sentiment, and no accepted leadership in public affairs. Political action is largely a matter of personal interest and secret intrigue. The country is ramified with various secret societies; some of which are radical, others reactionary or conservative. Mysterious negotiations and tortuous plotting are the favorite methods of procedure.

"Diplomats, and foreigners generally," said Calhoun, "sit here like spectators at a play, watching and wondering what the next act in the unfolding drama is to be." [2]

The Anti-Imperialist Impulse in the 1911 Revolution. Though Chinese historians vigorously debate the causes of the Revolution, most agree that the anti-imperialist impulse played a central role. It could scarcely have been otherwise, inasmuch as Chinese politics often revolved around the question of China's international status. Being a Chinese nationalist implied opposition to the whole structure of semi-colonial arrangements governing China's relations with the Treaty Powers. While patriots might disagree about the precise constitutional form of a sovereign national state and the tactics required to achieve it, every Chinese nationalist knew that the imperialists must one day be sent home: the foreign concessions, the special law courts, the spheres of influence, the Maritime Customs, the gunboats on the Yangtze, the whole foreign package. [3]

Anti-imperialist feeling, which was especially strong among patriotic students and merchants, found expression in the "rights recovery movement" during the final years of the Ch'ing dynasty. The diplomatic policies pursued—resisting the Germans in Shantung, the British in Tibet, the Russians in Outer Mongolia, the Japanese in Manchuria—rested upon the nationalist aspirations of the modern public opinion just then emerging in the treaty ports.[4]

Yet, the Ch'ing attitude toward the Treaty Powers was not entirely consistent; China's humiliation continued. Whatever the skill at managing barbarians, whatever the achievements of the late Ch'ing reforms, the dynasty could not altogether avoid the appearance of complicity. Modernization required money to be borrowed from foreign bankers, who usually insisted upon terms that further eroded Chinese sovereignty. In those halcyon days of *chemin de fer* diplomacy, the Ch'ing financed a certain number of railroads by bargaining away valuable economic concessions. Thus, there was a heavy mortgage on China's future.[5]

Railway policy of the Peking regime occasioned the revolutionary outbreak. Trouble began when Peking unveiled plans to nationalize the railway lines previously under provincial control. Built by imperialists, financed by imperialist money, now scheduled for expropriation by an alien dynasty, the railroad emerged as a potent political symbol.[6]

The Hukuang Railway, in whose financing the Taft Administration had successfully demanded a share, provided a target for the September riots in Szechwan. During the early months of the Revolution, the Peking government's Railway Minister, Sheng Hsuan-huai, was denounced as the venal puppet of the Treaty Powers. In the end, power flowed to Yuan Shih-k'ai precisely because most Chinese patriots regarded Yuan as the only leader capable of keeping the imperialists and their running dogs at bay.[7]

Yet, however much the Revolution owed to the anti-imperialist impulse, however much Chinese patriots might aspire ultimately to rid themselves of foreign domination, the time was not right. So, while denouncing the imperialists in their rhetoric, China's revolutionaries scrupulously avoided violence against foreign interests. Remembering the fate of the Boxers, they took every precaution, even when the exigencies of revolutionary warfare argued for another approach.[8]

The Treaty Powers. As was their custom, the Treaty Powers reacted with despatch. No Power appeared to shed tears for the crumbling dynasty, if only because the anti-imperialist policies of recent years had taken a certain toll. Certain Powers, notably Britain and Russia, believed they could get along better with a new regime. As a group, the Powers were determined to withhold formal diplomatic recognition from the new government until the Chinese Republic acceded to foreign wishes in the matter of loans, concessions, spheres of influence, and the like. In a sense, the 1911 Revolution presented an opportunity for the several Treaty Powers to recoup their recent losses and perhaps expand their interests. What fear there was regarding unilateral foreign military intervention—Russia or Japan being the Power most likely to intervene in extreme circumstances—involved the possible seizure of Chinese territory more than the restoration of the Ch'ing. (Only the Japanese seem seriously to have considered intervening in defense of the dynasty.) Where the revolutionaries established stable conditions—in the Yangtze Valley, for example, where British interests were paramount—the imperialists quickly came to terms with the new order of things, accepting the Revolution de facto precisely because it respected foreign interests.[9]

But the Treaty Powers did not expose themselves to undue risk. From the first sign of revolutionary violence down to the Manchu abdication and beyond, the Powers took concerted action to protect foreign life and property. To the usual foreign naval presence in the Yangtze Valley were added substantial reinforcements of gunboats and warships. The foreigners also intervened with military troops. Invoking the Boxer Protocol, the Powers announced in November 1911 that they would position numerous troops along the railway corridor connecting Peking and the sea. By the following spring, the forces numbered nearly 10,000 men, a troop level slightly lower than in 1900. Foreign naval vessels rode at anchor in the Yangtze, monitoring the battles between revolutionists and Manchus. Through their massive naval and military intervention, the Treaty Powers seemed to be telling the Chinese that they could jolly well have themselves a Revolution, if they wanted one, so long as it remained within certain limits. Meanwhile the Powers would maintain an attitude of strict neutrality and would suspend their banking services for the duration. The Treaty Powers cooperated, thus, to preserve the overall structure of foreign privilege.[10]

The American Role. The United States tagged along, as usual, contributing naval vessels for Yangtze duty and military troops for the Peking-Tientsin corridor. American naval commanders, army officers, consuls, and diplomats went along with the common policy, which tended to be made on the spot by consensus of the Powers.[11]

State Department policy, too, was largely derivative, as befitted a Power having few tangible interests to defend. Though American diplomats sometimes tried to take credit for enunciating the principles of concerted action, strict neutrality, and opposition to foreign intervention, these policy axioms were shared by the Treaty Powers generally, and if one nation deserved the glory, Great Britain was certainly the likeliest.[12]

It is therefore pointless to construct a blow-by-blow account of American diplomacy, for it was determined by policies made elsewhere. But the highlights deserve treatment in brief compass.

The United States reacted to the September Szechwan riots in the usual Treaty Power manner—by force of arms. On September 3, the Chargé in Peking, E. T. Williams, reported that the disorders posed danger to American citizens, mostly missionaries, and that they were "inspired by opposition to railway construction by foreigners." Williams, a former missionary, feared an outbreak of anti-foreignism on the Boxer scale. Assistant Secretary of State Francis M. Huntington Wilson, on September 7, thus, directed Admiral Murdock, Commander-in-Chief of the Asiatic Fleet, to "send gun-boats where they will afford the greatest security to

Americans." Two days later, the Admiral cabled the Navy Department from Shanghai that conditions throughout the Yangtze Valley were so unsettled that he had summoned the entire Asiatic Fleet, usually stationed in the Philippines, and that he would sail immediately for Nanking with three men-of-war.[13]

Then the storm broke. On October 11, E. T. Williams reported the Wuchang rising, in which the revolutionists "carefully avoided attacks on foreigners." Naval vessels guarded the foreign concessions, he wrote. The following day, Williams surmised that the rebellion was "undoubtedly the most serious since the Taiping." And, on October 13, Amos Wilder, Consul-General in Shanghai, cabled that the Revolution might well topple the regime.[14]

The direction of American policy was established almost immediately. Policy-makers chose a somewhat passive course, partly because they had no real option, partly because their most recent attempts at independent action, the various Manchurian moves of 1909–1910, had fallen short of success. By policy-makers the historian refers primarily to Huntington Wilson and to Ransford Miller, head of the Far Eastern Division, who together managed day-to-day affairs down to the end of the Taft Administration. During that year and a half, Secretary Knox and President Taft functioned primarily as distant supervisors of their more capable subalterns.[15]

The key document was drafted by Ransford Miller on October 14, a long memorandum to the Secretary of State setting forth a five-point policy developed in consultation with Huntington Wilson: 1) reliance on the Asiatic Fleet to protect American life and property in the Yangtze Valley; 2) removal of Americans from remote areas to the shelter of the foreign concessions; 3) "strict neutrality" as between the contending Chinese factions; 4) opposition to unilateral foreign intervention; and 5) adherence to a "common policy" developed by the concert of Powers. Such was the State Department's first definitive response ever to revolutionary Asian nationalism.[16]

The details were fleshed in during the following month. On October 17, President Taft, away on an extended political trip, gave hearty approval to the Department's policies. Ten days later, Secretary Knox, wiring Taft in Chicago that the fate of the Manchu dynasty hinged on Yuan Shih-k'ai and that the international banking consortium had suspended financial negotiations inasmuch as the times seemed "impolitic and inopportune" for further cash advances, went on to suggest that the Pacific Fleet, as well, might prove useful in Chinese waters. Taft issued the order to Navy Secretary Meyer the following morning. And, on November 23, Knox informed Minister Calhoun that the President was preparing to despatch 2,400 men from Manila to Tientsin as part of the international expeditionary force. Knox instructed Calhoun to proceed quietly, avoiding any "conspicuous position of initiative."[17]

In December, the focus of American policy shifted from the military plane to the diplomatic when it became clear that the Chinese revolutionaries were likely to win. It was important to establish working relations with the rebels who now controlled Shanghai and the Yangtze Valley. Rejecting advice from Calhoun that the Powers should lend Yuan enough money to crush the rebellion, and a suggestion from Japan that they promote a constitutional monarchy, the United States held fast to the "cooperative policy," which at that time meant working closely with Britain. The Department reaffirmed its commitment to "strict neutrality" in a circular note of December 12, discouraged all foreign loans, and, on December 18, joined with the other Powers in an identic note to the belligerents meeting in peace conference at Shanghai.[18]

Meanwhile, American naval commanders and consuls in the Yangtze Valley, Shanghai, Canton, and other areas of revolutionary strength, were opening channels to rebel authorities. Soon the State Department took steps to inform itself regarding the provisional government in Nanking, which, early in 1912, seemed likely to dominate the future. On January 22, the Department commissioned Admiral Murdock and Charles D. Tenney, a former missionary serving as Chinese-language Secretary in the Peking Legation, to visit Nanking and report back on "the solidarity of the revolutionary movement" and the question "how far the provisional government at Nanking is representative of the will of the Chinese people."[19]

Seeing Nanking at a time of revolutionary euphoria, when the power and prestige of the Republican cause was at its height, the American observers developed high regard for Wang Ching-wei, Huang Hsing, Sun Yat-sen, and the swarm of foreign-educated students and other patriots assembled in the rebel redoubt. On January 26, Admiral Murdock cabled that the Republican government, whose leaders were "capable but inexperienced," "undoubtedly represents the will of the great majority of the people in China." His final report, on February 12, described Sun as "a man of character and force" and expressed high hopes:

> As a general result of my visit to Nanking, I am impressed with the sincerity and ability of the officials in charge of the revolutionary government and with their confidence of eventually establishing an elective government for China, capable of controlling the country and developing peace and prosperity.[20]

Tenney also was enthusiastic. Though familiarity with conditions in the Peking area, where the revolutionary struggle enjoyed relatively little support, led Tenney to caution that a Republic would encounter many problems, he favored early diplomatic recognition. Just as the Manchus were departing, on February 11, Tenney cabled Calhoun:

> In reply to Department of State, my opinion is that revolutionary movement represents firm purpose of Chinese people and that Nanking Government meets general approval. People determined to try Republicanism. I think success doubtful, but nothing can prevent trial. As soon as North and South have settled I think Provisional Republic should have immediate recognition.[21]

But the advices of the observer team were ignored in Washington. While de facto relations obtained immediately upon the exit of the Manchus, formal recognition was delayed pending settlement of the outstanding questions, financial and otherwise, between China and the Powers.[22]

Moreover, the Chinese political situation soon began to deteriorate. As power passed from Sun Yat-sen in Nanking to Yuan Shih-k'ai at Peking, it became clear that Yuan, though widely regarded as China's most capable leader, would find it difficult to establish and maintain order. Adding to the political uncertainties was the fact that President Yuan had no roots in the democratic tradition. Though he agreed to go along with Nanking's plans for free elections and a Parliament, Yuan's relations with Republican institutions were always tenuous. Also he was broke: no money to pay his troops—the latter reacted by laying waste certain districts near Peking in early March—and no money for routine government operations. Within weeks after assuming office, Yuan therefore asked the consortium for a loan of £60 million sterling. At the same time, Yuan, holding power by virtue of his reputed ability to manage the barbarians, showed little inclination further to compromise Chinese sovereignty.[23]

Moving cautiously, the concert of Powers decided to delay diplomatic recognition until the domestic situation had stabilized, the details of the reorganization loan (or Six-Power loan) were fixed, and other matters were adjusted. The State Department, eager to preserve the "cooperative policy" and the American Group's share in Chinese finance, followed suit once again. Responding to a memorandum from the Japanese Ambassador in Washington, Acting Secretary of State Huntington Wilson on February 27 agreed in principle to refrain from recognizing the Chinese Republic until the Powers collectively determined that foreign interests enjoyed adequate guarantees. This did not happen until autumn 1913, after the Chinese had acquiesced to stiff conditions regarding the reorganization loan, had acceded to British wishes in Tibet, to Russian desires in Mongolia, and so forth.[24]

Their policies wedded to those of the other Powers, American diplomats now cultivated a general pessimism regarding China's future. During the remainder of 1912, reports from Peking to Washington rejected the sanguine view: the deepening rift between south and north, the devolution of power to provincial authorities, the increasingly bitter division between Yuan and the Republican idealists, anti-foreign sentiment, the impracticality of Sun, the treachery of Yuan, the venality of practically everyone—such were the new themes. As the dust settled, there was general agreement that China was unsuited for democratic institutions.[25]

Charles Tenney, staying on at Nanking as American Consul, soon lost his Republican enthusiasm. By summer 1912, Tenney was reporting to Minister Calhoun that "the animus of the Republican leaders is strongly anti-foreign," a point that somehow escaped him earlier, and, by the following February, his despatches tended to conservatism and even reaction. Characterized as "a protest against the inefficiency rather than the tyranny of the Central Manchu Government," the Chinese Revolution could not "be closely likened to any of the European revolutions of the 18th and 19th centuries with which we are familiar." Tenney continued:

> From the motives that have led to the Revolution and the establishment of the Chinese Republic, we should not expect greater liberality and friendliness towards foreigners, but rather less; we should not expect greater care in respecting treaty stipulations, but rather an increased tendency to evade treaty obligations. It is by a study of the motives that have inspired both the classes of the Chinese Republicans outlined above that we can understand also the lamentable dearth of administrative honesty and disinterested patriotism among the new leaders. The young foreign educated Chinese Republicans have not been actuated by a longing to improve the conditions of the Chinese people but rather by the childish desire to "save face" for China in her relations with the outside world by the magical results which they suppose will follow the adoption of Western governmental forms and machinery. The Chinese literati and gentry who have espoused Republicanism are still less actuated by any wish to improve the lot of the people. They are utilizing the change in government to strengthen their hands in the exercise of the local tyranny which they have always tried to exercise over the common people for their own selfish good.

"So in the minds of both classes of Republican leaders," Tenny concluded, "there have been lacking those high motives which ennoble the thoughts and stimulate to unselfish patriotism." Though in certain ways the most perceptive analysis of the 1911 Revolution to emerge from the American official mind, the historian suspects it was less than forthright, and obviously it was insensitive to Chinese nationalism.[26]

Other American diplomats, except at Canton and a few locations where Chinese Republicans were seen to behave particularly well, generally inclined toward the critical view. Minister Calhoun kept his own counsel. In May 1912, Calhoun reported that popular support for the Republic was "a matter of great uncertainty." "The storm whipped the surface of the sea into angry whitecaps," he wrote, "but that it touched or stirred the deeper currents is much debated. In the treaty ports, and along the coast and throughout a large part of the Yangtze Valley, the revolutionary sentiment seemed strong, and the enthusiasm for the republic fervent; but in the interior, among the far off hills, in the remote valleys, the unbroken silence of the centuries still broods over the people." Maintaining that "indifference" and "passive silence" remained the leading Chinese characteristics and that President Yuan was "far from being a great statesman," Calhoun concluded: "To establish a republic upon such an uncertain foundation is like building a house upon the shifting sands."[27]

Assessments of this kind, typical of American diplomatic reporting between February 1912 and March 1913, reinforced the State Department's resolve to continue its policy of collaboration with the other Treaty Powers.[28] This policy, if it had as its principal object the tangible interests of the United States, might also be seen to evince that considerable loss of diplomatic innocence which was inevitable under the semi-colonial Unequal Treaties. In any event, American East Asia policy did nothing for Republican China. For these reasons, the policy encountered a mixed reception, which later coalesced into active opposition, on the part of the foreign-policy public.

THE PUBLIC REACTION

The foreign-policy public generally viewed the Republican Revolution in a favorable light. Though the majority of the American population may have remained indifferent to this as to most other overseas events, citizens who made a response usually gave themselves over to what Henry May has termed "vast visions of hope." The cultural historian has written, "No event of the period was subject to more incessant moral interpretation."[29]

Eventually, this movement of opinion, guided by the Missionary Mind, turned sharply against the China policy pursued by the Department of State.

Yet it should be noted that the Chinese Revolution did not lack its American detractors.

Businessmen and Old China Hands. One may generalize that businessmen and old China hands tended to maintain a certain critical distance. As early as October 1911, the *Wall Street Journal* complained that the Revolution "upsets the railway concessions, endangers the currency reform, interrupts trade, and imperils the lives and property of American citizens in China. . . . In this world of hard facts, it is not difficult to discern in what direction our national sympathy will finally gravitate." In December, the *Journal of the American Asiatic Association* wrote of the Revolution: "Apart from the losses of the battlefield, it has plunged a majority of the provinces into poverty and famine; it has arrested all trade and commerce, crippled agriculture and industry, and diverted practically every penny of tax revenue from the purpose of peace." If businessmen did not altogether welcome the Revolution, this was primarily because it was bad for business.[30]

Moreover, businessmen as a group seemed rather unappreciative of the Revolution's anti-imperialist point. Never exactly sympathetic to Chinese national aspirations, businessmen generally feared that matters might get out of hand if the more radical element attained power. As between Sun Yat-sen and Yuan Shih-k'ai, businessmen preferred the strong man, trusting Yuan and his retainers to respect foreign interests. In November, the Asiatic Association hailed Yuan as "the man of the hour" and "nearly the Dictator of China"; the following month, it decried the emergence of Sun and the radicals as fresh evidence of "the pathos of the situation." Regarding the Hukuang loan, the trade association maintained that "reason has been on the side of the Central Government."

During the last months of 1911, it expressed the hope that the struggle would result in a constitutional monarchy.[31]

Yet, it would be wrong to conclude that businessmen were wholly reactionary. More pragmatic than ideological, American businessmen in China soon accommodated themselves to the new situation. Those in Shanghai, where Republican sentiment ran deep, discovered that it was possible to do business as usual with patriotic Chinese merchants, and this was what mattered. If the Asiatic Association remained relatively jaundiced in its successive estimates of the Chinese Republic, even it eventually was forced to admit that "the republican form of government is, after all, the one that divides Chinese the least." On the Pacific Coast, the leading commercial organizations, including the San Francisco Chamber of Commerce, apparently came to believe that the Chinese Revolution might, in some perhaps not easily definable way, prove beneficial to trade.[32]

But the better-connected businessmen in New York and East Asia generally remained pessimistic about the Republican experiment, and a number evinced a kind of nostalgia for the Ch'ing. Willard Straight, principal negotiator for the American Group, wrote from Peking in December 1911 that he did not believe "that the Manchus deserve the celerity with which they have been tin-canned." Warning his correspondent not to adopt the optimistic assessment enjoying currency among Chinese patriots and a certain class of foreigners, Straight observed with acid sarcasm: "I am told on all sides that the situation is extremely interesting, that we are seeing the awakening of a great people, and that autocracy, corruption, squeeze, cowardice, avarice, intrigue, and all the evils inherent in any oriental administration . . . are about to disappear, and the equality, fraternity, and honesty, hitherto hidden beneath the blushes of a modest Chinese proletariat, are to become the watchwords of national development." Striving after effect, Straight said he worried that the Nanking rebels would seek "a panacea for all China's ills in an orgy of hot air and republican nonsense. . . . The old crowd were bad enough," he sighed. "The Rebels are infinitely worse. When it comes to a choice between the most reactionary

Manchu and that ass, Wu Ting-fang, I should prefer the Manchu every time."[33]

Whatever their retrospective judgment on the Ch'ing, men doing business with East Asia generally refrained from sentimental effusion regarding the new Republic (Pacific Coast merchants, again, represented a partial exception). The critical, even pessimistic mentality was perhaps most pronounced among old China hands, whose estrangement from the general current of American opinion was much remarked by the Asiatic Association. Quoting such a one, unidentified by name but broadly hinted to be the estimable historian H. B. Morse, the Association endorsed his observation that the central questions between China and the United States

> will be answered in China's favor by ninety-nine out of every hundred Americans, and just there lies the danger. The teaching of history is not known to them, and even the hundredth American is quite ready to accept as a fact that the doings of October, 1911 to February, 1912 [Chinese Revolutionary Rebellion] have completely transformed a great Asiatic race and modified its inherited character.[34]

Republican institutions being unsuited to the genius of an Oriental people, old China hands refused to be swept away by an alien enthusiasm. W. W. Rockhill, connoisseur of traditional Chinese culture and architect of the Open Door, was among the Chinese Republic's enemies. Writing from Constantinople in the summer of 1912 to the venerable Dr. Morrison, longtime London *Times* correspondent in Peking, Rockhill observed: "Better than anyone you know the position of the present Government of China, hardly yet established, not recognized by any of the Treaty Powers, up to its neck in financial troubles . . . with no man of tried ability but lots of spectacled, frock-coated young dreamers fresh from the United States, Japan or Great Britain, full of Utopian dreams of universal and immediate reform, etc., etc." The following year Rockhill told an American diplomat that a certain development "will not help the Republic (Thank God! for I am absolutely opposed to its maintenance a day longer than is necessary)."[35]

Certainly, businessmen and old China hands, whatever the

regional variations or individual exceptions, held attitudes toward
Republican China markedly different from those of the Protestant
missionaries.

China Missionaries and Their Public. For missionaries and their
constituents, the Revolution of 1911 was a dream come true.
Everything they had worked for suddenly seemed possible. Though
most missionaries probably had limited experience of revolutionary
events, a few, notably Christian college teachers and Y.M.C.A. secretaries, found themselves in the midst of the struggle. Y.M.C.A.
officials looked on as Chinese merchant and student members
joined the patriotic movement. The President of North China Union
College, Howard Galt, reported to the American Board that the
Revolution "stimulated the students to eloquence as fiery as that
of William Pitt or Patrick Henry," and that it was "indeed a test
of patience for some of our hot-headed young revolutionaries to
sit supinely by while young men in the south seemed to be accomplishing so much for the popular cause." [36]

To many Chinese Christians the temptation proved irresistible,
and they thereby placed the missionaries in a delicate position; for,
however liberal their theology, however radical their Social Gospel,
missionaries could not with impunity take that final step to violence nor encourage it among their charges. The reasons were at
once idealistic and pragmatic: idealistic in that missionaries found
it difficult to countenance the use of force; pragmatic because their
legal rights under the Unequal Treaties depended upon scrupulous
abstention from Chinese politics. So Howard Galt had little choice
but to shut down his college after an undergraduate was arrested
(later executed) for plotting the assassination of a Manchu prince,
just as Lyman Peet, President of Foochow College, took similar
action when his students, "their minds preoccupied with a desire
to help in throwing off the Manchu yoke," demanded that they be
allowed to "drill with firearms." Peet, in his annual report to the
American Board, expressed relief that, "so far as known, no one
took part in the destruction of life and property by the throwing
of nitro-glycerine bombs." [37]

Only a handful of missionaries overcame their scruples and

plunged into the revolutionary struggle. Their activities, if always relatively tame, naturally embarrassed American diplomats as the latter pursued their policy of "strict neutrality." In January 1912, the Peking Legation, responding to a complaint that American missionaries in Shanghai were openly proclaiming sympathy with the Republican cause, directed Consul-General Amos Wilder to monitor the situation closely. Wilder immediately called in the leading political types—E. W. Thwing, the anti-opium crusader; Gilbert Reid, the foreign light of the 1898 Reform; and Bishop James Bashford—and requested they cultivate a discreet silence. Yet, Wilder's entreaties were perhaps only partially successful, for, while they made a sensible impression on E. W. Thwing, the Reverend Reid soon decided upon a personal mission to the court of Peking, whither he repaired for ten days in order to persuade the Ch'ing to abdicate. Bishop Bashford, meanwhile, was in the slough of despond. Wilder found the Methodist Bishop of Peking sulking in Shanghai because a notorious local radical group called the "Dare-to-Die" squadron seemed over-represented with Methodist youth. "At present he is perturbed by the presence in Shanghai of seventeen female patriots," Wilder wrote, "ten of them of his Foochow mission schools. They have come to join the bomb-throwing brigade, and thus far have not been dissuaded." Even the most political of missionaries drew the line at nitroglycerine.[38]

Yet, missionary opinion, while far from incendiary, expressed general support for the Revolution. Without confusing the views of articulate liberal-Social Gospel types in the treaty ports with those of their more numerous colleagues in the hinterlands, some of whom remained rather oblivious of the upheaval, the historian concludes that, among missionaries who held informed opinions, approval of the Revolution was virtually unanimous. Missionaries emerged early as partisans. In November 1911, the *Chinese Record-er* of Shanghai, principal voice of China missions, was already exulting that "the sunrise of a new era seems to have dawned . . . a simultaneous budding of new life 'under heaven,'" and two months later the journal published a five-page editorial observing that "this break with the corrupt and outworn system of the past means the presence and power of a new life, a life destined to raise and remake this nation, and set it one day with the other nations of the world as an equal." That the anti-imperialist movement might have implications for their own privileged position under the Unequal Treaties did not seem to occur to the missionary enthusiasts. "The opposition to railway concessions is based on serious political reasons well known to all Chinese, who are resolved to be masters in their own house," wrote one American missionary to the folks back home. "The deepest root of the rebellion," he observed, "is the self-respect of the Chinese." [39]

Since it was the nature of missionaries never to give themselves halfway to a cause, nor understate the truth, missionaries made every effort to spread the good news about China throughout the United States. Interest in China ran high as missionary-minded Americans followed the Revolution closely from its earliest days. In mid-October 1911, Arthur Judson Brown, head of the Foreign Missions Conference of North America, an umbrella organization, wrote the State Department that "the more than twenty millions of Protestant Christians in the United States who are the constituents of our Foreign Missions are flooding us with inquiries." Sometime later, Homer Stuntz, Secretary of the Northern Methodist mission board, told President Taft: "Many thousands of devout men and women are earnestly praying that you and your advisors may be guided in this great crisis in the affairs of China." [40]

China missionaries were extraordinarily vocal. Through speeches, letters, articles, and books they disseminated fact and opinion. More than usual, they were able to claim credit for the world's progress. "The ideas that have awakened this great people, slumbering for millenniums," wrote the Louisville *Christian Observer,* "have been introduced into China by missionaries." While their message was overly simple, so that the man in the pew heard less about anti-imperialism and nitroglycerine than about more comforting themes, it did not lack sympathy for China. "The rebellion has been skillfully planned and financed, and proves that the Chinese have awakened and desire progress," observed the influential *Missionary Review of the World:* "The leaders are educated and capable and are carrying the masses of the people with them." That Sun Yat-sen was a Christian man did not go unnoticed. But the missionaries were realists, so that, when Sun was eclipsed by Yuan, the American Board's *Missionary Herald* made bold to say, "May the God who knew King Cyrus and girded him . . . gird and guide Yuan Shi Kai!"[41]

In view of this enthusiasm, the historian may surmise that the 300 or so China missionaries home on furlough, determined to reach as many of their 5 million base constituents as possible, gave somewhat more than their annual average of 30,000 speeches. In any event, China missionaries were much in demand as speakers on college campuses, at church conventions, and in local churches during the period of the Republican Revolution. Even the sea lanes of the North Pacific provided no hiding place from the missionary message. Aboard the SS *Mongolia* of the Pacific Mail Line, a few days out of Yokohama, bound for San Francisco, businessman Robert Dollar recorded in his diary that he and his fellow passengers had heard one James W. Bashford deliver a "very fine lecture on the effects of the revolution in China."[42]

The Republican Revolution, in sum, received highly favorable notice among China missionaries and the foreign-missions public in America.

Newspaper Editors and Others. Newspaper editors gave great coverage to the 1911 Revolution. The Szechwan riots, the Wuchang uprising, the battle of Hankow, the recall of Yuan Shih-k'ai, Sun's inauguration, the Manchu abdication—the unfolding narrative dominated the front pages of major American dailies. And editorial writers commented frequently. This pattern obtained among newspapers of every kind. If the sensational *San Francisco Examiner* beamed the dramatic developments day after day—on November 16 the Hearst paper gave over its entire front page to China—and much the same coverage characterized the *Chicago Tribune,* the historian will find no diminution of interest among quality papers, such as the *Boston Transcript* and the *New York Times.* For example, during the Revolution proper, the *Times* found room on page 1 for China news 39 mornings, published 31 editorials and ran 7 articles in the Sunday Magazine. The Chinese Revolution was its biggest foreign story of the year.[43]

It is notable that small-town papers also seemed absorbed. The *Walla Walla Union,* serving a primarily agricultural community in Washington state, ran China stories on the front page for 35 consecutive days. The recall of Yuan Shih-k'ai rated a four-inch banner. Even the Six-Power loan negotiations made front page news. For a season, China seemed as important in Walla Walla as the price of wheat on the Portland Grain Exchange.[44]

Whether in Walla Walla or Manhattan, editorial writers declared early for the Republican cause, and the *Literary Digest* has left us a convenient summary of the movement of opinion. In its October 28 issue, the magazine reported that most newspapers, including the *Boston Transcript,* the *New York Tribune,* the *Washington Times,* the *Indianapolis News,* and the *St. Louis Globe-Democrat,* were saying China was truly ready for a Republic, and on November 11 the *Digest* wrote that "our editors see very clearly a China for the Chinese, ruled by a real Parliament." Among the newspapers now celebrating "this greatest of latter-day revolutions" were the *New York Herald* and the *Louisville Courier-Journal.* On January 13, 1912, the *Digest,* in a piece entitled "The Newest and Greatest Republic," featuring a picture of Sun Yat-sen, observed that "China, not Japan, is now the Land of the Rising Sun." The magazine continued:

> Japan will no longer be the most Occidental nation in the Orient, it is remarked, if the Chinese succeed in establishing a federal republic modeled upon the Government of the United States, with leaders imbued with Western ideas through their education in Europe and America. The press of this country are looking with wonder.

Though certain editors seemed to fear that the Republic would encounter rough going, the hope was general that the Chinese Revolution might, as the *St. Louis Post Dispatch* expressed it, "lead the way to the redemption of all Asia."[45]

The Manchu abdication, on February 12, occasioned much comment from editors, who interpreted it as one of the great events of world history. Even the New York *Journal of Commerce,* not usually given to hyperbole, observed that it was the most significant event since the fall of the Roman Empire, and the *New York Times,* noting that the Chinese Revolution might prove more important than the French, stated that "there has been nothing so tremendous in itself or so pregnant with possible consequences in the history of the world in many generations."[46]

The generous assessment of the 1911 Revolution, so different from the calculated pessimism of the professional diplomat, businessman, or old China hand, seemed common not only among newspaper editors but among a large segment of the opinion elite generally. Owing, one presumes, to their slight acquaintance with East Asian affairs coupled with sentimental influences, many of those one would expect to articulate the sense of the community appeared to embrace the uncritical view of the Chinese Republic. Some seemed to regard democracy in China as an established fact. Of fifteen distinguished Americans asked by the *New York Times* to list the year 1911's greatest achievements, nine singled out the Chinese Revolution, in phrases such as "the movement in China for free and honest government," "the triumph of democracy in China," "the triumph of the progressive movement in China," and "the growth of political democracy in China."[47]

That their views may have reflected, in some degree, the Missionary Mind, is suggested by the strikingly different attitude toward the Revolution adopted by members of the ethnic communities.

Ethnic Americans. As one might perhaps expect from their lack of philanthropic activity in East Asia, Roman Catholic Americans, in particular, seemed to take relatively little interest in the Chinese Revolution. While Protestant eyes were riveted on China, Catholic attentions, to the extent that they had an overseas focus, directed themselves toward Europe. Among Catholic intellectuals, France generally appeared to be of paramount importance. The intellectual *Catholic World,* which every month published a ten-page section on foreign affairs, placed France first and China last throughout the years 1911–1913, and its commentary on China lacked all sense of republican commitment. The Manchu abdication rating a short, bloodless paragraph, the editors noted dryly that "there is every reason to think that the body of the people have had very little to do with the recent change." The *Catholic World* seemed to reserve its passion for the struggle between church and state in France. Meanwhile, among ordinary Roman Catholics, events in Ireland, Italy, even Spain, appeared to command more attention than those in China. In the Archdiocese of Boston, for example, the weekly *Pilot* did not cover the Chinese Revolution from October through December 1911, and a brief January article described Sun Yat-sen merely as "China's present dictator." Yet there was no lack of interest in Irish Home Rule.[48]

If Catholics may have paid scant attention, the Chinese Revolution seemed even less compelling in the Jewish community. In the sweatshops and tenements of the Lower East Side, as in the drawing rooms of German Jewish patricians uptown, China was generally quite remote. For American Jews, the most important foreign issues were Russian government restrictions on Jewish emigration and, to a lesser extent, Palestine. Reading through a Jewish newspaper, say the Boston *Jewish Advocate,* the historian finds the problems of Russian Jewry featured prominently, but little word of Republican China.[49]

Yet, there was one ethnic group to whom the Chinese Republic really meant something—Chinese-Americans, who played a leading role in its financing and who followed the revolutionary drama closely. On October 15, the *San Francisco Examiner* reported that "the excitement in Chinatown is intense, and the bulk of the influential men of the quarter are sympathizing with the revolutionists." On November 5, following the battle of Hankow, the community gave itself over to a day of banquets and parades said to be the greatest ever in Chinatown, San Francisco. The one thousand or so Chinese studying at American colleges and universities, members of the Young China generation, many of them genuine democrats, many of them Christians, also supported the cause. Among the more remarkable was the Columbia graduate student and later Chinese Foreign Minister, V. K. Wellington Koo.[50]

But besides Chinese, who had no vote, ethnic Americans, at

least those who were not Protestants, demonstrated little support for the Republican Revolution.

Public Opinion and the State Department. By the end of February 1912, Chinese news largely had disappeared from the front pages, and events in East Asia were once again obscured from public view. The military intervention of the Treaty Powers, Yuan Shih-k'ai's vicissitudes, the founding of the Kuomintang—these events and others largely escaped the attention of a people inclined to look upon the Chinese Revolution as a *fait accompli*. And, though Chinese politics no longer dominated the headlines, China, probably because it continued to be mentioned in church, remained on the mind of many. With pro-Chinese sentiment somehow deepening during 1912, the foreign-policy public eventually turned against the China policy followed by the Taft Administration. Vocal public opposition was a new and potentially troublesome element in East Asia policy. In brief, the foreign-policy public, lacking the stabilizing influence one associates with a responsible and informed opinion leadership, came to demand unilateral recognition of the Chinese Republic and withdrawal of the American Group from the Six-Power consortium.

The Department received a flood of letters and telegrams on the recognition issue. Except for a single Cleveland racist, all urged recognition at once. The movement of opinion is interesting in several ways. Chinese-Americans and missionary groups dominated the early flow, with other church organizations—individual congregations, denominational groups, the Federal Council of Churches—joining as the year 1912 progressed. By year end and during early 1913, there developed something like a mass movement, so that Rotary Clubs, civic and commercial groups, even the establishment Republican Club of New York, felt compelled to take a stand. By early 1913, apart from the Asiatic Association and a few other diehards, virtually no opinion leaders in the country were still in favor of the Department's China policies. At Delmonico's in October 1912, Seth Low observed that "public opinion in this country is substantially unanimous in desiring the recognition of the Republic of China."[51]

China being a grass-roots cause, many letters finding their way to the Department issued from persons or groups who presumably had little or no abiding interest in foreign relations apart from this single issue. A religious organization in Elmira, New York; the Presbyterian churches of Newark; the Rotary Club of Harrisburg, Pennsylvania; the Cleveland Y.M.C.A.; missionary institutions in Cincinnati and Indianapolis; the Rotary Clubs of San Antonio and Pueblo, Colorado; a civic association in Helena; the Chautauqua Assembly at Pacific Grove, California; the Women's Missionary Social Union of Everett, Washington—these and hundreds more told the State Department its China policies should be abandoned. In February 1912, Congressman Lafferty of Oregon sent the Department a prize-winning essay entitled "Why the United States should be the First Nation to Recognize the New Republic of China," the effort of a thirteen-year-old Portland schoolgirl expressing "the sentiment of a great number of the people of Oregon." "The people out there," Mr. Lafferty explained, "are heartily in sympathy with the struggling Chinese."[52]

As months passed and the Department still would not act, many citizens interpreted the delay as a function of the American Group's involvement in the Six-Power consortium. Fed by missionary and journalistic criticism, and powered by instinctive hostility to Wall Street (which many citizens held in low regard in 1912, year of the Pujo Committee hearings on Capitol Hill), public opposition to the Department of State's financial diplomacy steadily widened. Even the terms of the reorganization loan—hypothecation of the so-called salt gabelle, its foreign administration, along with other stringent controls—received close scrutiny. "It had been charged," recalled Willard Straight in an address to the East Asiatic Society of Boston in 1913,

> that the "Six Power" Group was forcing China to borrow enormous sums which she did not require; that the bankers were endeavoring to secure a monopoly of China's loan business for thirty years to come; that the terms demanded by the Group affronted China's national dignity, interfered with her administrative independence and threatened her territorial integrity; that in order to obtain this security bankers

were fastening upon the Chinese people an iniquitous and antiquated tax, and that through their machinations they had obliged their respective governments to withhold recognition of the Chinese republic until the loan had been concluded. The American Government and the American Group, moreover, in addition to their equal share in this general denunciation, were accorded particular attention as being the venal tools of European diplomacy. [53]

The Department received a considerable flow of mail on the Six-Power loan, virtually all of it critical, from persons such as the missionary leader Arthur Judson Brown, from the Massachusetts Women's Christian Temperance Union, the Lord's Day League of New England, even the San Francisco Labor Council (no friend of California Chinese), and others. "The 'six-power loan' is not in good repute with us," wrote David Starr Jordan, President of Stanford: "The Chinese people are afraid of 'power loans,' and their experience justifies this caution. Not only must China pay the common usury exacted of debtor nations, but the transaction is likely, somewhere, to cut deeply into her sovereignty." In a populist flourish, Jordan noted that the "money-lenders hunt in packs when concerted action best serves this interest." The Department also was stung by comparable attacks from humbler quarters, such as the Peoria mechanic who dipped his pen in venom and wrote:

> Since the death of John Hay, former Secretary of State, the course pursued by our government with China has been shameful.
> We have joined with other nations in a policy of exploitation and robbery, and seemingly for the purpose of continueing [sic] that policy we are declining to recognize the new "Republic of China."

It is doubtful that many other international financial negotiations have generated this level of interest and concern among ordinary citizens. [54]

Naturally, the bankers affiliated with the Department did their best to defend themselves. Though China did not matter much in the material sense, Wall Street had no desire to see this issue added to the litany of public grievance. The bankers had their reputations to think of, and they owed their friends an explanation. So, in October 1912, Thomas W. Lamont of Morgan invited President

Eliot, a summer neighbor at Bar Harbor and consortium critic, to come down and discuss things with H. P. Davison, Jacob Schiff, Paul Warburg, Frank Vanderlip, and Willard Straight over dinner at the Metropolitan Club. Bankers also felt obliged to explain themselves to mission-board officials. In February 1913, responding to a request from H. P. Davison's wife, who seemed to become exercised upon reading in one of her mission journals that the American Group was behaving contrary to the interests of China, bankers quickly arranged a conference in New York to explain their motives.[55]

It is notable that the East Asia policy of the Taft Administration also came in for criticism from academic circles. At the November 1912 Clark University conference on Asia, the China experts of the day, such as they were, questioned Washington's approach. Albert Bushnell Hart, who if not a Sinologist was at least a Harvard historian, gave a paper comparing the concert of Powers in Eastern Asia to the reactionary Holy Alliance ("worse than nonsense" was the Asiatic Association's view of this effort). Moreover, Willard Straight's paper in defense of Administration policy was poorly received, as was that of his British friend J. O. P. Bland, an estimable old China hand, who defended opium-smoking as one of those settled habits of a great Asiatic people. Straight left an amusing account of the Worcester meeting, that "rough neck conference" in "wildest Massachusetts," where the food was bad and the papers worse, "the villagers" gathered round to sample the half-baked opinions of A. B. Hart, "the whiskered progressive," and C. C. Wang, "the young Christian soldier," and where a certain evangelical ambience was present. "They put Bland and myself in an overheated 2x4 hotel," Straight wrote, "where we created a terrible sensation by asking for a cocktail, which we were caustically informed the hotel did not sell."[56]

Bland, in his diary, was even more caustic: "They put us up at a vile temperance and godliness hole called the Standish—We dined out at some psalm-singing Club . . . nothing but water to drink . . . Then to a reception at the President's house, which was exactly like an American missionary gathering in China—the high nasal voices, the twaddle and gush about things as they *aren't,* the hideous women and the *Chin-less* men." Bland also recorded the conference's working session:

> I followed a missionary speaker who by much deliberate suppressio veri won the hearts of the good folks of Worcester. He described a purely unreal Chinese Republic—and a happy contented Chinese people—
>
> I told 'em the truth about opium—not welcome in this sanctified atmosphere—Prof. Blakeslee said 'well done' but the audience was glum.

Bland and Straight, their thoughts out of season, their expertise neglected, "swore that never again would we come to Worcester, Mass."[57]

The academics, like the other groups in the foreign-policy public, no longer had confidence in the China policies of Taft and Knox.

THE POLITICIZATION OF CHINA POLICY

The years 1912–1913 saw China, perhaps for the first time, become a domestic political issue in the United States. Sensing a widening gap between official policy and public feeling, leaders of the political opposition to the Taft Administration manipulated the China issue for personal and partisan gain. Made possible in large measure by the absence of an informed, articulate, responsible body of citizens concerned with the American national interest in East Asia, politicization was to become a China-policy tradition.

Though the China issue really belonged, for social and cultural reasons, to the Republicans more than the Democrats—the Republican Party having its natural base in the missionary-minded towns of the Middle West[58]—those in a position to exploit it now were Democrats.

In early 1912, the national Democratic Party, after nearly two decades of wandering the political wilderness, was positioned to recapture the federal establishment. When the Sixty-second Congress returned for its second session on January 3, Democrats effectively dominated Capitol Hill. Having done well in the 1910 congressional elections, the party now controlled the House of Representatives, and, though Republicans still organized the Senate, Democrats usually could find the votes for their legislative priorities. Relations between the Taft Administration and the congressional leadership, Republican and Democratic, were badly frayed, particularly in foreign affairs. Taft-Knox dollar diplomacy being in bad odor on the Hill, there was lacking that intimate collaboration between the executive and the key congressional committees, House Foreign Affairs and Senate Foreign Relations, on whose sufferance the successful pursuit of American foreign policy may be said to depend. The year 1912 was a presidential election year, and the Democrats were thought to have an excellent opportunity to regain the White House. A number of able Democratic candidates threw in their hats. President Taft, meanwhile, entered 1912 uncertain of receiving his party's renomination. There was also the possibility of a third-party challenge, further dividing Republican ranks.[59]

In this political context, the Democratic Party seized upon American China policy as a means to embarrass and further weaken the Republican Administration. First on Capitol Hill, and eventually in the recaptured White House, Democratic leaders played politics with China to maximum political advantage.

This did not lack its effects on foreign policy.

Pressure from the Hill. In the first days of 1912, almost as soon as they got off the train at Union Station, congressional Democrats positioned themselves to exploit public dissatisfaction with Administration policy. Having spent the months since adjournment in their home districts, Members of Congress were doubtless aware that a sizeable bloc of their constituents had reacted to the Chinese Revolution in what might be called the missionary manner and would be receptive to a like-minded congressional initiative.

The day Congress reconvened, January 3, the gentleman from New York, Mr. Sulzer, the distinguished Chairman of the Committee on Foreign Affairs, introduced a bill congratulating the people of China for what was said to be their assumption of a Republican form of government and calling upon the President to extend formal diplomatic recognition. In an interview with the *New York Times,* Sulzer, who as veteran Representative of the Lower East Side had long known the politics of Russian Jewish emigration, spoke now of China as a "new republic evolving from centuries of oppression and being heroically constructed on the ruins of a tottering despotism." Perhaps with one eye on the governorship of New York, which he went on to win that November, Sulzer added,"Public sentiment in America favors the Resolution."[60]

Representative Sulzer's move, taking the form of a concurrent resolution, was a bold challenge to a China policy based on the principles of "strict neutrality" regarding the Chinese belligerents and cooperative action with the other Treaty Powers. Inasmuch as the Ch'ing dynasty did not abdicate until February 12, the resolution, as the Asiatic Association pointed out, amounted to American interference in a Chinese civil war. With the support of the House leadership, the resolution was reported out of committee on February 28, went next day to the floor where, over strong Administration objections (and following a brief debate in which Representative Sulzer said, "Long live the Republic of China!"), it passed unanimously on a voice vote. The Senate also moved expeditiously. The resolution went to the other body on March 1 and, the Republican leadership being powerless to stop it, the bill was marked up in the Foreign Relations Committee. A clean bill, reported out by Chairman Lodge, passed the Senate unanimously a few days later. Even the supporters of Administration policy would not go on record against the Chinese Republic in an American election year. "Congress has spoken," said Congressman Sulzer: "Let the President act accordingly."[61]

This massive pressure from the Hill—not a single vote for Administration China policy in either house—naturally caused considerable dismay downtown. "The question of future formal recognition of the republic of China being susceptible of use as a matter of politics," as Huntington Wilson put it, the State Department had somehow to demonstrate its control over events in order to regain the policy initiative.[62]

Early in February, Huntington Wilson decided to accomplish

this in the traditional manner, by reaffirming the legendary Open Door policy. Done the proper way, with plenty of publicity, a media event of this kind might enable the Department to conduct its business, once again, above the din of partisan strife. The diplomatic historian will add that the idea was also rooted in international politics. In fact, the proposal for a new American *démarche* originated in Germany. Fearful that China's weakness might lead Japan to intervene militarily in Manchuria, German diplomats approached the American Ambassador in Berlin late in January, suggested that the United States despatch a circular note codifying the cooperative policy theretofore observed by the Treaty Powers, and urged that no independent action be undertaken without mutual consultation. Washington, which had often found Berlin a useful informal ally in East Asia, accepted the suggestion and issued such a note on February 3.[63]

Yet, its domestic political purpose was also clear from the fact that Huntington Wilson laid elaborate plans for public relations. Announcing the move to the press when it could more easily (and more properly) be kept secret, and publicly releasing the replies of the Powers, State generated front-page headlines for a day—"Hands Off China, Knox Says to World; Kaiser Backs U.S." read the lead article in the *San Francisco Examiner*—and received favorable editorial comment. But the success soon faded as the foreign-policy public continued to clamor for recognition, and the Department again found itself on the defensive.[64]

Fearing that Congress was prepared to force the Administration's hand, the Department tried to defuse the issue by proposing an alternative congressional resolution to that of Representative Sulzer. A new bill for this purpose, drafted by Ransford Miller on February 19, would extend congratulations to the Chinese people for having embraced the Republican form of government but remain silent on diplomatic recognition. "It seems to the Division," wrote Miller to Huntington Wilson, "that some such resolution as this would go far towards satisfying the public sentiment in this country . . . and at the same time permitting the executive branch of the Government to follow a conservative course in regard to the formal recognition of the new government at the proper time as well as to maintain an entirely consistent attitude with respect to cooperating with the other powers." [65]

Moreover, in declaring its intention to follow the cooperative policy regarding recognition, first announced on February 27 in a memorandum to the Japanese Ambassador, the Department carefully allowed for the contingencies of American domestic politics. The memo reaffirmed "the principle of concerted action" and stated that the United States "agrees in principle to the application of that policy to the recognition of the Republic of China . . . so long as this course shall entail no undue delay." Explaining the exact language to President Taft, Huntington Wilson emphasized that "the draft is intended to leave a loophole through which you could recognize the Republic if it were found that the policy of waiting for the other powers was entailing an undue delay which might cause trouble with Congress." [66]

All during this period, there was fear that Congress would force a policy change through some legislation more forcible than a concurrent resolution. In another attempt to take the heat off at home, the Department decided in mid-July to despatch a circular note to the Powers formally recommending recognition of the Chinese Republic. Huntington Wilson, Ransford Miller, that veteran bureaucrat Alvey Adee, even Secretary Knox (whose work day rarely exceeded two hours) devoted themselves to the project. Its motives seemed wholly political; certainly the proposed move was not based on the reports flowing from Peking, which continued to be pessimistic. [67]

Whatever its results—and diplomats appeared to entertain no real hopes for its success—the very fact of having tried would serve as evidence of good faith toward Republican China, or at least suggest the absence of bad faith. "While we may get no credit if we send it, we may get a lot of blame if we do not," said one senior official. It was especially important to forestall further criticism from missionaries and missionary groups. When the Department got wind in July that Representative Sulzer had arranged to meet in New York with the mission-board secretaries, who were said to be considering a nationwide campaign for China recognition, it took more than routine notice. Concern regarding missionary influence on public opinion prompted Secretary Knox, on July 17, to hand over to Bishop Bashford the secret American circular proposing recognition.[68]

Attached to the circular note issued by Secretary Knox on July 20 were the following instructions for the chiefs of missions: "In handing the foregoing textually to the Minister for Foreign Affairs, you may in strictest confidence intimate that public opinion and sympathy in this country are so far in favor of early recognition that there is great probability that a strong demand for such recognition will be made through the Congress, should action by the Executive be unduly delayed." To Ambassador Whitelaw Reid in London the Secretary wrote: "Considerable pressure is being brought to bear upon the Administration to secure prompt recognition of the Republic of China, and it is highly desirable to avoid any issue between the President and the Congress."[69]

Though the move produced polite refusals from all the Powers, it did buy time at home. By fuzzing the issue, the Department was able to salvage its steady policy. During the autumn of 1912, Congress having adjourned *sine die,* members were in their home districts campaigning for re-election, and national attention was focused on the three-way struggle for the presidency, which was dominated by domestic concerns. Taft, having been humiliated at the polls, eloquently defended his East Asia policies in his annual message to Congress in December, but public pressure continued to mount, and after the new Congress had organized, in January 1913, there was a final effort to force a policy change. Led by Senator Augustus Bacon of Georgia, ranking Democrat on the Foreign Relations Committee, the move was resisted successfully by the Republicans.[70]

A fresh approach to East Asia policy had to await the Democratic Administration then preparing to assume power.

New Policies Downtown. Inaugurated on March 4, 1913, President Woodrow Wilson produced the final act in America's response to the Chinese Revolution. This change of direction in China policy, much discussed by diplomatic historians, occurred within weeks of the President's taking the oath of office. On March 18, Wilson broke with the financial diplomacy of his predecessor by announcing that the State Department would withdraw support from the American Group. On April 2, Secretary of State William Jennings Bryan summoned the diplomatic corps to inform them that the United States had decided to formally recognize the Republic of China. One month later, the Chargé in Peking, E. T. Williams, called upon President Yuan and the deed was done.[71]

The reasons for this abrupt policy change, amounting to a kind of distancing from the other Treaty Powers on two specific issues, but no root-and-branch repudiation of imperialism, have received much study. Students of diplomacy are inclined to remark the amateurishness of policies undertaken in the absence of adequate consultation with the other Powers, who learned in the newspapers of United States withdrawal from the Six-Power consortium. Yes, these were the salad days of Wilsonian diplomacy. Moreover, it was doubtless true that the President, while refusing to sanction further Wall Street participation in Chinese finance for the time being, did not intend to retard or impede American economic relations with China or to repudiate the doctrines of political economy near to his heart. It also seems likely that Woodrow Wilson, the principled foe of the Mexican dictator Huerta, misperceived the Chinese situation in his haste to recognize the regime of Yuan Shih-k'ai.[72]

Yet, the President's own participation in the Missionary Mind must also have had a certain effect on his framing of the policy questions. Much remarked by Arthur Link and other scholars who have interpreted Wilson's initial China policies as a species of "missionary diplomacy," what the historian may call the missionary element in the President's thinking surfaced early and often. As early as January 16, 1913, the President-elect was telling Bryan, "I warmly concur in your judgment that I ought to send to China and Japan men of pronounced Christian character. These nations are very much on my mind, and I think there are certain distinct services which we can render them." A notable feature of the 1911

Revolution, Wilson noted several weeks later, was that "the men now most active in establishing a new government and a new regime for China are many of them members of the Y.M.C.A., and many of them also men trained in American universities. The Christian influence, direct or indirect, is very prominently at the front and I need not say, ought to be kept there."[73]

The missionary ingredient in Wilson's makeup found classic expression in his repeated efforts to persuade John R. Mott to serve as American Minister in Peking. Writing to Bryan on February 5, Wilson observed that the missionary leader "has as many of the qualities of statesman as any man of my acquaintance." When Mott, then leading evangelical revivals in China, replied that he could not see his way clear to accept a diplomatic post, Wilson, citing "my duty to the public interest," urged him to reconsider: "The interests of China and of the Christian world," the President argued, "are so intimately involved." Again Mott refused, on account of his religious commitments, but the President wired back on March 21: "It would help rather than interfere with your work as representative of this government if you retained your post of guidance in your present work. . . . I am eager to unite what you represent with what this government means to try to represent."[74]

Yet, regardless of the President's undoubted missionary idealism, one may observe that his new direction in China policy served also to consolidate his domestic political base. Wilson, like many elected public officials, was capable of operating simultaneously on several levels of reality.

The historian sees an example of this mental agility in Wilson's reaction to Yuan Shih-k'ai's mid-April appeal for Christian prayer. As noted in Chapter 1, Wilson was deeply moved on the level of the religious affections. Rejecting the cynical interpretation advanced by one Cabinet member, Wilson insisted he was going to be praying and he urged the others to join him. But the President was also a politician. The Chinese appeal for prayer, coming at a time when the United States had promised diplomatic recognition but had not yet delivered, was an obvious play for American public opinion, and the President was deeply sensible of this. Following the Cabinet meeting on April 18, Navy Secretary Daniels recorded in his diary: "The President said there had come into his mind a suggestion which might seem irreverent but which was not at all irreverent, i.e., that people would say if we pray that China may become a peaceful and progressive republic, why does not this country help answer its own prayers by immediately recognizing China? Secretary Garrison [the Secretary of War] thought the country would say that you better recognize China first and pray afterwards."[75]

Given Wilson's political instincts, the historian may surmise that his decision to chart a new course in East Asia policy was not wholly devoid of domestic considerations. Mott in Peking would satisfy a certain constituency, and one may presume that Wilson, like many new presidents, needed to demonstrate leadership in foreign affairs soon after taking office. What better way to do this than in China policy, where such initiative was certain to gain overwhelming approval from Congress and the foreign-policy public? Moreover, the shakiness of Wilson's political base—he was a minority President without experience on Capitol Hill—added weight to this option. Where later Democratic Presidents would worry about the political danger of *losing* some one or another East Asian country, Woodrow Wilson had the opportunity to gain one.

Whatever the mix of motives, the new East Asia policy clearly enhanced the Administration's political standing. This first bold stroke of presidential initiative abroad met with the approval of newspaper editors representing what the *Literary Digest* called "a diversity of sectional and political allegiance." The withdrawal from the consortium, the decision to recognize China, and the offer of Peking to Mott made front page news all across the United States. As Willard Straight explained the move to J. O. P. Bland, "The press throughout the country is hailing it with delight. Their attitude is exactly that of our friends at the Worcester Conference." The White House experienced an avalanche of mail. "Your Chinese policies are great," wrote a citizen of Breese, Illinois: "God knows we need them as much or more than the poor Chinese." From Manhattan, the President's friend Cleveland Dodge confided that "the mere fact of your wishing to have Mott in China has made a great impression both here and abroad, and has announced to the world, more definitely than anything else could have done, the kind of policy which you intend to adopt in your dealings with China."[76]

Yet, in certain quarters, notably the Asiatic Association, the new East Asia policy encountered criticism. Some informed businessmen and others observed that the Wilson Administration approach was merely a substitute for a policy, possessing negative capability only, and would upset relations with the other Treaty Powers without doing anything tangible to solve China's problems. Quipped a political cartoonist in the *New York Herald,* "He asked for bread, and you gave him a hot-air balloon." In Peking, the British Minister, Sir John Jordan, terming the American move "as outrageous as anything they have done," tended to blame Secretary Bryan. "I travelled once with him for four days," wrote the veteran diplomat, "and he told me a good deal about China which I did not before know." Willard Straight, in New York, taking the long view, wondered if it would ever be possible to pursue a coherent and consistent East Asia policy in a democracy "where even the amenities of, let alone the conduct of international relationships must always be subordinated to the exigencies of domestic politics."[77]

EXPLAINING PUBLIC OPINION

In October 1911, William T. Ellis, a frequent writer on East Asian affairs, said of the American public's reaction to the Chinese Revolution: "Not one man in a hundred has the least idea of what the present disturbance is about." Yet, one year later, the well-connected Seth Low, as noted earlier, told the Asiatic Association that public opinion was "substantially unanimous" in desiring a new American China policy.[78]

How is the historian to account for this seemingly new policy consensus on the part of the interested public? Without denying multiple causation or the inevitable complexity of events, there is a strong case to be made for the decisive influence of the Missionary Mind.

Again, there is the argument from exclusion: only the Protestant missionary enterprise possessed both the sustained will and the communications system required to effect such a massive movement of public opinion. From the evidence presented earlier in this chapter one would not expect decisive influence to flow from the business community, whose opinions of the Revolution, if not always reactionary, were generally the opposite of sentimental; moreover, the business community, then as now, had relatively little control over the foreign-policy views of ordinary citizens. Clearly, Chinese-Americans and Chinese undergraduates, though enthusiastic about the new China, could not have had more than limited local influence on American opinion. Newspaper editors, though favorable to the Revolution as it was happening, relegated China to the inside pages after the Manchu dynasty abdicated and the real drama appeared to be over: this was in February 1912, yet pro-Chinese opinion continued to build during the following year and more. Moreover, if newspaper editors had in fact been responsible for creating the new public consensus, then one would expect to find the sentimental view circulating among newspaper readers and citizens generally, including Roman Catholics and other ethnic Americans, who somehow remained rather indifferent to the Chinese Revolution. In addition, the diplomatic historian is disinclined to seek the original source of the new, missionary-minded policy consensus in that body of well-to-do, educated, urban professional men who, though knowledgeable about Europe, were ignorant of East Asia, and who instinctively concentrated on American interests rather than the interests of some foreign nation. Historians familiar with elites will remain skeptical that the new policy consensus was some sort of spontaneous public upwelling of republican virtue: republican virtue there was—"I should like to live long enough," wrote one citizen, "to see all the monarchical forms of government abolished all over the world"[79]—but in order to achieve political effect, first in Congress, then in foreign policy, such sentiment would need to be channeled, focused, led.

Finally, the argument from exclusion poses a question: What could have compared, in its ability to reach people and its will to do so, to the missionary enterprise with its 300 China partisans giving 30,000 speeches annually to a constituency numbering millions?

Yet the case for the Missionary Mind rests also upon direct evidence, both quantitative and qualitative.

There is direct evidence that China missionaries, many of them abandoning their traditionally apolitical posture, functioned as foreign-policy opinion leaders at home during the period of the Republican Revolution. Fortunately for the historian, the State Department saved its mail on the China recognition question and related issues, and a statistical survey of this correspondence yields the data listed in Table 9:

TABLE 9 Occupations of China Opinion Leaders, 1911-1913
(%)

Missionaries, Ministers, or Religious Workers	30
Businessmen	17
Lawyers	9
Academics	8
Editors or Journalists	3
Other	13
Unidentifiable	20

Source: Correspondence in U.S. Department of State Decimal File 893.00/634, National Archives.

One may note that the considerable presence of businessmen and lawyers, though rather less weighty than usual, fits in generally with what is known about the foreign-policy elites. One may also remark the relatively low percentage accounted for by editors and journalists—it may be that most members of this occupational group knew from experience that public officials took their published views seriously as a matter of course, so that there was little reason to write letters—and the relatively high percentage, perhaps higher than was usual, of academics, who in many cases were reflecting the views of their Chinese undergraduates. The China opinion leaders who were missionaries, ministers, or related religious workers (30 percent) represented the largest single occupational grouping.

The degree of China-missionary influence on the foreign-policy public becomes clear when the researcher tracks down the source of the views advanced by the persons in the State Department sample. Though most businessmen and lawyers, and all missionaries, basically relied on their own judgments, large numbers of those whose occupation was "other" or "unidentifiable" cited or deferred to the opinions of missionaries. An analysis of this kind yields the results in Table 10:

TABLE 10 Sources of Views Advanced by China Opinion Leaders, 1911–1913
(%)

Missionaries	47
Businessmen	17
Lawyers	9
Academics	5
Editors or Journalists	4
Other	9
Unidentifiable	9

Source: NA 893.00/634

That missionaries accounted for the opinions of nearly one-half the sample—nearly three times the number influenced by businessmen, and twice the number affected by businessmen and lawyers combined—may suggest an even wider impact on public opinion generally.

Yet, the most telling evidence comes from the sensitive contemporary observer. The eye, especially the foreign eye, can see the essentials of a situation, including those matters an insider may take for granted. This is particularly true in cultural affairs.

Our Tocqueville in this regard may be J. O. P. Bland, sometime secretary to Sir Robert Hart of the Chinese Imperial Maritime Customs, sometime secretary to the Shanghai Municipal Council, longtime London *Times* correspondent, author of *Verse and Worse* and several volumes of history, the latter written in collaboration with Sir Edmund Backhouse, that enigmatic personality recently unmasked by Hugh Trevor-Roper: Bland, that is, was one of the greatest old China hands of his generation. [80]

Bland spent the autumn of 1912 and the first months of 1913 in the United States. He gave a paper at the Worcester Conference; delivered the Lowell Lectures in Boston; spoke at Cornell, the Colony Club in New York, the University Club in Detroit; searched the bookstores of Chicago for a copy of his most recent work, and was told that "Chicago folks won't read heavy books"; he traveled around and took it all in. [81]

Bland's American sojourn led him to certain definite conclusions about American public opinion, which he shared on more than one occasion with the editors of the *New York Times*. On the China recognition issue he observed: "I have heard some of the most important men in America express themselves in favor of such a recognition without delay, but the proposition does more credit to the heart than to the head of those who made it." Regarding the sources of this innocence, he considered: "The opinion so generally held here reflects well the instinctive American love for the underdog and the reassuring optimism of a class of your people to whom optimism is a vocational necessity. I refer to the missionary body, which is largely responsible for the exuberant hopes for young China." [82]

On New Year's Day, 1913, Bland called on President Taft at the White House. He recorded the meeting in his diary: "As to U.S. policy in China, Taft said he had had difficulty in restraining the sentimentalism, led by missionaries, wh[ich] w[oul]d immediately recognize the Chin[ese] Republic." [83]

FIVE

Nonrecognition:
American Policy-Makers and the Twenty-one Demands

Confronted with a difficult situation in international politics, the Missionary Mind could be sternly righteous. It tended to view the world as a struggle between darkness and light. In the Missionary Mind, that sense of the moral ambiguity of political affairs, which comes naturally to most officials responsible for conducting them day in and day out, usually gave way to the more sweeping sense that good must be championed and evil must not be recognized.

The tension between these two mentalities—what Max Weber calls "the ethic of responsibility" and "the ethic of ultimate ends" —was by no means peculiar to American East Asia policy. The universal historian might observe that the conflict is to be found in every age or civilization. The historian of American foreign relations might well write the general history of his subject in terms of this creative tension. For Americans in particular—senior officials included—have persistently violated Weber's trenchant dictum that you should not go into politics if you value the salvation of your soul. [1]

Yet, the sense of righteousness, the impulse to express outrage regarding perceived injustices or immoralites, was more characteristic of American East Asia policy than of any other, and the Missionary Mind was largely responsible for this state of affairs. Not only did the Missionary Mind exercise considerable sway over the foreign-policy public, but also it could influence and even determine the choice of policy options made by the officials directly responsible for the foreign relations of the United States.

No doubt the Missionary Mind's most abiding diplomatic legacy was the so-called "nonrecognition doctrine," according to which the United States formally withheld acknowledgment or approval of certain situations in East Asia. The framing of the nonrecognition doctrine involved something more willful than simple misperception and more emotional than routinized bureaucratic procedure: the deliberate refusal to countenance certain developments, the attempt to embarrass and even shame the party deemed responsible (that is, the Japanese Empire).

The nonrecognition policy was a peculiar instrument of international politics, productive of little tangible good, some tangible harm, and often quite baffling to foreign friends. To interpret this doctrine as the product of rigid insistence on the Open Door policy raises more questions than it answers, for the historian is then led to ask how and why a workaday policy about trade was transformed into the international vehicle of moral obligation. To the extent that American officials, like members of the foreign-policy public, viewed the Open Door as a symbol of missionary duty to East Asia, the Missionary Mind may be said to have shaped the overall course of American diplomacy.

And, to the extent that missionary impulses, of a more or less explicitly doctrinal nature, may be discerned in the making of the nonrecognition policy, the historian may conclude that this instrument was the diplomatic artifact of the Missionary Mind. American East Asia policy, thus, had American Protestantism for its cultural matrix.

The nonrecognition policy has its proximate origins in the United States' response to a major episode in international relations: the famous, in some quarters notorious, Twenty-one Demands of Japan upon China, in 1915. This chapter focuses on American policy toward that situation.

What follows is perhaps a conventional diplomatic history, conventional in more senses than one. Here are the usual cables, memoranda, *démarches* and procès-verbaux. Though certain of the interpretations advanced here may be somewhat novel, especially as regards William Jennings Bryan and Robert Lansing, the narrative flows through well-established channels. The term Missionary Mind does not often appear in the coming pages; yet, for all that, it may be the unseen guest.

THE TWENTY-ONE DEMANDS AND THE OFFICIAL MIND: THE POLICY OPTIONS

One way to estimate the range of choice open to the American official mind is to imagine that the year is 1915, that you are head of the Far East Division, and that an aide has just entered your office, somewhat excitedly no doubt, with the news that Japan is reported to be making certain proposals, twenty-one in number, to the authorities in Peking. What would you do? What course of action would you recommend for the United States?

The official mind's first obligation would be to ascertain the precise character of the Japanese desiderata and determine their possible bearing on United States interests in China. When the verbatim text became available from the Japanese Foreign Office, one would need to authenticate an English-language version with the State Department linguists and then proceed to subject it to very close scrutiny.

Scrutinizing the Text. Looking over such a text, the official mind would see that the Japanese propositions were collected in five different groups. Going through them one by one, and determining the exact political significance of each, would be the logical next step.

Had the official mind operated in this way, it might have recognized something like the following:

Groups I and II related solely to South Manchuria, Eastern Inner Mongolia, and Shantung—areas which, in fact, already belonged to the Japanese sphere-of-influence. The items regarding Shantung, where the Japanese recently had replaced the Germans by force of arms, ran as follows: that China formally agree to transfer to Japan the former German concessions in that province; that China pledge not to alienate additional territory in or near Shantung to any third power; that China grant Japan a certain railway concession; and that China agree to the establishment in Shantung of additional treaty ports. The demands with respect to Manchuria and Inner Mongolia were of similar tenor. The specifics involved extension of the leases on certain Japanese-owned railroads; granting of land tenure rights to Japanese subjects; permission for Japanese subjects to live, travel, and do business throughout these provinces; agreement that all foreign mining rights be reserved for Japanese nationals; agreement that China consult Japan on all matters involving foreign participation in railway construction, finance, or public administration; and, finally, the transfer to Japanese management of a particular provincial railroad. All in all, Groups I and II amounted to a certain extension of Japanese interests in three geographical areas where Japanese power or influence were already well entrenched. The American official mind might also perceive an attempt to regularize the new configuration of power in those provinces brought about by Japan's successful war against Germany and by the relative wartime withdrawal from China of the remaining Allied Treaty Powers. Yet, an objective observer could not, without the aid of extraneous influences and a certain amount of imagination, discern in the text of Groups I and II any proposed restrictions on American material interests. Indeed those articles were silent on the Open Door for trade. [2]

The articles in Group III dealt exclusively with the Hanyehping industrial complex in the Yangtze Valley. An American official might recall that this company, while it lay within the geographical area claimed by the British for their sphere-of-influence, was, in fact, Japan's major source of iron ore. He might also remember that Japanese businessmen had long been involved in the company's operations and that Japanese capital investment in the Hanyehping already amounted to something like $15 million. Though the Japanese articles proposing that the Hanyehping be placed under joint Sino-Japanese management, and that the Hanyehping enjoy first option on all mining rights in the area, had no bearing on the economic activities of Americans, these matters no doubt would receive careful attention at the British Foreign Office. [3]

If Group III appeared harmless to the United States, the single article in Group IV would seem even less menacing. There Tokyo was demanding that the Peking regime refrain from ceding, leasing, or otherwise alienating any additional territory along the China coast to any of the Western Treaty Powers. [4]

Moreover, the official mind would find it exceedingly difficult, except perhaps in one particular, to locate any threat to American national interests in Group V. The seven articles in Group V contemplated the following developments: employment of increased numbers of Japanese nationals as advisors to the Peking government; confirmation of the right of Japanese charitable institutions to own land in the Chinese interior; establishment of joint Sino-Japanese police forces in certain unspecified localities; China's undertaking to fill a substantial percentage of her arms and ammunition orders in Japan or, alternatively, China's agreement to establish a joint Sino-Japanese munitions factory on Japanese soil; the granting to Japan of certain specified railway concessions in the vicinity of the Yangtze Valley; China's agreeing to consult Japan before negotiating any foreign loan for internal improvements in Fukien province; finally, the granting to Japanese Buddhist missionaries of the same rights and privileges enjoyed by Christian missionaries from the West. Surveying Group V, the official mind might well observe that only three articles dealt with economic matters—those relating to arms, Yangtze Valley railroads, and loans for Fukien—and that the first two were unrelated to American interests. The demand relative to arms might be seen as an attempt by Tokyo to replace Berlin as the major supplier of weapons to China; and the demand relative to railroads doubtless would be of interest to London. But, from the perspective of official Washington, probably only the Fukien article might seem at all relevant in a theoretically material way. (The Bethlehem Steel Company from time to time had expressed interest, though nothing more, in the possibility of a naval-related project at Foochow to be backed, it was hoped, by American finance capital.) [5]

Calculating American Interests. Having gone over the demands seriatim, having scrutinized each proposition for its possible bearing on American economic interests—an exercise the reader may repeat by turning to the Appendix (pp. 203–205)—the official mind would be led to conclude that the document as a whole posed no real problem for the United States. Apart from the Fukien article, which may be considered a special case, the document is more remarkable for the foreign economic interests it scrupulously respects, and passes over in silence, than for those it intends to adjust. For example, there is no indication that the Japanese wished to interfere with the Maritime Customs or to impede the trade in kerosene, cotton piece goods, wheat flour, tobacco, or any other existing item of exchange. There is no intimation of harm to American investment in the International Settlement at Shanghai, or existing foreign investments elsewhere in Chinese territory. From a Wall Street perspective, it is notable that the document is silent on the Hukuang Railway.

The official mind seeking to validate the conclusion that the Twenty-one Demands were economically harmless to the United States could easily have found such confirmation in the business and financial community. One or two phone calls would have established that the leading American interest groups saw no cause for alarm. The American Asiatic Association, for example, observed that "a good deal of unnecessary heat has been engendered by the newspaper discussion of the Sino-Japanese negotiations" and that, so far as the business community was concerned, "those who should be best informed on the subject entertain the fewest misgivings about the outcome of those *pour-parlers.*" Later, when the issues had been resolved, the trade association lamented the "alarmist comments with which the course of the negotiations was so plentifully bestrewn." The other major American interest groups to which the official mind would pay attention—the Pacific Coast Chambers of Commerce and the American Association of China at Shanghai—maintained silence on the Twenty-one Demands. Apart from the assumption that these commercial bodies somehow had become blind to their own interests, or that they suddenly had developed an unwonted reticence to sound the alarm in response to imminent danger, this silence might seem deafening.[6]

So the official mind with reason would conclude, tentatively, that the Japanese demands on China had little economic bearing on American interests. The diplomat would remain alert for any solid indication to the contrary, but, for the moment, he would surmise that the Japanese, not wishing to alienate their major trading partner, had drafted their proposals very carefully so as to avoid material effect on the United States.

Turning from the purely economic to the political level, the American official mind might also reasonably gather that Japanese diplomats had framed their demands in conformance with the Open Door policy. To be sure, these specific propositions amounted to one big demand for legal acceptance of the considerable increase in Japanese economic and political influence in China which had taken place during the World War. One could now speak of the Japanese preponderance in East Asia, Japan having replaced Britain as the paramount power.[7]

But the Open Door was a separate question altogether, and the American official mind must need a certain amount of ingenuity to interpret the Japanese demands as a violation of that concept. To the extent that the Open Door involved the maintenance of a uniform or nondiscriminatory tariff on foreign goods entering Chinese territory, the Twenty-one Demands seemed consistent with that policy. There is no indication that the Japanese sought revision of the tariff structures in Manchuria, Inner Mongolia, Shantung, Fukien, or elsewhere. In this sense, Japan continued to preserve the Open Door for trade.[8]

To the extent that the Open Door might be construed to apply to investment as well as trade, the issue would become more complicated. Yes, the Japanese were asking for preferential treatment with respect to certain railroads, certain financial transactions, and the like. But most of these demands were to take effect in regions regarded as belonging to or claimed for the Japanese sphere-of-influence: Manchuria, Inner Mongolia, Shantung, and Fukien. The remaining economic demands—the Yangtze Valley articles—might be viewed as bearing on the British sphere. This was the way the imperialists played their game in China. The sphere-of-influence idea was commonly accepted: the United States had seemed to accept it at times, in fact if not in law, and all attempts to challenge this principle diplomatically had been unsuccessful. So, to interpret the Japanese demands as infringing the principle of equal investment opportunity the official mind logically would have to reject all foreign claims to spheres-of-influence in China—a proposition unlikely to win speedy acceptance at the British Foreign Office or the Quai d'Orsay.[9]

The demand relative to arms and ammunition purchases might seem a borderline case with respect to the Open Door for trade, but China was a peculiar country, and in the practice of that time and place such matters were sometimes considered to belong under the rubric of "concessions" rather than foreign trade properly speaking. The American official mind might well wish to ponder the fact that the Central Powers previously had enjoyed what the Japanese were now demanding. And, rechecking the text of the demands, an official could plainly see that Tokyo had left a loophole for itself, in the event of any question about the Open Door for trade, by providing for the establishment of a Sino-Japanese arsenal on Japanese soil.[10]

Considered in its economic aspect, therefore, the Open Door could easily be seen to remain open regardless of the specific matters the Japanese were now eager to discuss with China. A common tariff, collected by the Imperial Maritime Customs, would continue to be applied in Manchuria, Inner Mongolia, Shantung, Fukien, and elsewhere; this, doubtless, was the principal reason for the American business community's general lack of alarm. The non-trade matters of interest to the Japanese were consistent with the sphere-of-influence idea, and the Open Door policy provided no solid basis in international law for discriminating against a Japanese sphere-of-influence while accepting the spheres claimed by the white Treaty Powers. To construe the Japanese economic demands as closing the Open Door, in sum, one logically would be forced to so interpret all foreign claims to spheres-of-influence in

China—a can of worms that the prudent official might have preferred not to open at that time.

Moreover, the American official mind, scrutinizing the text of
the Japanese propositions, could not detect any technical violation
of that Chinese territorial or administrative integrity that the Open
Door Policy was calculated to preserve. Japan was not asking for
ownership of any territory; Japan was not demanding that any
agency of Chinese public administration be run from Tokyo the
way the Indian Civil Service, say, was run from London. The document is notably silent on the administrative apparatus whose
integrity the Open Door aimed originally to preserve, the British-
dominated Imperial Maritime Customs.[11]

Certain of the Japanese demands might seem troubling—especially those relative to arms, advisors, and police—and the document as a whole may be said to contemplate the further erosion of
what little remained of Chinese sovereignty or effective political
independence. But the Open Door policy, so far from guaranteeing
such sovereignty or independence, undermined it in fact as in law.
Though respecting China's territorial or administrative integrity
after its fashion, the Open Door policy did not insure sovereignty
or independence as those terms ordinarily were understood in the
civilized world. This being the case, the American official mind
would have to consider the questionable cases here—the arms,
advisors, and police—in the context of the phrase "administrative
integrity" or "administrative entity." The man of affairs could
easily envision his Japanese counterpart arguing that the Chinese
government had long employed numerous foreign advisors, including Americans, that the munitions factory and the constabulary
would be in the nature of joint ventures—and that, in all cases,
China, her administrative integrity not impaired but strengthened,
would retain final authority. As the *New Republic* observed: "The
integrity of China will be preserved—for exploitation by Japan. . . .
Japan will not interfere with the treaty rights of other powers because, if for no other reason, she will need foreign capital with
which to develop the resources of China."[12]

Once again, Japanese diplomats might be seen to have framed

their demands with some precision, carefully respecting the standards of international law. Perhaps Tokyo had not altogether forgotten that the preservation of the Open Door was one of the objects of the Anglo-Japanese alliance.

Considering Policy Alternatives. If the American official mind could not clearly perceive the Japanese agenda as involving any technical violation of the Open Door policy, and if in addition those proposals seemed to have little bearing on American economic interests—what then? How should the United States react, if at all? What policy choices must be considered?

While retrospective decision-making is often vaguely irresponsible at best, there were indeed choices to be made at the time, choices that other governments had also to make. One way to estimate the range of policy options available to American officials would be to survey the choices perceived at some other foreign office, for example, that of Great Britain.

Briefly, the historian may observe that the British seemed to take the Twenty-one Demands fairly well in stride. There was generally a certain distance. "It is a pity for this unfortunate country as it was just beginning to find its feet again under Yuan Shih-k'ai's guidance," wrote Sir John Jordan, British Minister to China, on January 26, 1915: "However, it is largely to blame for its own weakness, and might is right in these days." Sir John, who as dean of the diplomatic corps could be expected to appreciate every turn of the screw, even managed to see the lighter side. On March 5, Jordan wrote: "The Japanese Minister told me that Baron Kato could not repress a smile when he formulated the demands for Japanese churches, hospitals, etc., and there is a touch of humour about the idea of a Japanese conversion of China."[13]

But the humor soon gave way to the stiff upper lip and the sober calculation of interest. For certain of the demands, particularly the Hanyehping items and the articles contemplating what Sir John called "the barefaced plunder of our Railway concessions," had a bearing on the British sphere-of-influence in the Yangtze Valley and on British investments elsewhere. The British had invested more than £100 million sterling in China.[14]

What to do?

As described in a March 19 letter to Sir John from a senior official at the Foreign Office, London perceived two possible frameworks for its East Asia policy: siding with its allies the Japanese; or playing a passive role, except insofar as actual British interests were at stake. The issue was much debated in the Cabinet and at the Foreign Office. One group wanted Britain "to side with the Japs and to use our influence with Yuan, monetary assistance and if absolutely necessary Weihaiwei, as assets to secure some measure of control over Japanese activities." But this group was overpowered by another, led by Sir Edward Grey, the Foreign Secretary, who believed that "our right policy is to efface ourselves over the demands, as far as is consistent with any actual British rights which they may affect, and bide our time in China till the war is over." In general, British policy, with certain exceptions, followed the passive course. The (theoretical) option to side with China or oppose Japan never was seriously considered. The British had too much at stake.[15]

In view of the British example, the historian may suggest that the American official mind would have done well to consider the advantages and disadvantages likely to flow from several alternative courses of action in East Asia. One can distinguish four such possible frameworks for American policy:

Option #1 would be to side with the Japanese. This would secure the overall interests of the American business community, probably would facilitate opening of new markets for investment capital, might lead to some kind of financial understanding on Fukien, and might even induce the Japanese to revise the freight-rate schedule on the South Manchuria Railway, that habitual grievance of the American cotton-goods exporters.[16] Supporting Tokyo might also reduce Japanese pressures regarding the immigration issue, and in general its contribution to the relaxation of tensions across the Pacific would be considerable. But this policy option, though perhaps the most compelling from the narrowest view of the American national interest, could never be sold to a missionary-minded Congress and public. And there were other objections.

Option #2 would involve doing nothing, or at least very little. The State Department would watch the situation closely but would keep out of it, except where American economic interests might possibly be involved. In the event of any question in this regard, the Department could ask Tokyo to clarify the article or articles at issue. In the event of some perceived threat to trade or investment, the United States could inform Japan of the specific interests at stake and ask for additional clarification. Any perceived threat to Chinese territorial or administrative integrity, however defined, might be discussed in the same responsible and discreet manner. In general, the State Department would try to maintain a low profile. This option would have the advantage of distancing the United States from a delicate and potentially dangerous situation in which it had few tangible interests, economic, political, strategic, or otherwise. The axis of tension between Tokyo and Peking had its own integrity, and there might be little that any third party could do to reverse the course of events. No doubt the British, however self-effacing in the largest sense, could be expected to salvage as much of the status quo as was possible under the circumstances, and this was perhaps the surest guarantee of American interests in China. Moreover, by maintaining a low profile, the United States would avoid the appearance of responsibility for a situation which might easily deteriorate into war or revolution or some combination thereof. In a worst-case situation, such deniability would prove useful. Denying all responsibility might not prevent a political firestorm of criticism at home, but the latter would be preferable to the assumption of international responsibilities which in time would force the United States to choose between war and diplomatic humiliation—choices that would prove even less palatable to the American public. So there was a good deal to be said for keeping hands off.

Option #3 would be to encourage, facilitate, possibly even mediate a diplomatic solution to the points at issue between China and Japan. American officials could reason that the United States possessed long-term national interests in addition to interests of shorter duration. The principal long-term interest could be thought to be a stable structure of international relationships in East Asia that recognized the legitimate interests of all. The foundation for such a structure must be amicable relations between Tokyo and Peking. While this would not come about easily, or quickly, in time the old British-dominated system of Unequal Treaties would prove unable to contain the rising forces of Chinese nationalism and Japanese expansion. The long-term goal of American diplomacy, thus, must be to prevent collision of these two powerful movements. Perhaps the United States, precisely because its interests in China were relatively insubstantial and were unlikely to be threatened in any case, might play a uniquely useful role in promoting peaceful relations throughout the region. Such a role, which might be visible or not, and which might be more or less active as situations dictated, of course would depend upon absolute neutrality as between China and Japan, a high order of East Asian expertise, extreme delicacy in word and deed, patience, and willingness to get one's hands dirty. It might or might not involve some measure of political responsibility. Such an approach would possess the advantages, material and immaterial, present and future, likely to result from increased stability in the Pacific basin. One possible disadvantage would be that Japan might take offense, interpreting such a move as yet another attempt, more sophisticated than formerly, to frustrate her ambitions in East Asia.

Option #4, the final policy choice available, would be to side with China. The man of affairs may object that the official mind should rule this out immediately. Chinese and American interests were by no means identical; they coincided only in certain special situations, and in the largest sense they diverged somewhat sharply and even opposed one another. American interests in China were protected by the Unequal Treaties; the latter were in China's interest only in a very roundabout way, if at all, and, from a strict Chinese nationalist perspective, they were an abomination. Ingratiating Chinese diplomats, who could be expected to proclaim friendship for the United States in direct proportion to their ability to influence this country, no doubt would fuzz the issue, and Chinese diplomats do make good friends, but the experienced

American official would recognize the old game of playing off the barbarians for what it was. Moreover, any attempt to side with China would be likely to exacerbate the already considerable tensions in American-Japanese relations, a condition which might not augur well for American business interests or for national security. The United States might not necessarily welcome Japanese paramountcy in East Asia, but it lacked the raw power to reverse that development and it lacked clear authority in international law for a diplomatic challenge. Certainly the United States could invoke the Root-Takahira agreement and make its opinions known about this and that, but to carry any weight, and to stand any chance of support from other Treaty Powers, such a representation would necessitate an airtight case that Japan had flagrantly violated the Open Door concept. For reasons described above, this was not possible, as Japanese diplomats had been too careful.

Under the circumstances, any attempt to implement Option #4 would require a rhetorical or moralizing posture which, while it might make use of specious arguments regarding the Open Door or adduce disingenuous references to purely theoretical interests, was more or less missionary in character.

Yet this, the missionary role, is precisely the one the United States decided to play.

THE PRUDENT FRIEND

The making of American East Asia policy took place in a particular bureaucratic setting. Though President Wilson exercised creative supervision over the direction of policy, elements of "bureaucratic politics" were not lacking. Within the bureaucracy there were certain tensions, certain differences, certain distinct lines of influence.

The diplomatic historian can distinguish three lines of force along which policy recommendations were borne to the President. Each had its moments of influence and effectiveness. One ran direct from Secretary William Jennings Bryan. In general that was the weakest. Another ran from Far East Division head E. T. Williams through Counselor Robert Lansing to the President. That tended to acquire greater influence as Lansing successfully ingratiated himself with Wilson, on European matters even more than East Asian, at Bryan's direct expense. A third line of force, perhaps the most consistently effective, ran direct to the Oval Office from Minister Paul Reinsch in Peking.

Reinsch. Reinsch was a leading academic intellectual of the Progressive era. Born the son of a Lutheran pastor, educated in Lutheran schools, later Professor of Political Science at the University of Wisconsin, Reinsch rarely had ventured outside the German-American culture of Madison and Milwaukee before going to Peking. Much of his surviving correspondence is in German. Though he did not read Chinese or Japanese, Reinsch was an academic authority on East Asia, having published full-length studies of the region's politics and intellectual development.[17]

Reinsch was the first in a long line of political scientists who have played pivotal roles in our East Asia policies. Like certain of his successors, Reinsch found it possible to preach representative government while embracing an authoritarian regime. Reinsch did nothing to discourage Yuan Shih-k'ai from terminating the Chinese experiment with free institutions; yet Reinsch, who was active in Progressive politics at home, insisted on seeing Yuan as a kind of East Asian embodiment of the Wisconsin Idea. As American Minister, Reinsch quickly came under the spell of American-educated Chinese officials, particularly the able young diplomat V. K. Wellington Koo, and he developed considerable hostility toward the Japanese. "The American Minister," wrote Sir John Jordan in 1914, "is very suspicious of Japanese doings."[18]

As Minister to China, Reinsch tended to formulate and implement his own personal policies whenever possible. Though his relations with the State Department, particularly with Secretary Bryan, were rather strained, Reinsch believed he could count on the support of President Wilson, a fellow political scientist, with whom he corresponded privately. Down to the Twenty-one Demands episode, Professor Reinsch, realizing that a more aggressive American role in China hinged upon development of more substantial American material interests than presently existed, made every effort to encourage greater United States trade and investment.

Reinsch cabled the State Department its first word of the Japanese demands on January 23, 1915. "Serious tension again exists between Chinese and Japanese governments," he wrote: "The Japanese Minister has submitted a long list of demands, at the same time pledging the President and Ministers of State not to divulge the character of the demands to other powers on pain of serious consequences to China. The demands are stated to be such as could not be granted without abandoning entirely the open door policy as well as independence in political and industrial matters." Though Reinsch could as yet provide no details, his cable concluded with allusions to the possibility of further Chinese "revolutionary movements," of Japanese "military occupation," and of ultimate Chinese "vassalage to Japan."[19]

Reinsch would sound these themes practically every day for the next four months. No doubt he was sincere in his purpose. But the student of Reinsch's cables may observe that these documents, so far from being dispassionate reports, were essentially rhetorical effusions calculated to produce a certain emotional resonance in official Washington. Generally they were long on ideas and other abstractions and thin in factual detail. An overheated, even hysterical tone was not uncommon. In his private papers, Reinsch, who ended his career as American lobbyist for the Chinese government, left evidence that his behavior during the Twenty-one Demands period was based upon a personal agreement with Wellington Koo. The two met every night, under cover of darkness, conspiring to thwart the ambitions of Japan. The historian surmises that Wellington Koo, that complete Chinese diplomat, perhaps was manipulating Reinsch, who carefully concealed his activities from his own government. Wellington Koo seems to have been less than forthcoming with Reinsch on the precise terms of the demands. From his American sojourn, Wellington Koo well knew the American vulnerability to the hallowed phrases of the Open Door. In Reinsch's January 23 cable noting that the demands "are stated to be such as could not be granted without abandoning entirely the open door policy," one may detect the fine hand of Wellington Koo, who might be expected to understand what made the Americans tick. Through the medium of Reinsch's cables, the Chinese enjoyed effective access to American policy-makers throughout the crisis.[20]

On January 24, Reinsch made the first of several policy recommendations on behalf of his Chinese friends. Apparently puzzled by Sir John Jordan's lack of perturbation, Reinsch cabled that the United States should initiate an "exchange of views with Great Britain" looking toward the establishment of a concerted effort "to safeguard the integrity of China." Wellington Koo seemed to be exerting maximum leverage in return for a minimum of information, releasing the details drip by drip. Indeed the most Reinsch could offer the Department was a vague reference to "Shantung, exclusive mining rights in two provinces, and three railways." Yet Professor Reinsch did not hesitate to conclude that the Japanese proposals "constitute the greatest crisis yet experienced in China."[21]

Williams. Reinsch's alarums produced an immediate reaction from E. T. Williams. A former American Board missionary who entered diplomatic service late in life, Williams was Chargé in Peking during the Republican Revolution and had supervised the Far East Division since 1913. A man of deep learning and profound sympathies, he possessed every quality one might hope for in a man of his station save a clear sense of the distinction between Chinese and American interests and an ability to appreciate the legitimate ambitions of the Japanese Empire.[22]

In reaction to Reinsch's first cables, Williams busied himself for more than a week churning out action memoranda. His first memo to Secretary Bryan, on January 25, began: "A very critical situation exists in China, and unless Japan is checked, military operations are probable and the overthrow of the Chinese Republic very possible." His policy proposal went well beyond Reinsch's. Williams reasoned that, because of war in Europe, Britain would have little room for maneuver in East Asia. He therefore suggested that the United States, citing the Root-Takahira agreement as legal basis, intervene directly in the Sino-Japanese negotiations by informing Japan that this country wished to be consulted on the points at issue. "The United States," Williams wrote, "is the custodian of the Open Door in China. We initiated the policy and obtained the pledges of the other powers to observe it. This policy is essential to the protection of our commercial interests in China and is favorable to our educational and missionary enterprises there. Japan is among the nations pledged to support this policy." Williams concluded: "It seems to me that we are under moral obligation to the Powers whose pledges are registered with us to permit no violation of these pledges to pass without protest."[23]

Bryan. Bryan, though in some ways the policy-maker closest to the pure missionary type, did not share the view that the United States was the custodian of East Asia or that America had a moral obligation to protest against Japanese ambitions in that part of the world.

It can be argued that William Jennings Bryan has not received adequate credit for his services to the Republic as Secretary of State. True, by comparison with a member of the Yale Club or the Knickerbocker, Bryan must seem a rustic. But rustics are sometimes quite sophisticated about politics, and Bryan, who singlehandedly had dominated the Democratic Party for nearly twenty years before handing the 1912 presidential nomination to Governor Woodrow Wilson of New Jersey, had a reasonable claim to an understanding of the political world. The diplomatic historian might argue that an acquaintance with domestic politics, which thrives on the frank recognition of concrete interests, the instinct for compromise, and a sense for the common good, is a useful background for international politics—as useful, in its way, as time spent on Wall Street, in some law firm, or in a university lecture hall. Moreover, it is by no means clear that Bryan's so-called pacifism was inconsistent with his diplomatic office. To the extent that diplomacy is the alternative to war, every diplomat is in a certain sense a peacemaker; and one cannot doubt that Bryan would have been the first to bear arms in the event his country had been invaded. Though Bryan may have dispensed a certain amount of patronage while at the State Department, modern Secretaries also have been known to take political connections into account when staffing the upper echelons at Foggy Bottom. Certainly Bryan, who resigned in the wake of the *Lusitania* crisis when it became clear that President Wilson was deliberately seeking confrontation with Germany, was very far from being a venal careerist. In fact, Bryan's principal offense as Secretary of State, if offense it be, was that he was absolutely neutral as between Britain and Germany.[24]

Bryan also was neutral as between China and Japan. Though hopeful regarding China's evolution toward Christian democracy, Bryan was sensitive to Japan's aspiration to be accepted as the equal of the modern West. Throughout his tenure of office, Bryan engaged in extensive discussions with the Japanese Ambassador, Viscount Chinda, on the status of Japanese immigrants in California and elsewhere. On several occasions, Bryan received sharply worded notes from Japan to the effect that the 1913 anti-Japanese legislation in California was in violation of the 1911 Treaty of Commerce and Navigation. Bryan came to recognize the potential for danger in the drift of American-Japanese relations, and he developed the ability to conceptualize the problems of the East Asia and Pacific region as a whole. In Bryan's view, the American national interest required friendly relations both with Japan and with China and the promotion of good relations between Tokyo and Peking. For this reason, his own relations with Reinsch and E. T. Williams, while formally correct, were less than intimate. Indeed, Bryan conducted a personal correspondence with the Ambassador to Tokyo, George Guthrie, in order to balance Reinsch's anti-Japanese reporting. Over time, Bryan acquired an impressive grasp of policy detail. One might say that Bryan approached the international politics of the Pacific basin much as he had approached the political infighting of the Democratic Party—with an eye toward compromise and consensus.[25]

On January 23, when the first of Reinsch's cables arrived bearing news of the demands, Bryan reacted with utmost circumspection. Believing that Reinsch was deliberately exaggerating the situation, and that the President might be vulnerable to such misrepresentation, Bryan attempted to shift Wilson's attention to the issue of

Japanese immigration. When Reinsch's cable came in, Bryan immediately drafted a letter to the President describing his most recent discussions with the Japanese Ambassador on the racial-equality issue. Explaining that Japan had indicated an interest in negotiating a new treaty with the United States, one of whose provisions would insure better treatment for Japanese immigrants, Bryan asked for permission to begin exploratory talks at once. Also Bryan enclosed, without comment, a copy of Reinsch's cable. Bryan was playing for time, certain that the Chinese situation would seem more complicated or ambiguous when all the facts were in. He also knew that any possible American involvement would seem less offensive to Japan if the United States simultaneously signaled a willingness to yield some ground on the immigration issue.[26]

Wilson. The President replied to Bryan four days later. One cannot know exactly what passed through Wilson's mind during this period. Yet one may speculate that any thinking Wilson did about East Asia was sandwiched in between his domestic worries and his preoccupation with the war in Europe. At that time Wilson was spending grueling, agonizing days as he searched for the proper American response to German submarine warfare.[27]

Thus, the President was quite busy, and his knowledge of East Asia was fragmentary. Like most members of the national elite, Wilson knew very little about the region apart from what he heard in church or learned from China missionaries, who numbered among his most frequent correspondents. The personal letters from Paul Reinsch tended to reinforce these sentimental influences. Of Japan Wilson knew practically nothing.[28]

The historian may intuit that, under these circumstances, Wilson would tend to rely on his various instincts. Reinsch and the Far East Division were convinced that big trouble was brewing: it would be necessary to give them some satisfaction. Bryan need not be taken seriously. Moreover, the American China constituency, especially in the hinterlands, would expect the United States to do something. A presidential election year, 1916, was impending, and the Republicans would be just as capable of exploiting the

China issue then as the Democrats had been in 1912. Meanwhile, there was the likelihood of pressure from the Hill. There would be newspaper editorials, and China missionaries would make known their opinions far and wide. To lose China in 1915 would not be good.

Perhaps the President's thinking ran along political lines like these. No doubt the President also believed there was a genuine community of interest, of a kind, between China and the United States which must be maintained. Wilson had a sentimental attachment to the Chinese Republic. Just as a German attack on a British passenger vessel in time of war could be regarded as an attack on the rights of American citizens, so could the Japanese demands on China be perceived as inimical to American rights and interests. In both situations, the United States might base its position on international law. More telling than the letter of the law, however, would be the ultimate identity of the client.

On January 27, Wilson informed Bryan of his decision that the United States would side with China. Wilson's letter indicated an unwillingness seriously to consider any other policy option. Wilson rejected Bryan's proposal for negotiations with Japan on the immigration issue. No racial liberal, and perhaps unwilling to risk the loss of California in 1916, Wilson considered that the time was not "opportune." The idea might be good in theory, he wrote, "But there are many things to consider first: among the rest are Japan's present attitude and intentions in China and her willingness or unwillingness to live up to the obligations she has assumed towards us with regard to the open door in the East." Then, in a move reminiscent of his posture toward European affairs, the President said: "I would be very much obliged if you would ask Mr. Lansing to prepare . . . a memorandum explicitly setting forth just what obligations in this sense she did undertake." While it is notable that the President did not request a full policy review, or even a legal analysis of the demands then known, and that the President suggested a certain lack of familiarity with the statutes he was preparing to invoke, the course to be followed by American diplomacy was clearly and firmly set. And Mr. Lansing was to be its grey eminence. [29]

Lansing. Robert Lansing had what one might call a pin-striped mind. He knew the rules, he played by the rules, his thinking took place within orderly pre-established confines, and he dressed the part. A government lawyer, Lansing was quick and thorough, ticking off the statutory justifications for a given course of action immediately after it had been decided on by higher authority. He was cautious and given to succinctness of expression. Perhaps he was also a shrewd bureaucratic player of the modern type. At that time, Lansing was making himself indispensable to President Wilson by providing the latter with legal arguments for the desired confrontation with Germany. In bureaucratic-political terms, Lansing was driving a wedge between Wilson and Bryan, isolating Bryan generally, and positioning himself to succeed the Secretary of State in due course. [30]

In general, Lansing positioned himself with respect to the Twenty-one Demands so as to faithfully execute the President's wishes and provide a clear alternative to Bryan. This he did by siding with the radically pro-Chinese E. T. Williams. On January 28, after Bryan informed Lansing of the President's request for a memo on the Open Door, the Counselor immediately assigned the task to Williams, who was not a lawyer. From that time forward, Lansing delegated almost all his East Asian assignments to missionary Willaims. Lansing's desk diary records conferences with Williams at least once a day, on average, over the following three months. Usually Lansing just rubber-stamped whatever Williams came up with and sent it on its way. By allying himself with Williams, Lansing minimized Bryan's room for maneuver. On January 28, Williams worked very quickly, and within a few hours had completed his assignment, in Lansing's exact words, "to collect the various statements of the Japanese Government relative to the 'open door' policy." Williams codified his substantial collection in a memorandum which Lansing read carefully, underlining key passages, then Lansing rushed it to Bryan, who looked it over and, having little alternative, sent it on to the White House. The legal brief was in the President's hands less than twenty-four hours after Wilson ordered it. [31]

Yet, it would not be entirely correct to interpret Lansing's alliance with the Far East Division as nothing more than a cynical exercise in bureaucratic cunning, for there is no evidence that Lansing disagreed, in any significant way, with the pro-Chinese views of Williams (or the President). Indeed Lansing, though he thought like a lawyer, might also be regarded, metaphorically speaking, as a card-carrying participant in the Missionary Mind. Like the President, Lansing was a devout Presbyterian; he taught Sunday School, served as Elder, had even done home mission work among factory workers in upstate New York. During his early life in Watertown, New York, Lansing had known Ernest J. Weekes, his home church's missionary to Canton. In his Washington years, Lansing came under the influence of the missionary-minded John W. Foster, his law partner and father-in-law. Whatever the wartime exigencies compelling Lansing to negotiate the Lansing-Ishii agreement in 1917, the historian may well doubt that Lansing's public career, taken as a whole, witnessed any consistent endeavor to improve relations with Japan. His differences with the President over East Asia policy may be viewed as those, largely of style and tone, that may arise naturally between the lawyer and the academic intellectual as they work together for some common goal. In his memoirs, Lansing recalled that the basic purpose of American policy toward those "unconscionable" demands of 1915 had been "defeating Japan's aggressive designs." The policy documents that have survived offer no real indication that Lansing ever wavered from that purpose.[32]

The First Move. On January 28 and 29, the President decided he must take some action. Reading over the Far East Division memo, Wilson could see that Japan indeed had entered into numerous agreements to maintain the Open Door. Yet, almost every day he received a fresh cable from Paul Reinsch (the cables were rushed to the White House on receipt) stating that the Japanese demands (the details of which were still unknown) were calculated to violate those accords. On January 29, Wilson learned from Reinsch that the Sino-Japanese negotiations would begin shortly and that "an early decision as to American policy is therefore indispensable."

Writing to Bryan later that day, Wilson proposed a "very early appointment" for that purpose. [33]

Among the President's principal foreign-policy advisors there was wide disagreement over how the United States should proceed at this juncture. Bryan apparently believed that the State Department should take no action until it received the verbatim text of the Japanese proposals. Lansing's bureaucratic ally, E. T. Williams, favored an immediate approach to Japan. "In our own interest and in that of the powers who have at our request entered into the 'Open Door' Agreements," he wrote on January 27, "it seems to be our duty to ask explanation from Japan and insist firmly upon our rights." Williams reiterated: "I believe that any lack of firmness will but encourage further disregard of our rights. . . . Our present commercial interests in Japan are greater than those in China," he conceded, "but the look ahead shows our interest to be a strong and independent China rather than one held in subjection by Japan." Williams concluded: "China has certain claims upon our sympathy. If we do not recognize them, as we refused to recognize Korea's claim, we are in danger of losing our influence in the Far East and of adding to the dangers of the situation." Paul Reinsch recommended an even more aggressive measure in his cable of February 1: that the United States encourage China to disregard the Japanese injunction of secrecy and make the demands known to the world—with the United States pledged to "assume moral and consequent political responsibility" for the Chinese *démarche*. The United States should take this action, Reinsch argued, "in its own interests as well as in those of China which it has hitherto loyally championed." But Colonel Edward M. House of Texas was more cautious. House, who would be away in Europe on special presidential assignment during the remainder of the crisis, warned the President in late January that the East Asian situation posed dangers he would do well to avoid. [34]

Faced with the perceived necessity to do something, the President, probably reflecting the caution of Colonel House, decided the United States would maintain a low profile for the time being.

On February 2, Wilson directed Bryan to make discreet inquiries at the British Foreign Office and asked Mr. Lansing to summon the British Ambassador for a full and frank discussion. On February 8, Wilson explained his move in a personal letter to Reinsch:

> I have thought a great deal about the present situation in China, in view of the Japanese demands, and I have been doing what I could indirectly to work in the interest of China. I have had this feeling, that any direct advice to China or direct intervention on her behalf in the present nego-tiations would really do her more harm than good, inasmuch as it would very likely provoke the jealousy and excite the hostility of Japan, which would first be manifested against China herself. I have been try-ing to play the part of prudent friend by making sure that the repre-sentatives of Great Britain realized the gravity of the situation and just what was being attempted. For the present I am watching the situation very closely indeed, ready to step in at any point where it is wise to do so.[35]

But Washington's approach to Japan's East Asian ally was un-successful, for the British were loath to take the American cousins into their confidence on so delicate a matter. London had never exactly admired the point, much less the techniques, of American East Asia policy. On February 2, Bryan instructed Ambassador Walter Hines Page to call at the Foreign Office and to state that Washington had received reports about certain demands, which "are probably exaggerated," and to ask for any information. Sir Edward Grey replied that London had been in contact with Tokyo regarding the matter, but he refused to elaborate. Lansing's inter-view with the British Ambassador on February 11 was equally un-availing. From this reticence certain American officials concluded that, while Britain's interests in China certainly were threatened by the demands, London's hands were tied because of the war, and the United States therefore would have to go it alone in East Asia. Ruling out the possibility of any coordinated action at the moment, American diplomats did not bother to contact London again until the closing days of the East Asian imbroglio.[36]

On February 9, some time after the basic direction of American

East Asia policy had been determined, the State Department received what purported to be the verbatim text of the Japanese demands.[37]

A VERY WEIGHTY STATE PAPER:
THE DECISION TO PROTEST GROUP V

During most of February, there was considerable confusion in Washington and other capitals as to the exact nature and extent of the Japanese proposals. The document handed to Secretary Bryan on February 8, a few days after negotiations had commenced in Peking, by Japanese Ambassador Chinda, listed only eleven items. The following day the Department heard from Ambassador Guthrie in Tokyo that the Japanese Foreign Office had given an identical memorandum to Britain, France, and Russia with the assurance that the demands "are not contrary to China's integrity or to the rights and interests of other nations."[38]

The initial memorandum apparently was a diplomatic blunder on the part of the Japanese, for, by failing to mention the items in Group V, it gave the color of truth to suspicions entertained in some quarters that Japan was double-dealing. Two weeks later, following intense speculation in the Western press and a flurry of diplomatic activity on three continents, the Japanese Foreign Office issued a second memorandum, this one listing the full agenda of demands, including those in Group V. Though the Japanese explained that the items in Group V had been omitted because they were in the nature of requests or desiderata as distinct from demands, a certain amount of damage had been done. While Secretary Bryan accepted in good faith Ambassador Chinda's statement (apparently true) that Tokyo had kept him in the dark regarding Group V, pro-Chinese officials such as E. T. Williams concluded that Japan's behavior had been "intentionally misleading."[39]

Throughout the middle weeks of February, President Wilson faced mounting pressure to take some kind of action. Owing to the press-relations efforts of Wellington Koo and Paul Reinsch, the newspapers were full of alarming stories, and official Washington was alive with rumor. On February 10 and again on February 18, resolutions were introduced in the House of Representatives aimed at forcing the Administration's hand. Soon newspaper editors throughout the country were declaring their sympathy for China and were calling for some decisive American move.[40]

The heretofore prudent friend of China decided during the Cabinet meeting on February 19 that the United States would intervene directly in the Sino-Japanese negotiations by making its views known on the matters at issue. Specifically, the President decided to acquiesce in the demands listed in the Japanese memorandum of February 8 but to single out for harsh criticism certain of the more ambitious articles in Group V. Wilson settled on this course of action on the strength of Paul Reinsch's February 15 recommendation that the United States move boldly to extract from Japan a "definite unequivocal assurance that her demands will be limited to those specified in the memorandum." In Reinsch's view, as in that of E. T. Williams, who seconded the Minister's suggestion, the initial Japanese agenda—the articles relating to Manchuria, Inner Mongolia, and Shantung—could be passed over in silence because of what Williams called "Japan's special interest in these regions." But Wilson would lodge formal protest against certain unspecified desiderata in Group V. Writing to Bryan on February 25, Wilson defined the goal of American East Asia policy as "taking advantage of the opening to present to Japan very frankly our views on her 'suggestions' or 'requests'." The President added: "I think those views can be made very weighty and conclusive. We shall not have uttered a more important state paper."[41]

A Rear-Guard Action at State. As the President's attention returned to other issues, pro-Chinese officials at the Department devised a move calculated to extract diplomatic concessions from Japan in return for United States acquiescence in some of the more modest demands. The idea was to require a quid pro quo for American acceptance of the original Japanese agenda—and then proceed to lodge formal protest against the more controversial desiderata in Group V.[42]

This policy proposal, which advertised itself as a "bargain" in a transparent move to mollify Secretary Bryan, was the work of missionary E. T. Williams. On February 22 or 23, Williams was asked by Counselor Lansing, who in turn had been asked by the President, to draft the formal representation to Japan. But, when Williams started to work, he found that he could not justify allowing Groups I through IV to pass without comment. So, reversing his own policy recommendation of February 15, Williams suggested that the United States obtain concessions from Japan in return for American acquiescence in Group II of the demands (those relating to South Manchuria and Eastern Inner Mongolia). "Before the Department decides definitely to make no objections to the 'demands' as distinguished from the 'requests' which Japan has presented to China," Williams wrote on February 26, "I respectfully suggest the propriety of obtaining a quid pro quo since we shall be surrendering valuable treaty rights." The putative bargain was to be as follows: the United States would formally consent to Group II if Japan undertook to reaffirm the Open Door principle, revise the freight-rate schedules of the South Manchurian Railway, and raise no further objection regarding the California statute expropriating the lands of Japanese farmers.[43]

Lansing, after consultation with Williams on February 26 and discussions with Bryan on February 27 and March 1, concluded that these policy suggestions "are worthy of careful consideration." Expanding on Williams's proposal to include Groups I, III, and IV in the package deal, Lansing wrote to Bryan on March 1:

> If a bargain along these lines could be struck, it would relieve us of the vexatious California land controversy, and prevent in large measure future disputes which seem almost inevitable if the "demands" of Japan are permitted at the present time to pass unchallenged. In any event, can there be any harm in attempting to reach a reciprocal understanding, such as the one outlined above? We would certainly be no worse off than we were before; and I think, even if our proposal is rejected, we would be in a far better position to discuss Japan's conduct when a more propitious time comes to take up with other interested powers the question of the "Open Door" and the respective rights of the Powers secured through application of that principle.[44]

This bureaucratic package, again, was simply a hard-line method of implementing the President's basic decision to oppose Japan. Though it had the veneer of diplomatic realism, it was realism in the service of moralistic purpose. There is no evidence that Lansing and Williams ever intended to dissuade the President from his determination to protest Group V. Moreover, there is the suspicion that Lansing and Williams wanted the United States to float the proposal precisely because they expected the Japanese to reject it. In effect, the pro-Chinese subalterns were proposing that the United States agree to recognize the Japanese sphere-of-influence in China if Japan agreed to drop the racial-equality issue. Lansing and Williams being well-informed diplomats, they might have been expected to know that Japan would find such a proposal insulting. The whole package rests, after all, on the assumption of some invidious distinction—in immigration matters as in Great Power politics—between Japanese nationals and white people.

Perhaps Lansing and Williams believed Japan might be prepared to humiliate itself in this manner before the world. Certainly this was no "bargain" in any meaningful sense, nor was it calculated to improve the climate of Japanese-American relations. The diplomatic historian may speculate that its framers, understanding that Japan was now the paramount power in East Asia, would expect Tokyo to see that the proposal demanded a great deal in return for very little—and therefore would reject it immediately. On this assumption, Lansing and Williams, when called upon later to draft the formal protest against Group V, might throw in Groups I through IV for good measure. Or they might find some alternative method to deny legal recognition to the entire Japanese agenda, so that the United States would occupy the optimal position "to discuss Japan's conduct" at the anticipated postwar peace conference. The subsequent behavior of Lansing and Williams regarding the Twenty-one Demands is fully consistent with this interpretation.

Bryan as Diplomat. While Lansing and Williams were preparing to extract the last pound of diplomatic flesh from Japan,

Secretary Bryan's thinking was moving along different lines. Bryan was arguing that American East Asia policy should promote a diplomatic settlement of the issues between China and Japan.[45]

As soon as he received the full official text of the demands, Bryan drafted a four-page analysis of Group V and sent it to the President. "Our telegram to Tokyo had the desired effect," he wrote on February 22: "It brought out the fact that the additional concessions were presented as *requests*—not as demands." Working entirely on his own, Bryan then suggested certain textual revisions of the articles in Group V which he hoped would prove acceptable to the Chinese and Japanese negotiators. Two of the seven articles —those relating to the land tenure rights of Japanese charitable institutions in the Chinese interior, and to the status of Buddhist missionaries—Bryan deemed "unobjectionable," inasmuch as they aimed to place Japanese subjects on a plane of equality with Western nationals. Aware of Japanese sensitivities on the race issue, Bryan suggested that the article dealing with China's government advisors be rephrased to the effect that China would not "discriminate" against Japan when selecting such officials. Bryan held that compromise was possible on the article regarding joint Sino-Japanese police forces, which he believed the Japanese had submitted because of understandable anxiety over the maintenance of public order in Manchuria; he reasoned that the Japanese probably would not insist on joint policing in other regions if their vital interests in Manchuria received adequate safeguard. Secretary Bryan also offered suggestions on the desiderata respecting Fukien, arms purchases, and the Yangtze Valley railway concessions. Though certain of the articles in Group V did seem troubling in their pristine form, Bryan remained confident there was ample room for compromise and a peaceful settlement between China and Japan.[46]

Bryan wanted the projected note to Tokyo to embody his suggested revisions of Group V rather than some categorical protest that might strain relations between the U.S. and Japan. But Bryan understood that any attempt to make known America's views on the Twenty-one Demands could be constructive only if Japan was convinced that Washington was acting in good faith. So as to ease any Japanese apprehensiveness in this regard, Bryan again tried to persuade Wilson to yield some ground on the immigration issue. On March 8, the Secretary drafted a three-page proposal for a comprehensive diplomatic settlement of the matter. Bryan hoped to begin negotiations with Japan at once. He told Wilson: "I believe it would go far toward restoring harmonious relations."[47]

There is no evidence that Bryan was interested in the Lansing-Williams plan that would induce Japan to back down on the racial-equality issue.

The March 13 Note. The President stuck to his guns. Rejecting Bryan's proposal to encourage compromise on Group V while negotiating an agreement with Japan on the immigration issue, Wilson also turned down the Lansing-Williams plan to demand concessions for American acquiescence in Groups I–IV. "I think we ought to go straight at the matter of the requests," the President reaffirmed on March 4. The Williams-Lansing proposal, he considered, in an apparent reference to the way its successful implementation might appear to others, "would seem like bargaining away some of the rights of China in exchange for relief from some of our own difficulties."[48]

The note took shape between March 4 and March 12. E. T. Williams spun out a draft nearly twenty pages long, basically a cut-and-paste of his previous memoranda. After many revisions, Williams on March 11 showed a final draft to Lansing, who spent a few minutes going over it. The following day, Bryan, after a conference with Lansing, wrote an introduction and conclusion to his liking and sent the entire document on to the President, who looked it over, made "a few verbal changes," pronounced the overall effort "thorough and satisfactory," and asked the Department "to despatch it promptly." Next day, Bryan summoned the Japanese Ambassador, delivered the note, and sent a brief summary out over the wires to Tokyo and Peking.[49]

The excessive length of the March 13 note was due primarily to its extensive legal paraphernalia. Citing chapter and verse from the Open Door notes, the document referred also to the Anglo-German understanding of 1900, the Sino-Russian Manchurian Convention of 1901, the Anglo-Japanese Alliance of 1902, "the Japanese Declarations at the opening of the Russo-Japanese War, the British-Japanese Treaty of 1905, the Russo-Japanese Treaty of Portsmouth of 1905, the Franco-Japanese Entente of 1907, and the Russo-Japanese Treaty of 1907," not to mention the Root-Takahira agreement of 1908. The point was to remind Japan of her commitment to the Open Door and to emphasize why "the United States feels itself under a moral obligation to the Powers whose pledges are deposited with it not to pass over in silence any threatened violation of these pledges." [50]

In addition to America's custodial role in East Asia, the note invoked certain American "interests" and "treaty rights" to justify a diplomatic representation. These were described somewhat vaguely. Pride of place went to the religious interest: "For two generations," the document intoned, "American missionaries and teachers have made sacrifices in behalf of religious and educational work in China." To be sure: "American capital has been invested and industries have been established in certain regions," not merely in direct investments but "in the economic development of China along broader lines," financial undertakings including "certain public improvements, such as the Huai River conservancy, the Hukuang Railway project, etc." The document cited long passages from the Sino-American treaties of 1844, 1858, 1868, and 1903 to prove that the United States enjoyed most-favored-nation status. [51]

The note was deliberately ambiguous with respect to the legality of Groups I and II, which in effect demanded recognition of the Japanese sphere-of-influence in Manchuria, Inner Mongolia, and Shantung. "While on principle and under the treaties of 1844, 1858, 1868 and 1903 with China the United States has ground upon which to base objections to the Japanese "demands" relative to Shantung, South Manchuria, and East Mongolia," read the key passage, "nevertheless the United States frankly recognizes that territorial contiguity creates special relations between Japan and these districts. This Government, therefore, is disposed to raise no question, at this time, as to Articles I and II of the Japanese proposals." At best, this might be interpreted as a kind of grudging de facto acceptance of the Japanese sphere. The historian may speculate, however, that, by locating those "special relations," as distinct from special interests, in "territorial contiguity," as distinct from power, and by including the limiting phrase "at this time"— all this with the clear understanding that what the Japanese were attempting was in fact objectionable both "in principle" and in law—the note was calculated to leave open the door for a possible legal challenge at some later and more propitious time. The close student may detect here the return of the Lansing-Williams "bargain" in somewhat repressed and attenuated form. If the Lansing-Ishii agreement could be seen to be based on this March 13 passage as precedent, so could the Lansing caveat of May 11, 1915.[52]

The sting of the March 13 note—its essential hostility to Japanese ambitions in East Asia—perhaps can best be felt in its treatment of Group IV (no further alienation of territory on the China coast to Western Treaty Powers) and Articles 2 and 7 in Group V (the right of Japanese philanthropic organizations to own land in the Chinese interior, and equal rights for Japanese Buddhist missionaries). Had he wished to express a minimum of friendliness toward Japan, Williams might have welcomed Group IV as a step in the direction of preserving Chinese territorial integrity and administrative entity, and might have accepted those two articles in Group V as very wholesome indeed, inasmuch as they endeavored to place the schools, hospitals, churches, and missionaries of all nations, including Japan, on a plane of equality. Instead, Williams lumped all these items together with Article 5 of Group V (the Yangtze Valley railway concessions), reluctantly observing that "this Government perceives no special menace."[53]

If its handling of Groups I through IV might be termed somewhat niggardly, the March 13 note tended to wander away into abstractions or extraneous matters when commenting on the four items in Group V to which it took specific exception: Articles 1, 3, 4, and 6. Article 4 (regarding arms purchases) and Article 6 (in effect, demanding recognition of a Japanese sphere in Fukien), as examples, are condemned on the ground that they "would, if they should become operative, be violations of the principle of equal opportunity for the commerce and industries of other nations." While some reference to Bethlehem Steel's corporate plans for Fukien would have been understandable in a full and frank discussion, the note raised instead the gratuitous issue of freight rates on the South Manchuria Railway.[54]

The discussion of Articles 1 and 3 in Group V was also somewhat wide of the mark. The document briefly observed that Article 1 was unnecessary, inasmuch as Japan already supplied six of China's twenty-five foreign advisors, and that any attempt to extract a promise that China would not discriminate against Japan in this regard must be superfluous. And it dismissed Article 3, providing for joint Sino-Japanese police forces in certain localities, with the observation that this development might lead to increased "friction" between Chinese and Japanese residents. "But what is more important," the note concluded,

> is the fact that these proposals, if accepted by China, while not infringing the territorial integrity of the Republic, are clearly derogatory to the political independence and administrative entity of that country. The same is in a measure true of Paragraph 4 of Article V relative to the purchase of arms. It is difficult for the United States, therefore, to reconcile these requests with the maintenance of the unimpaired sovereignty of China, which Japan, together with the United States and the Great Powers of Europe, has reaffirmed from time to time during the past decade and a half in formal declarations, treaties and exchanges of diplomatic notes. The United States, therefore, could not regard with indifference the assumption of political, military or economic domination over China by a foreign Power, and hopes that your excellency's Government will find it consonant with their interests to refrain from pressing upon China an acceptance of proposals which would, if accepted, exclude Americans from equal participation in the economic and industrial development of China and would limit the political independence of that country.

Here Williams was straining to find some impeachable offense which, "while not infringing the territorial integrity of the Republic," might nevertheless be viewed as somehow alien to the spirit of the Open Door. The international lawyer might observe that the abstractions to which Williams appealed must have possessed considerable totemic significance.[55]

Perhaps the most constructive passage in the March 13 note was the conclusion, drafted by Secretary Bryan. Expressing "friendship and esteem" toward "the aspirations of Japan in the Far East," the conclusion attempted to reassure Japan regarding the motives of American policy. "This Government cannot too earnestly impress upon your excellency's Government," the note said, in a passage which may seem ironic, "that the United States is not jealous of the prominence of Japan in the East or of the intimate cooperation of China and Japan for their mutual benefit. Nor has the United States any intention of obstructing or embarrassing Japan, or of influencing China in opposition to Japan."[56]

As President Wilson predicted, the views expressed in the March 13 note were "very weighty," so weighty that the State Department was reduced to sending the full twenty pages by mail to the Japanese Foreign Office. Japanese diplomats are reported to have found those views unintelligible. Whatever its cathartic value, the American representation in defense of China apparently gave rise to a certain amount of humor on the Tokyo cocktail circuit.[57]

CHAMPIONS OF CHINA

The United States received no written reply to the March 13 note. Though Ambassador Chinda explained the Japanese position in full to Secretary Bryan on several occasions, the Foreign Office in Tokyo made no direct response. Meanwhile, negotiations in Peking continued for nearly two months.

During this period, the United States often appeared to lack a coherent and consistent policy. For some time, American East Asia policy, while seeking no direct confrontation with Japan, nevertheless seemed to imply that future relations between the two countries hinged upon Japan's willingness to drop the four articles in Group V that the United States regarded as objectionable (Groups I through IV might be countenanced). Yet the American Minister in Peking seemed to be following a rather different policy, contemptuous of all Japanese ambitions, while the Secretary of State in Washington was promoting diplomatic compromise between China and Japan. Then, compounding the confusion, American diplomats seemed suddenly to change the direction of policy as the Sino-Japanese negotiations entered their final phase.

The Bryan Mediation Effort Regarding Group V. If there was any opportunity to improve Japanese-American relations during this period, or to promote the stability of the East Asia and Pacific region, that opportunity slipped away when the President, Mr. Lansing, E. T. Williams, and Paul Reinsch neglected to adopt Secretary Bryan's various proposals or refused to consistently support his initiatives. Following the March 13 note, as earlier when he sought approval for a new round of negotiations between Washington and Tokyo and suggested certain compromises on Group V, Bryan maintained his faith in diplomacy as an instrument of peace. He remained scrupulously neutral as between China and Japan. "The thing that disturbs me most in this eastern trouble," Bryan told Wilson, "is the feeling of suspicion on both sides—a feeling that does not give assurance of peace." On another occasion, Bryan articulated his conception of the East Asian situation as follows: "As Japan and China must remain neighbors, it is of vital importance that they should be neighborly, and a neighborly spirit cannot be expected if Japan demands too much, or if China concedes too little." After due allowances for folksiness, there remains a clear-sightedness which is enviable.[58]

Bryan's efforts actively to promote a diplomatic settlement of Group V began on March 17 when Ambassador Guthrie reported from Tokyo that the Japanese might be interested in discussing the Fukien issue. It may be recalled that Fukien was quite possibly the one item on the Japanese agenda bearing directly on American interests (or potential interests) and that the March 13 note had objected to it. Bryan learned that this article, and the article forbidding alienation of additional territory along the China coast to any Western Power, arose primarily from Japan's suspicions of American ambitions—suspicions deriving in the first instance from Secretary Hay's attempt to acquire a naval base in Fukien and by no means dispelled by persistent rumor to the effect that the Bethlehem Steel Company contemplated some naval-related project at Foochow. "It is evident," Bryan wrote, "that the suggestion made by Secretary Hay as to a coaling station has been in the back of the Japanese head ever since." Ambassador Chinda, when he called at the Department on March 22, explained further that Fukien was a matter of much importance because of its territorial propinquity to the Japanese province of Formosa.[59]

Bryan, aware that the Bethlehem interest was potential rather than actual, and eager "to relieve the anxiety of the Japanese people," proposed a substitute article that he thought would serve Chinese interests no less than Japanese. Bryan reasoned that Japan might be willing to drop its insistence that Fukien belonged to the Japanese sphere-of-influence if the United States demonstrated sensitivity to Japan's national security interests in that area by adopting a self-denying ordinance. This, in turn, would be contingent upon acceptance by both China and Japan of a revised article in Group V, excluding all foreign powers (and all foreign capital) from the ports of Fukien. Bryan had the documents drawn up.[60]

Next, Bryan turned to the three remaining items in Group V: arms, advisors, and police. Again he suggested substitute articles designed to achieve what he took to be the legitimate aims of Japanese policy without sacrificing the equally valid interests of China. Carefully investigating the particulars of each situation, Bryan refrained from facile moralizing. On the arms matter, for example, the Secretary observed that, while in the largest sense unfortunate, the Japanese request was in another way "not unnatural," inasmuch as "China has been buying her arms of Germany and Austria." More articles were drawn up, and Bryan incorporated them in a draft telegram to Tokyo and Peking.[61]

With what one may suppose was a certain degree of trepidation, Bryan on March 25 laid his Group V compromise on the President's desk. In addition to the new Fukien article, there were revised articles providing that China agree not to discriminate against Japan when choosing foreign advisors or purchasing arms and ammunition abroad, and that China establish a joint Sino-Japanese constabulary in certain areas of South Manchuria and Eastern Inner Mongolia heavily populated by Japanese nationals. The President scheduled an appointment with Bryan for the following day. Here was Group V, redrafted by William Jennings Bryan in accordance with his conception of a fair adjustment of Chinese and Japanese interests, consistent with American interests and the Open Door policy: Yes or No? [62]

For reasons that may forever remain opaque, the President said Yes. From the White House Bryan phoned Lansing and ordered that the cable go out immediately to Tokyo and Peking. [63] Upon reading Bryan's cable, Paul Reinsch exploded. Mediation, particularly on the notorious Group V, was not at all what the political scientist had in mind. Moreover, Reinsch's relations with Bryan, never very good, had taken a nasty turn in recent weeks because the Secretary had expressed displeasure at finding the Minister's confidential cables quoted in the American newspapers. But Bryan's attempt to facilitate a diplomatic settlement of Group V was the last straw. On March 30, Reinsch sent the Secretary a blistering despatch: "From my knowledge of the attitudes of the Chinese government and people," he wrote, "I feel it my duty to inform you that the compromises suggested . . . would definitely set a term to the existence of China as a free country. Should they become aware that the American government favors an adjustment . . . I fear that such knowledge would produce in the minds of the Chinese a conviction that the United States had betrayed its historic friendship and its moral responsibility in respect to principles of China's administrative integrity and the open door. If it is not the policy of the United States to take any preventive action in the present crisis, I beg to submit that it would at any rate be more expedient to follow a course of passive acquiescence rather than to intervene in such a manner as could scarcely fail to cause revulsion of Chinese feeling against the United States." Knowing that his cable would be read by the President, Reinsch pulled out all the stops. The diplomatic historian may speculate that Reinsch's Chinese associates, of whom Wellington Koo remained principal, may have been less interested in the United States as agent of mediation than as object of manipulation. [64]

In any event, the Reinsch telegram worked. President Wilson, whose view of Group V had never been sanguine and who may not fully have understood what Bryan was up to, immediately reined him in. In a sharply worded letter on March 31, Wilson told the Secretary that the Peking cable "had given me a good deal of concern" and that Bryan henceforth should take care to "set the matter in the right light alike in Reinsch's mind and in the mind of the Chinese." Bryan got the message; there was no further effort to mediate. [65]

The historian does not wish to make too much of this episode. It may be that the United States had too few interests at stake in China, and had behaved too irresponsibly in the situation, for Japan to take her views at all seriously. Perhaps the tensions in U.S.-Japanese relations over the racial-equality issue precluded any useful American input. Yet it is worth noting that one of the Bryan substitutes, the Fukien article, soon appeared on the negotiating table in Peking, was agreed to by both sides, and was incorporated in the new Sino-Japanese treaty. [66] As an act of international statesmanship the Bryan mediation effort regarding Group V compares quite favorably with the March 13 note—and the extraordinary moves to follow.

Policy Shift: Opposing the Entire Japanese Agenda. In April, the President, abandoning his February decision to protest against Group V while acquiescing in Groups I through IV, shifted American policy into wholesale rejection of the Japanese agenda. Even the most innocuous demands—the rights of Buddhist missionaries, for example—were included in the general condemnation. Preoccupied with European affairs, Wilson may not have been altogether familiar with the Japanese proposals. But he forged ahead anyway, determined that the United States appear to be playing a leadership role in East Asia. Since an element of the irrational was not lacking, this policy shift may be an example of that tendency in foreign policy, identified by Ernest R. May, whereby the "calculated" element in the decision-making process gives way to the "axiomatic." [67]

Yet Woodrow Wilson's axioms, on China as on other issues, had a way of corresponding to domestic political advantage. Wilson's political advisors would not have argued that a decision to oppose the entire Japanese program would cost him many votes in the 1916 election. Indeed, this course seemed to be exactly what most members of the foreign-policy public wanted. As the veteran Japan missionary Sidney Gulick observed, "Since my return to the United States I have become amazed at the suspicion at Japan's motives and policy. Apparently mischiefmakers have succeeded in poisoning the opinion of vast numbers of our best citizens, making them believe that Japan contemplates the 'looting of China'." At this time, *Outlook* complained that the mail from its usually sophisticated readers amounted to "expressions of feeling rather than contributions to the discussion," and even Willard Straight's friends, much to his dismay, gave themselves over to "bombastic conversation." If the foreign-policy elites were agitated, the China missionaries and their constituents seemed even more so. At one point, a group of prominent missionaries in Peking, denouncing the Japanese demands as "international highway robbery," sent the President a lengthy cable (costing $7,000 and paid for by Chinese friends) asking Wilson to do his duty "in compliance with the high mandate of the Christian Civilization of the Twentieth Century." The missionaries also were most active at home, as during the Chinese Republican Revolution. Though the Asiatic Association assured its business members that Japan's demands on China involved "no great change in the relations previously existing between the two Powers," the influential *Missionary Review of the World* published the text of the "high-handed demands" and called upon Protestants "to pray that the great republic, which is apparently earnestly seeking the light, may be guided so that the progress of the Kingdom of God may not be hindered." Even if, as an article in the *New York Times* reported, "the news fell unheard and unappreciated upon a hyphenated country and a hyphenated press," among Roman Catholics and immigrants, that is, there were editorials in papers from Boston to Walla Walla, and concern was voiced in all sections of Protestant America, that the

United States express diplomatically its vigorous opposition to Japan. "I get the same sentiment from many quarters," confided Wilson to Interior Secretary Franklin Lane on April 12.[68]

Moreover, Reinsch's cables, to which the President remained peculiarly vulnerable, now took on a histrionic edge. Reflecting what may have been a more intransigent negotiating posture on the part of the Chinese, and legitimate concern for the stability of the Peking regime during a period that saw the beginnings of the nationalist May Fourth Movement, Reinsch depicted the situation in somber tones. Warning now of Japanese control throughout the Yangtze Valley, now of violent revolution, now of anti-white race hatred throughout East Asia, his cables placed the worst possible interpretation on events sufficiently difficult in themselves.[69]

On April 14, Reinsch cabled some news appearing in the violently anti-Japanese *Peking and Tientsin Times* as "first evidence of the success of Japanese efforts to alienate Chinese confidence in the United States." The clip was said to quote "a prominent Japanese" as gloating that "'the Secretary of State is so much under the influence of Baron Chinda that he is not saying a word against the wishes of Japan.'" The newspaper reporter, presumably a Chinese, was said to observe that "the American Government seems to have abandoned its championship of the open door policy." Following this item, Reinsch, who in February suggested the policy adopted ultimately by the President, now went on to urge that the United States register disapproval of the entire Japanese program. "It is to be feared that unless our Government unmistakably dissociates itself from the appearance of acquiescence in the unconscionable demands of Japan," he warned, "persistent flagrant misrepresentations of its motives, such as cited above, will embitter Chinese public opinion against it." Without mentioning that Chinese diplomats already had formally accepted some of the demands, Reinsch begged permission to reassure Peking that the United States "has not abandoned either its material interests or its moral obligations in respect to China." Reinsch concluded, "Meanwhile I am taking appropriate steps through friendly Chinese to prevent the spreading of misrepresentations."[70]

The cable drew an immediate response from the President. "I am very uneasy about what is going on, as reported by Mr. Reinsch," Wilson told Bryan, "and I must frankly admit that I do not credit the assurances the Japanese have sought to give us." The President directed the Secretary to summon the Japanese Ambassador for the first of what were to be several full and frank discussions of "grave concern," told Bryan to cable Reinsch instructions that he indeed reassure the Chinese, and seized the opportunity to shift American East Asia policy into an even more aggressively anti-Japanese course. "Has Reinsch been told definitely that it is not true that we have acquiesced in any of Japan's demands?" Wilson asked, perhaps rhetorically. Wilson then sketched the new policy he intended to follow: "In short, I feel that we should be as active as the circumstances permit in showing ourselves to be champions of the sovereign rights of China, now as always, though with no thought of seeking any special advantage or privilege. In this way only can we make good this message to Reinsch."[71]

The President reaffirmed his policy shift on April 16. Reacting to yet another despatch from Reinsch, Wilson told Bryan that the United States should "try in every practicable way to defend China." Said Wilson in reference to an item completely overlooked in the March 13 note, "Her [China's] position in the matter of the Han-Yeh-Ping is certainly justified by every consideration." The President urged the Secretary to call in Ambassador Chinda for another "very candid talk." Wilson continued: "I think you will be justified in showing him that we take it very seriously and are very much concerned, seeing in such things a very decided infringement of the principle of the open door and also of China's administrative and economic integrity." The missionary-minded President concluded that the United States should "be very chary hereafter about seeming to concede the reasonableness of any of Japan's demands or requests."[72]

Events now came with a rush. The East Asian situation took a dramatic turn during the last week of April and the first week of May. On April 26, the Japanese negotiators in Peking announced they were withdrawing Group V from consideration. In addition, the Japanese no longer insisted on the Hanyehping demand relative to mining rights in the Yangtze Valley. The revised Japanese agenda, which included modifications of the demands regarding Eastern Inner Mongolia, was not unlike the original memorandum issued at the Japanese Foreign Office in early February. Responding to the negotiating skill of the Chinese, certain suggestions from their ally Britain, the American moral protest, and criticism from within the Tokyo foreign-policy elites, Japan's "elder statesmen" (*genrō*) had insisted successfully that the government assume this more modest position. Moreover, Japanese domestic political pressures had eased after the late March elections to the Diet, so that the ruling party was no longer obliged to maintain such a forward posture on the China or continentalism issue. "We have all along believed," observed a senior official at the British Foreign Office, "that political pressure was in the main responsible for the very stiff attitude adopted, just as in the United States the Government in power must before the Presidential Election twist the Lion's tail a little with the object of conciliating the Irish or the German vote." [73]

Yet, an atmosphere of crisis now surrounded the Peking negotiations, for the Japanese were claiming that the revised agenda represented their final offer, while the Chinese were saying that these terms were totally unacceptable. For several days, rumors of war enjoyed currency. On May 4, it became known that Japan was preparing to issue an ultimatum. Three days later, Japan informed China that she had until May 9 to accept the revised demands—or face the most serious consequences. In London, meanwhile, fear of war between Japan and China led policy-makers to revise the policy of relative "effacement" pursued since January. Sir Edward Grey warned Tokyo and Peking, in no uncertain terms, that Britain could not abide a war in East Asia. To Tokyo Sir Edward counseled moderation; to Peking, capitulation. On May 9, China agreed to Japan's terms; two weeks later a new treaty was in force. Chinese officials, whose last-minute stalling was a familiar ploy, are said to have expressed a degree of satisfaction with the outcome. Indeed Yuan Shih-k'ai was heard to claim that it had been a diplomatic triumph for China. [74]

The United States behaved rather strangely in these circumstances. President Wilson, determined that the United States appear as the champion of its Chinese client, during a Cabinet meeting on Arpil 26 decided upon the following specific steps: 1) a public statement dissociating the State Department from acquiescence in any of the demands; 2) a new letter to the Japanese Ambassador protesting those items; and 3) a diplomatic initiative to enlist support among the Allied Treaty Powers for a joint representation to Tokyo. These three measures, the President told Bryan on April 27, represented "the only means we have of reassuring China, our own people, and other governments less free than we to protest."[75]

Bryan continued to seek the middle ground. The impulse to do so received considerable reinforcement on April 27 when Bryan heard from Peking that the Japanese had dropped Group V and one of the Hanyehping items and had toned down the Mongolian proposals. Though Paul Reinsch tried to explain away this move as yet another example of Japanese duplicity, "designed primarily to mislead other nations and give the semblance of moderation, whereas essentially the demands remain as heretofore, unacceptable by any independent nation," the Secretary of State professed to see certain significant changes. On April 30, Bryan began work on a detailed analysis of the revised Japanese agenda. Most of the remaining articles, concluded the seven-page Bryan memo, were calculated to place Japan on an equal footing with the major Western Treaty Powers. Writing to Wilson on May 3, Bryan opined: "Taking the document as a whole, and considering the concessions which Japan has made, I think we are justified in believing that she will modify such of the demands as are still unreasonable."[76]

Though the President retained his resolve, Bryan, by dint of a certain rough-hewn guile, moved deftly to temper Administration policies. Volunteering to draft the communiqué on the Twenty-one Demands, Bryan put together a document that was pointedly evenhanded. Released at the Department on the evening of May 6, its key passage read as follows:

This Government has not only had no thought of surrendering any of its treaty rights in China, but it has never been asked by either Japan or

China to make any surrender of these rights. There is no abatement of its interest in the welfare and progress of China, and its sole interest in the present negotiations is that they may be conducted in a manner satisfactory to both nations, and that the terms of the agreement will not only contribute to the prosperity of both these great oriental empires [*sic*] but maintain that cordial relationship so essential to the future of both, and to the peace of the world.

Bryan, who the day before had shown this statement to the Japanese Ambassador, along with a little letter he had written, expressed gratification that Baron Chinda "found no fault."[77]

Also on May 6, Bryan made one last effort at mediation in East Asia. Believing the road to peace ran through Tokyo and Peking rather than the Foreign Offices of Europe, Bryan despatched urgent cables to those East Asian capitals counseling "a spirit of patience and friendliness" and imploring that the negotiations be continued "until an amicable solution of the existing disputes is found." The Secretary considered that "China and Japan because of their geographical position must remain neighbors and because of their mutual interests must be friends." Bryan also sent a personal message to Prime Minister Okuma.[78]

Meanwhile, President Wilson and his pro-Chinese subordinates continued to champion their East Asian client. On May 6, the United States, implementing a presidential decision made late in April at Paul Reinsch's behest, made formal approaches to London, Paris, and St. Petersburg contemplating a joint representation to Tokyo in protest of the already modified Japanese agenda. The American *démarche* stirred disbelief and worse wherever (China excepted) it did not generate anger. "The move which the U.S. Government made at the eleventh hour was as ill-timed as their policy in regard to China in the past would have led one to expect," observed a senior British official. In Tokyo, the British Ambassador called at the Japanese Foreign Office and reported afterward, "I have rarely seen Baron Kato so vexed." Sometime later, the British Foreign Office was said to have breathed a sigh of relief that "the Americans had made their move too late to do any harm." Between May 7 and May 10, the United States received the usual polite refusals from the Powers approached.[79]

As the Foreign Offices of Allied Europe were drafting the renewed expression of their highest consideration, Robert Lansing
stepped into the breach. "In the event that the Allied Powers re-
fuse to unite in a joint representation to Japan, which I am afraid
will be their reply," Lansing wrote on May 7, "I think that we
should be prepared to act immediately." Though E. T. Williams
was away at the Coast entertaining a party of visiting East Asian
businessmen, Lansing was sufficiently familiar with the situation
to devise a move calculated to achieve what he and his pro-Chinese
colleague apparently had wanted all along. Lansing continued, enclosing a formal note to this effect, which he had drafted:

> I suggest, therefore, that a notice in the sense of the one annexed be
> sent to Tokyo and also to Peking. While it might not prevent Japan
> from carrying out her purpose of coercing China to submit to her de-
> mands, it would constitute a complete reservation of all possible rights
> affecting American interests and Chinese interests as well, so that any
> agreement forced upon China at the present time could properly be-
> come the subject of discussion in the future when the conditions are
> more propitious. [80]

The Secretary of State, more concerned with preventing war
than with planning for the peace conference, seemed basically opposed. Writing to Wilson on May 7, Bryan said: "I am sending you
a suggestion which Mr. Lansing makes in regard to the Eastern situation. I hope that an agreement is going to be reached and that it
will not be necessary for us to send it." [81]

Even though an agreement in fact was reached two days later, the
President considered that Mr. Lansing's note should go out anyway. Minister Reinsch in his May 9 cable had called for "continued
watchfulness," inasmuch as the Japanese regarded Group V as
"unfinished business to be negotiated later," and the sinking of
the *Lusitania* on May 7 had suggested the importance of reaffirming American rights generally. "In view of the situation as a whole
(I mean the situation of the world, politically)," wrote Wilson to
Bryan on May 10, "I think that it would be wise to file such a
caveat as Mr. Lansing suggests. It will not do to leave any of our
rights indefinite or to seem to acquiesce in any part of the Japanese

plan which violates the solemn understandings of the nations with regard to China." The President hoped this checking move would "favorably affect the Japanese official mind with regard to the wisdom of postponing the discussion of Group V for a very long time indeed."[82]

The American official mind having decided, late in January, upon the wisdom of defending China rather than of siding with Japan, promoting a diplomatic settlement, or doing nothing; the United States, moreover, having pursued its missionary policy first by lodging moral protest against Group V, then by protesting against Groups I through IV after Group V had been withdrawn; the champions of China, in the final days, having tried to drive a wedge between Britain and Japan; the missionary head of the Far East Division having confused American and Chinese interests; the missionary-minded President having reaffirmed publicly, on April 21, his commitment to "this vision of that great sleeping nation [China] suddenly cried awake by the voice of Christ";[83] the Secretary of State, Ambassador of the "Prince of Peace" on the Chautauqua circuit, having pursued missionary policies of another kind; the zealous Minister in Peking having accomplished his mission with more than the usual ambassadorial enthusiasm; even the realist Robert Lansing having declared, on May 3, "I consider myself of the orthodox school which look upon the Bible as containing the history of the true religion, and of God's relation to man, and which consider repentance toward God and belief in Jesus Christ to be the only means of salvation"[84]—all these having happened, the United States announced on May 11, 1915:

> that it cannot recognize any agreement or undertaking which has been entered into between the Governments of Japan and China, impairing the treaty rights of the United States and its citizens in China, the political or territorial integrity of the Republic of China, or the international policy relative to China commonly known as the Open Door policy.[85]

We are assured on all sides that the making of foreign policy is not a Sunday School picnic. Yet perhaps this was not always exactly the case.

Conclusion

What is the point of this history, the meaning of this epiphany?

The Protestant missionary movement began to wane in the 1920s and, despite periodic atavism and latter-day nostalgia, the decline continues to this day. The development may be said to reflect the growing secularism of the bureaucratic and professional classes, the increasingly pluralistic composition of the governing elites, and other factors perhaps best reserved for discussion in another place.

A culture hero before World War I, the missionary by the 1920s sometimes was held up to public ridicule, as in the popular stage adaptation of Somerset Maugham's *Rain* (1922). Soon, a section of the Protestant religious community embraced the once-famous volume *Re-thinking Missions* (1932), whose central idea ran to the effect that Christianity was no better than any other religion. Clearly, a traditional civilization was in decay. Despite overseas efforts by American Catholics and fundamentalists during the intervening years, the missionary enterprise, as a religious phenomenon, could never regain its former prestige. Even so, the idea of mission retains its vitality, albeit in secularized form. It is one of the fundamental structures of the American civilization.

Of the Christian missionary as a cultural type it is impossible, at so close a range, to form an opinion that might possess any degree of accuracy. During the past two generations, the cultural situation has changed so often and so rapidly that the historian hesitates to venture an assessment. Yet, one perhaps may observe— after the necessary qualifications regarding racial attitudes, ethno- centrism, and the like—that the missionaries, taken as a group, were among the more remarkable men and women of their genera- tion. They believed in something, they had their integrity, they had boundless energy for practically everything they regarded as right, and they seem to be living forever (the number still alive and active is truly extraordinary!). In *Man's Fate,* André Malraux saw this quality of vocation very clearly when he wrote of the fictional Pastor Smithson, a China missionary, that "this man *lived* his idea: he was something more than a restless bundle of flesh." Persons of this type must always be taken seriously. Where are their heirs in our own day?

Yet, the historian must frankly recognize that the effect of the Protestant missionary movement on American East Asia policy, an effect that was essentially unintended, was nevertheless disastrous.

For, though the missionary enterprise started to collapse in the 1920s, the Missionary Mind lived on, metaphorically speaking, for another generation, giving our East Asia policies a missionary cast which was not in the national interest. In the early 1930s, Secre- tary of State Henry Stimson, recognizing his duty to Christian Civilization, invoked the moralizing Lansing nonrecognition doc- trine as an appropriate means to check the Japanese Army's seizure of Manchuria. Stanley Hornbeck, student of Paul Reinsch and former educator in China, maintained this ineffective, moraliz- ing policy toward Japanese aggression during the decade preceding Pearl Harbor. Eventually, moralism gave way to a species of tough- mindedness whereby economic sanctions were applied, the 1911 Treaty of Commerce and Navigation was abrogated, and Japan's supply of petroleum was shut off.

Meanwhile, Henry Luce, son of China evangelists and publisher of *Time, Life,* and *Fortune,* continued to project the missionary image of China onto the blank screen of the public mind. In time, the China issue became thoroughly politicized. Because of strong public support for the Republic of China, Congress in the years after 1945 mandated massive aid to Generalissimo Chiang, a member of the Methodist Church, for the Civil War against the Communists. Following the Communist victory in 1949, Congress maintained relentless pressure upon successive administrations to continue to recognize the diminutive Republic of China on Taiwan as the sole legitimate government of China and, more ominously, to isolate the Peking regime diplomatically. The Republican Party, one branch of which was rooted in the missionary-minded towns of the Middle West, generally took the initiative on the China issue. Republican China still plays a role in the fantasy life of the American Republican right.

Congressional opinion on East Asia entered the modern era in 1966, date of the televised "educational" hearings on China and Vietnam before the Senate Foreign Relations Committee. The central figures in the re-education of congressional and public opinion were J. William Fulbright and John K. Fairbank.

In the interim, a certain amount of damage had been done. "Who lost China?" Nobody knew for certain, but, just to make sure that nothing comparable would happen again, the State Department was purged of its China experts; South Korea, Taiwan, and Vietnam were redefined in relation to the vital interests of the United States; and American East Asia policy acquired a rigidity and moralistic point unsuited to the challenges of modern international politics. Secretary of State John Foster Dulles, the earnest Presbyterian layman who refused to shake hands with Chou En-lai at the Geneva Conference of 1954, was, on East Asian matters, the faithful heir of his uncle Robert Lansing. Secretary Rusk, the last in this apostolic succession, was a transitional figure.

The diplomatic historian does not mean to leave the impression that this American policy record, which belongs most properly to the field of abnormal psychology, was solely the product of the Missionary Mind. Sheer ignorance played a large part, as did racism, commercial greed, simple anti-communism and, above all, the actions of others: perhaps the universal historian would observe that no power in the East Asia and Pacific region had, over the long run, behaved particularly well. But much of the American contribution to this international failure can be traced precisely to the selective recognition and willful misperception—the dangerous good intentions—of the Missionary Mind.

Writing in the October 1955 issue of *Foreign Affairs,* Stanley Hornbeck, principal architect of American East Asia policy in the 1930s, observed: "The American polity is rooted in a belief in the reality of a corpus of natural, moral or divinely ordained law and a practical application of principles evolved and expounded in the corpus of Christian doctrine." Certainly this man was in a position to know.

Appendix
Notes
Bibliography
Index

Appendix: The Twenty-one Demands

THE CHINESE MINISTER TO THE SECRETARY OF STATE.

Group I

PROPOSED FOR THE PURPOSE OF PRESERVING PEACE IN THE FAR EAST AND STRENGTHENING THE FRIENDLY RELATIONS BETWEEN THE TWO COUNTRIES.

1. China shall recognize the transfer of all rights in Shantung acquired and enjoyed by Germany in accordance with treaty stipulations or other rights with reference to China, regarding which Japan expects to come to an agreement with Germany eventually.

2. China shall not lease to other countries any territory or island on the coast of Shantung.

3. China shall grant to Japan the right to construct a railway from Yentai or Lungkow to connect with the Kiaochow-Tsinan line.

4. China shall open without delay the principal important cities of Shantung to trade.

Group II

PROPOSED FOR THE PURPOSE OF SECURING TO JAPAN A POSITION OF SPECIAL DOMINANCE IN SOUTH MANCHURIA AND EAST MONGOLIA.

1. The lease of Port Arthur and Dairen, together with the South Manchurian Railway and the Mukden-Antung Railway, shall be extended to ninety-nine (99) years.

2. Japanese subjects shall have the right to rent and purchase land in South Manchuria and East Mongolia for uses connected with manufacture or agriculture.

3. Japanese subjects shall have the right to go freely to South Manchuria and East Mongolia for purposes of residence and trade.

4. The right to open and operate mines in South Manchuria and East Mongolia shall be granted to Japanese subjects.

5. China shall obtain the consent of the Japanese Government to actions of the two following kinds:

(a) Permitting citizens or subjects of other countries to build railroads in South Manchuria or East Mongolia, or negotiating for loans.

(b) Hypothecating the various revenues of South Manchuria and East Mongolia as security for foreign loans.

6. China shall consult Japan before employing advisors or instructors for conducting the administrative, financial, or military affairs of South Manchuria and East Mongolia.

7. Japan shall have control of the Kirin-Changchun Railway for ninety-nine (99) years.

Group III

1. China and Japan shall agree to act jointly, not independently, in the contemplated formation of the Han-Yeh-Ping Company.

2. Without consent foreigners shall not be permitted to open and operate mines in the neighborhood of the Han-Yeh-Ping Company's property; and anything affecting the company directly or indirectly shall be decided jointly.

Group IV

PROPOSED FOR THE PURPOSE OF EFFECTIVELY PROTECTING THE TERRITORIAL INTEGRITY OF CHINA.

1. China shall not alienate or lease to other countries any port, harbor, or island on the coast of China.

Group V

1. The Central Government of China shall employ influential Japanese subjects as advisors for conducting administrative, financial, and military affairs.

2. Japanese hospitals, missions, and schools established in the interior shall have the right to hold land in China.

3. China and Japan shall jointly police the important places in China, or employ a majority of Japanese in the police department of China.

4. China shall purchase from Japan at least half the arms and ammunitions

used in the whole country or establish jointly in Japan factories for the manufacture of arms.

5. China shall permit Japan to build railroads connecting Wu Chang with Kiukiang and Nanchang, Nanchang with Hangchow, and Nanchang with Chiaochow (Swatow).

6. In case the Province of Fukien requires foreign capital for railway construction, mining, harbor improvements, and shipbuiding Japan shall be first consulted.

7. Japan shall have the right to propagate religious doctrines in China.

Source: Memorandum from the Chinese Minister, n.d. [February 19, 1915], *FRUS, 1915,* pp. 93–95; the author has made certain minor textual changes to conform to modern usage.

Abbreviations Used in Notes

ABCFM   American Board of Commissioners for Foreign Missions
FO   Foreign Office Archives (Public Record Office, London)
FRUS   *Foreign Relations of the United States*
JAAA   *Journal of the American Asiatic Association*
MRW   *Missionary Review of the World*
NA   National Archives (State Department Archives)

Notes

CHAPTER ONE: THE MISSIONARY MIND

1. *Outlook,* 110 (May 12, 1915), 83; see A. T. Steele, *The American People and China* (New York, 1966), p. 1; and Harold R. Isaacs, *Images of Asia: American Views of China and India* (New York, 1972), p. 66 (originally published as *Scratches on Our Minds* [New York, 1958]).
2. For notable contributions to the discussion, see Akira Iriye, *Pacific Estrangement: Japanese and American Expansion, 1897-1911* (Cambridge, Mass., 1972), pp. 151-168, 185-201, 215-227; Iriye, "Japan as a Competitor, 1895-1917," in Iriye, ed., *Mutual Images: Essays in American-Japanese Relations* (Cambridge, Mass., 1975), pp. 86-92; and Michael H. Hunt, *The Making of a Special Relationship: the United States and China to 1914* (New York, 1983), entire work.
3. Martin E. Marty, *Righteous Empire: The Protestant Experience in America* (New York, 1970), pp. 166-187, 199-209; Henry F. May, *The End of American Innocence: A Study of the First Years of Our Own Time, 1912-1917* (New York, 1959), pp. 12-14, 95, 125-129.
4. See Pearl Buck, *Fighting Angel* (New York, 1936) and *The Exile* (New York, 1936), both passim; Irwin T. Hyatt, Jr., *Our Ordered Lives Confess: Three Nineteenth-Century American Missionaries in East Shantung* (Cambridge, Mass., 1976), entire work; Robert E. Speer, *Christianity and the Nations* (New York, 1910), pp. 17-54, 327-394; James L. Barton, "The Modern Missionary," *Harvard Theological Review,* VIII (January 1915), 17.
5. Clifton J. Phillips, "The Student Volunteer Movement and Its Role in China Missions, 1886-1920," in John K. Fairbank, ed., *The Missionary Enterprise in China and America* (Cambridge, Mass., 1974), pp. 98, 107;

May, *American Innocence,* pp. 251–269, 283–285; *MRW,* XXVII (February 1914), 87–105.

6. Ibid., 87, 102.

7. On this whole issue, see the illuminating discussion by William R. Hutchison, "A Moral Equivalent for Imperialism: Americans and the Promotion of 'Christian Civilization,' 1880–1910," paper presented at the 1981 Durham (England) Conference on Missionary Ideologies in the Imperialist Era, 1880–1920.

8. *MRW,* XXVII (February 1914), 87.

9. Basil Mathews, *John R. Mott: World Citizen* (New York, 1934), pp. 53–55, 61–62, 67–68, 70–71, 129–153; see Milton T. Stauffer, ed., *The Christian Occupation of China* (Shanghai, 1922); *MRW,* XXVII (February 1914), 87–98.

10. William James, *The Varieties of Religious Experience* (New York, 1958), p. 53 (first published in 1902).

11. See Robert T. Handy, *A Christian America: Protestant Hopes and Historical Realities* (New York, 1971), entire work, but especially pp. 117–139.

12. James A. Field, Jr., "Near East Notes and Far East Queries," in Fairbank, *Missionary Enterprise,* pp. 31–37, 50; Josiah Strong, *Our Country,* ed. Jurgen Herbst (rev. ed., Cambridge, Mass., 1963), pp. 219–256; *World Missionary Conference, 1910* (Edinburgh, 1910), IX: *The History and Records of the Conference,* 18–27, 35–71; see Hunt, *Special Relationship,* pp. 17–21, 99–108.

13. Valentin H. Rabe, "Evangelical Logistics: Mission Support and Resources to 1920," in Fairbank, *Missionary Enterprise,* pp. 58–69, 81–89; and Rabe's excellent full-length study, *The Home Base of American China Missions, 1880–1920* (Cambridge, Mass., 1978).

14. Rabe, "Evangelical Logistics," p. 88; Paul A. Varg, *Missionaries, Chinese, and Diplomats* (Princeton, 1958), pp. 52–67; U.S. Department of Commerce, Bureau of the Census, *Religious Bodies, 1916* (Washington, 1919), I, 96–97, 19–21, 31, 39–41; C.F. Remer, *Foreign Investments in China* (New York, 1933), p. 265.

15. *Literary Digest,* XLIII (December 30, 1911), 1234; ibid., XL (January 29, 1910), 187–188; Kenneth Scott Latourette, *A History of Christian Missions in China* (New York, 1929), p. 604; Tien-yi Li, *Woodrow Wilson's China Policy, 1913–1917* (New York, 1952), p. 15.

16. *Literary Digest,* XL (January 1, 1910), 20; *Pilot* (Boston), March 2, 1912, p. 1, and June 8, 1912, p. 3; *Catholic World* (New York) for the period; Sidney E. Ahlstrom, *A Religious History of the American People* (New Haven, 1972), pp. 827–843, 851–856; see Hubert Jedin et al., eds., *Atlas zur Kirchengeschichte* (Freiburg, 1970), pp. 98–99, 104–107.

17. *Pilot,* March 9, 1912, p. 4.

18. Ibid., March 8, 1913, p. 3, and February 24, 1912, p. 3.

19. *Reader's Guide to Periodical Literature* (White Plains, 1915), III, 1694–1702; see, for example, Carl Crow, "The Business of Christianizing the World," *World's Work,* 26 (October 1913), 632–652; H. W. Horwill, "The New Missionary Outlook," *Atlantic Monthly,* 107 (April 1911), 441–451; C. S. Lobinger, "America's Torch-bearing in Asia," *Review of Reviews,* 59 (December 1914), 714–717; E. A. Ross, "Christianity in China," *Century,* 81 (March 1911), 754–764; W.J. Bryan, "World Missionary Movement," *Outlook,* 95 (August 13, 1910); "Japanese View of Japanese Christianity," *Independent,* 74 (March 27, 1913); A. H. Gleason, "Christian Statesman," *Harper's Weekly* (March 21, 1914), pp. 10–11.

20. *Chicago Tribune,* April 27, 1913, VII, 5; May 6, 1913, p. 4; May 13, 1913, p. 3; see "The World in Chicago," *Survey,* 30 (July 19, 1913), 529–532.

21. *Literary Digest,* L (March 6, 1915), 480–481; *Outlook,* 106 (January 24, 1914), 154–155; *Independent,* LXXIV (January 23, 1913), 175–176.

22. Field, "Near East Notes," in Fairbank, *Missionary Enterprise,* pp. 31–38; Stuart Creighton Miller, "Ends and Means: The American Missionary's Justification of Force in Nineteenth Century China," in ibid., pp. 249, 269–280; Norman A. Graebner, "The 'New' China: A Missionary View, 1900–1910," paper presented at the 1972 Cuernavaca Conference on Protestant Missionaries in China and America; Paul A. Varg, *The Making of a Myth: The United States and China* (East Lansing, 1968), pp. 112–115; see Hunt, *Special Relationship,* pp. 182–189.

23. U.S. Bureau of the Census, *Historical Statistics of the United States: Colonial Times to 1957* (Washington, 1960), pp. 7–8; Tyler Dennett, "The Business Side of Foreign Missions," *Asia,* 19 (July 1919), 690–691; *MRW,* XXVI (December 1913), 902.

24. Rabe, "Evangelical Logistics," p. 83.

25. Robert E. Lewis, "The Vintage of the Colleges for the Foreign Field," *MRW,* XXIV (November 1911), 838–839; Phillips, "The Student Volunteer Movement," p. 98; Rabe, "Evangelical Logistics," p. 76.

26. May, *American Innocence,* pp. 12–14, 37–39, 51, 95, 106, 123–129, 303, 305, 333–354; *MRW,* XXVII (February 1914), 88; Handy, *Christian America,* pp. 117–151; Joseph R. Gusfield, *Symbolic Crusade: Status Politics and the American Temperance Movement* (Urbana, 1963), pp. 87–110; see William R. Hutchison, "Cultural Strain and Protestant Liberalism," *American Historical Review,* LXXVI (April 1971), 386–411.

27. *Historical Statistics,* p. 16; these numbers help make concrete the "constituency" mentioned frequently in Hunt, *Special Relationship.*

28. *World Missionary Conference, 1910,* IX, 246; Stauffer, *Christian Occupation,* p. 38; *Religious Bodies, 1916,* I, 108; Latourette, *Missions in China,* pp. 567–685.

29. Arthur H. Smith, *The Uplift of China* (New York, 1908), title page; Darwin F. Pickard to Lansing, December 18, 1914, Papers of Robert Lansing, Library of Congress.

30. Entries for April 21–30, 1912, MS Diary of James W. Bashford, Vol. 39, 8–9, Missionary Research Library, Union Theological Seminary, New York; Hunt, *Special Relationship,* pp. 26–27, 105–106, mentions in passing these characteristic activities.

31. See Selig Adler, *The Isolationist Impulse: Its Twentieth Century Reaction* (New York, 1962), p. 25.

32. "Interdenominational Mission Study Class" (Madison, N.J., 1913), pamphlet in NA 893.00/634.

33. L. H. Preston to Wilson, March 4, 1913; E. Fisher to Wilson, March 4, 1913; A.F. Fisher to Wilson, March 4, 1913; all in ibid.

34. *MRW,* XXV (September 1912), 661; ibid., XXV (August 1912), 618–619.

35. "Japan Mission Meeting at Arima, May 1910," typescript in ABCFM: 16.4.1, Vol. 36, number 320; James H. Franklin, "Results of a Tour of Asia," *MRW,* XXVII (January 1914), 7–16; Charles S. Macfarland, "Christian Internationalism," in Lindsay Russell, ed., *America to Japan* (New York, 1915), pp. 206–213; Gulick to Board, August 3, 1913, ABCFM: 16.4.1, Vol. 38, number 453.

36. Edward Dewey Graham, "American Ideas of a Special Relationship with China, 1784–1900" (PhD dissertation, Harvard University, 1969), pp. 166–222; *World Missionary Conference, 1910,* IX, 241; for background on American attitudes toward Japan in the latter nineteenth century, see Robert A. Rosenstone, "Learning from Those 'Imitative' Japanese: Another Side of the American Experience in the Mikado's Empire," *American Historical Review,* LXXXV (June 1980), 572–595.

37. Harlan P. Beach, "The Present Status of Missions in Japan," *MRW,* XXIV (September 1911), 690–694; John K. Fairbank et al., *East Asia: The Modern Transformation* (Boston, 1965), pp. 546–549; Mary C. Wright, ed., *China in Revolution: The First Phase, 1900–1913* (New Haven, 1968), pp. 1–63; Tetsuo Najita, *Hara Kei in the Politics of Compromise, 1905–1915* (Cambridge, Mass., 1967), pp. 142–184.

38. W. E. Griffis, "Christian Missions in Japan," *Century,* 82 (September 1911), 749–750; J. D. Davis, "Annual Report of the Japan Mission of the American Board, 1909–1910," ABCFM: 16.4.1, Vol. 36, number 322; G. S. Phelps, "Annual Report for the Year Ending September 30, 1914," ABCFM: 16.4.1, Vol. 36, number 94; Gulick to Barton, March 16, 1914, ABCFM: 16.4.1, Vol. 38.

39. See Handy, *Christian America,* pp. 110–124, 128–151.

40. Sherwood Eddy, "In the Wake of the Boxer Massacres in China," *MRW,*

XXIV (November 1911), 834–837; "Mott and Eddy Among the Students of China," ibid., XXVI (July 1913), 525–528; Harry S. Martin, Peking, "Notes on Governmental Conditions in China," December 1912, ABCFM: 16.3.12, Vol. 31, number 118; "China's Self-Government Begun," *MRW,* XXVI (June 1913), 402; Chargé Williams, Peking, to Bryan (cable), April 6, 1913, NA 893.00/1598; *MRW,* XXV (February 1912), 83; Arthur Smith, "A Year of the Republic in China," ibid., XXVI (January 1913), 3–4.

41. *World Missionary Conference, 1910,* Vol. III: *Education in Relation to the Christianization of National Life,* 122; "The Fight for Social Purity in Japan," *MRW,* XXV (July 1912), 482–483; ibid., XXIV (September 1911), 670; Gulick, "Recent Spiritual Movements in Japan," October 1913, ABCFM: 16.4.1, Vol. 35, number 298; Henry Loomis, "The Present State of Christianity in Japan," *MRW,* XXIV (September 1911), 665; H. W. Meyers, "Christ in the Slums of Japan," ibid., XXVI (April 1913), 287–289.

42. William R. Hutchison, "Modernism and Missions: The Liberal Search for an Exportable Christianity, 1875–1935," in Fairbank, *Missionary Enterprise,* pp. 116–123; M. A. Matthews to Bryan, July 2, 1913, NA 811.52/176; MacGillivray to Mackay, October 10, 1919, Presbyterian Church of Canada, Shanghai Mission, Archives of the United Church of Canada, Victoria University in the University of Toronto; A. P. Smith to Bryan, February 1, 1914, NA 811.52/37; John Higham, *Strangers in the Land: Patterns of American Nativism, 1860–1925* (rev. ed., New York, 1972), pp. 158–193.

43. Guthrie to Bryan, October 13, 1913, NA 811.52/214; Sidney Gulick, D. C. Greene et al. to Shailer Mathews, June 10, 1913, ABCFM: 16.4.1, Vol. 38, number 447; *Outlook,* 105 (November 1, 1913), 464–465; Ira V. Brown, *Lyman Abbott* (Cambridge, Mass., 1953), pp. 186, 211, 213; *New York Times,* April 19, 1913, p. 1; ibid., April 26, 1913, p. 2; ibid., May 24, 1913, p. 2; see ABCFM: 16.4.1, Vol. 38, number 472; Macfarland, "Christian Internationalism," pp. 206–213.

44. Jessie Ashworth Miller, "China in American Policy and Opinion, 1906–1909" (PhD dissertation, Clark University, 1940), p. 82; Gulick to Barton, June 15, 1915, ABCFM: 16.4.1, Vol. 38, number 477.

45. Shirley S. Garrett, *Social Reformers in Urban China: the Chinese Y.M.C.A., 1895–1926* (Cambridge, Mass., 1970), pp. 74–150 passim, especially 77, 85, 98, 108–109, 119, 128–129; Jesse G. Lutz, *China and the Christian Colleges* (Ithaca, 1971), 170–174; *China Mission Year Book, 1915* (Shanghai, 1915), pp. 103, 106–107, 111–112, 121–122; *The Christian Movement in Japan, 1913* (Yokohama, 1913), pp. 188–195, 205–208, 211–212, 221–222, 284; Sherwood Eddy, *The New Era in Asia*

(New York, 1913), p. 135; "Some Significant Signs of Progress in 1912," *MRW*, XXVI (January 1913), 1; "Yuan Shih Kai and the Y.M.C.A.," ibid., XXVI (April 1913), 243; compare Hunt, *Special Relationship*, pp. 190–198.

46. See Latourette, *Missions in China*, pp. 842–843; and Isaacs, *Images of Asia*, pp. 144–148.

47. *Christian Advocate* (Chicago), April 4, 1912, p. 2; *Daily Christian Advocate* (Minneapolis), clipping enclosed in Bashford to Knox, May 15, 1912, NA 893.00/634.

48. May, *American Innocence*, pp. 343–344.

49. *Literary Digest*, XLVI (May 10, 1913), 1064–1065; see Ernest P. Young, "Yuan Shih-k'ai's Rise to the Presidency," in Wright, *China in Revolution*, pp. 428–442; William McLeish, Peitaiho, to Eliot, July 14, 1913, Papers of Charles W. Eliot, Pusey Library, Harvard University.

50. *Literary Digest*, XLVI (May 10, 1913), 1064–1065; *New York Times*, April 18, 1913, p. 1; *Literary Digest*, XLVI (April 19, 1913), 878.

51. *The Cabinet Diaries of Josephus Daniels*, ed. E. David Cronon (Lincoln, Nebraska, 1964), pp. 40–42; Li, *Wilson China Policy*, pp. 14–15.

52. Bryan to Williams (cable), April 18, 1913, NA 893.00/1623; Williams to Bryan (cable), April 19, 1913, ibid./1624; Bryan to Arthur Judson Brown, April 19, 1913, ibid.; *Literary Digest*, XLVI (May 10, 1913), 1064–1065.

53. Ibid.

54. *New York Times*, April 28, 1913, p. 3; Louise Arthur to Tumulty, April 28, 1913, NA 893.00/634; clipping of prayer by George W. Hinman in ABCFM: 16.3.12, Vol. 32, number 200; *Literary Digest*, XLVI (May 10, 1913), 1064–1065.

55. See Paolo E. Coletta, "'The Most Thankless Task':Bryan and the California Alien Land Legislation," *Pacific Historical Review*, XXXVI (February 1967), 169–172; "Executive Joint Conference of the Senate and Assembly of the State of California (Sacramento, April 28, 1913)," typescript in Papers of William Jennings Bryan, Library of Congress.

56. *Pilot*, April 26, 1913, p. 1, and May 3, 1913.

CHAPTER TWO: THE BUSINESS MIND

1. *Historical Statistics*, pp. 550–551; for background on China, see Hunt, *Special Relationship*, pp. 4–8, 15–17, 92–99.

2. *JAAA*, XIII (March 1913), 35; ibid., XV (March 1915), 36; for an interesting case study of one segment of the East Asia market, see Sherman Cochran, *Big Business in China: Sino-Foreign Rivalry in the Cigarette Industry, 1890–1930* (Cambridge, Mass., 1980).

3. *Statistical Abstract, 1915,* pp. 716–717; *JAAA,* XIII (July 1913), 172–176; William C. Redfield to Bryan, April 24, 1913, NA 881.52/217.

4. Johannes Hirschmeier and Tsunehiko Yui, *The Development of Japanese Business, 1600–1973* (Cambridge, Mass., 1975), p. 145; *Statistical Abstract, 1915,* pp. 418–419; Thomas Sammons, "Record Year in Japanese Trade," *JAAA,* XIII (July 1913), 174.

5. Iriye, *Pacific Estrangement,* pp. 189–191; *Statistical Abstract, 1915,* p. 426; see Kang Chao, *The Development of Cotton Textile Production in China* (Cambridge, Mass., 1977), entire work.

6. Howard Ayers (President, Cotton Goods Export Association) to Secretary of Commerce, June 15, 1914, NA 711.94/209; *JAAA,* XI (February 1911), 1–2; ibid., XII (February 1912), 6; ibid., XIII (October 1913), 258; ibid., XIV (June 1914), 138–140; *Statistical Abstract, 1915,* p. 426; Hunt, *Special Relationship,* p. 176.

7. William C. Redfield, "The Progress of Japanese Industry," in George H. Blakeslee, ed., *Japan and Japanese-American Relations* (New York, 1912), pp. 122–123; see Hunt, *Special Relationship,* pp. 174–176.

8. Iriye, *Pacific Estrangement,* p. 192; Remer, *Foreign Investments,* p. 265.

9. See Chi-ming Hou, *Foreign Investment and Economic Development in China, 1840–1937* (Cambridge, Mass., 1965), pp. 125–127.

10. Remer, *Foreign Investments,* pp. 262, 265, 273, 353, 361, 642; see able survey in Hunt, *Special Relationship,* pp. 174–182.

11. See Noel Pugach, "Progress, Prosperity and the Open Door: the Ideas and Career of Paul S. Reinsch" (PhD dissertation, University of Wisconsin, 1967), pp. 288–289; Remer, *Foreign Investments,* p. 262; see Varg, *Making of a Myth,* pp. 48–50.

12. Mira Wilkins, *The Emergence of Multinational Enterprise: American Business Abroad from the Colonial Era to 1914* (Cambridge, Mass., 1970), p. 205.

13. Ibid., p. 94; Hirschmeier and Yui, *Japanese Business,* pp. 147–148; Mira Wilkins, *The Maturing of Multinational Enterprise: American Business Abroad from 1914 to 1970* (Cambridge, Mass., 1974), p. 28.

14. *JAAA,* XI (May 1911), 109–110; R. Ichinomiya, "The Foreign Trade of Japan," in Blakeslee, *Japanese-American Relations,* pp. 133–135.

15. Wilkins, *Maturing of Multinational Enterprise,* pp. 28–29.

16. Iriye, *Pacific Estrangement,* pp. 112–114; see Charles Vevier, *The United States and China, 1906–1913: A Study of Finance and Diplomacy* (New Brunswick, 1955).

17. *JAAA,* XIV (February 1914), 7–9; Straight to Reinsch, March 25, 1914, Papers of Paul S. Reinsch, State Historical Society of Wisconsin; Willard Straight, "The Politics of Chinese Finance: Address at the Dinner of the

East Asiatic Society of Boston" (Boston, 1913), pp. 13-14, 17-21, 26.

18. Vevier, *United States and China*, pp. 99-110, 113-115, 205; Thomas W. Lamont, *Henry P. Davison: The Record of a Useful Life* (New York, 1933), pp. 153, 155-156, 158, 170; Knox to H. P. Davison, February 20, 1913, NA 893.51/1342; Michael H. Hunt, *Frontier Defense and the Open Door: Manchuria in Chinese-American Relations, 1895-1911* (New Haven, 1973), p. 219; *New York Times*, March 6, 1912, p. 13.

19. Straight to Taft, December 26, 1912, Papers of William Howard Taft, Library of Congress; Hunt, *Frontier Defense*, pp. 239-240; Vevier, *United States and China*, pp. 106, 175-188, 203-205; Remer, *Foreign Investments*, p. 272.

20. *JAAA*, XIII (July 1913), 169; ibid., XIV (February 1914), 7-9.

21. See Noel Pugach, "Making the Open Door Work: Paul S. Reinsch in China, 1913-1919," *Pacific Historical Review*, 38 (May 1969), 157-175.

22. Reinsch to State (cable), January 23, 1914, NA 893.811/104; Bryan to Reinsch (cable), January 27, 1914, ibid.; Bryan to Reinsch (cable), January 28, 1914, ibid.; Straight to Reinsch, June 30, 1914, Papers of Willard Straight, Olin Library, Cornell University.

23. *Literary Digest*, XLVIII (February 28, 1914), 421-422; Wilkins, *Maturing of Multinational Enterprise*, pp. 15-16; Reinsch to Wilson, March 5, 1915, Papers of Woodrow Wilson, Library of Congress.

24. *New York Times*, February 21, 1912, p. 12; ibid., February 27, 1912, p. 5; ibid., February 28, 1912, p. 13.

25. Iriye, *Pacific Estrangement*, pp. 112-114; Hirschmeier and Yui, *Japanese Business*, pp. 145-147.

26. Cyrus Adler, *Jacob H. Schiff: His Life and Letters*, 2 vols. (New York, 1928), I, 215-216, 219-222, 225-226, 228-229, 239-240; *New York Times*, February 22, 1912, p. 11.

27. A. Whitney Griswold, *The Far Eastern Policy of the United States* (New York, 1938), p. 469.

28. *Statistical Abstract, 1915*, pp. 238, 352, 354.

29. Ibid., p. 730.

30. *San Francisco Examiner*, April 27, 1913, p. 77; San Francisco Chamber of Commerce to Secretary of State, April 12, 1912, NA 893.00/634; *Memoirs of Robert Dollar* (San Francisco, 1917), p. 255; *Private Diary of Robert Dollar on His Recent Visits to China* (San Francisco, 1912), p. 110; *Literary Digest*, XLVI (May 31, 1913), 1214.

31. C. B. Yandell (President, Seattle Chamber of Commerce) to Senator Wesley Jones, April 25, 1913, NA 811.52/71; *Memoirs of Robert Dollar*, p. 235; *JAAA*, XI (May 1911), 110; *New York Times*, February 23, 1911, p. 1.

32. *Statistical Abstract, 1915,* pp. 426, 442, 507; *JAAA,* XVI (March 1916), 35; Ralph W. Hidy and Muriel E. Hidy, *Pioneering in Big Business, 1882-1911* (New York, 1955), pp. 495, 528-529, 547; *JAAA,* XIII (July 1913), 174 and XIII (March 1913), 35; Hidy and Hidy, *Big Business,* p. 553.

33. *JAAA,* XIII (July 1913), 174; *Statistical Abstract, 1915,* p. 507; *JAAA,* XV (March 1915), 36; for general background on the silk industry, see Lillian M. Li, *China's Silk Trade: Traditional Industry in the Modern World, 1842-1937* (Cambridge, Mass., 1981).

34. See Wilkins, *Emergence of Multinational Enterprise,* pp. 59, 91, 107, 110, 203-204.

35. Max Winkler, "America, the World's Banker," *Foreign Policy Association Information Service,* III (special supplement number 3, June 1927), 57; *New York Times,* March 9, 1914, p. 15; ibid., March 12, 1914, p. 14; ibid., March 16, 1914, p. 11; Wilkins, *Emergence of Multinational Enterprise,* p. 201; Adler, *Jacob Schiff,* I, 211.

36. Memo of the Division of Far Eastern Affairs, January 2, 1912, Papers of Philander Knox, Library of Congress; *JAAA,* X (February 1910), 9; ibid., XI (December 1911), 325; ibid., X (May 1910), 118-119; here again are figures indicating the size of a "constituency," of the kind mentioned in Hunt, *Special Relationship.*

37. *Literary Digest,* XLII (March 4, 1911), 395-396, and XLVI (May 3, 1913), 991-994; *Boston Transcript,* May 1, 1915, part III, p. 2 and May 3, 1915, p. 10; Varg, *Making of a Myth,* pp. 62-69; *JAAA,* X (November 1910), 294; *New York Times,* March 23, 1912, p. 1; ibid., September 18, 1912, p. 1; ibid., May 24, 1913, p. 1; ibid., April 10, 1915, p. 10.

38. Portland Chamber of Commerce to Secretary of State, January 4, 1913, NA 893.00/634; *JAAA,* XIV (October 1914), 272-273; see Hunt, *Special Relationship,* p. 159.

39. Robert H. Wiebe, *Businessmen and Reform: A Study of the Progressive Movement* (Cambridge, Mass., 1962), p. 12; *JAAA,* X (May 1910), 118-119; ibid., XIV (February 1914), 2, 7-9, 12-13.

40. Howard Ayers, "Business Conditions in China," *New York Times Annual Review of Business* (January 1910), quoted in *JAAA,* X (Feb. 1910), 12-14; see Hunt, *Special Relationship,* pp. 97-98, 174-176.

41. See Varg, *Making of a Myth,* pp. 36-53; E. W. Douglas to Reinsch, September 11, 1913, Reinsch papers; Fred W. Scott to Representative A. J. Montague, February 13, 1915, Lansing papers; see, for example, L. R. Freeman, "American Trade with China: Possibilities and Limitations," *Review of Reviews,* 49 (February 1914), 227-229; *JAAA,* XIV (October 1914), 257-258.

42. See, for example, *JAAA*, X (December 1910), 322; ibid., XII (June 1912), 129-130 and 132-136; and ibid., XII (December 1912), 321.

43. On the structure of semi-colonialism, see Albert Feuerwerker, *The Foreign Establishment in China in the Early Twentieth Century* (Ann Arbor, 1976).

44. *JAAA*, X (June 1910), 132-139; ibid., XI (March 1911), 40-41; ibid., XII (December 1912), 322.

45. *Memoirs of Robert Dollar*, p. 192; Drew to Eliot, "Memo—China," October 1911, Eliot papers.

46. Jokichi Takamine, "The Japanese in America," in Blakeslee, *Japanese-American Relations*, pp. 28-31.

47. *Memoirs of Robert Dollar*, p. 158; Adler, *Jacob Schiff*, I, 213-241 passim; Schiff to Eliot, November 3, 1913, Eliot papers; *JAAA*, XI (May 1911), 109-110.

48. See *JAAA*, XIII (June 1913), 130.

49. U.S. Department of State, *Papers Relating to the Foreign Relations of the United States, 1911* (Washington, D.C., 1918), pp. 315-318; *Congressional Record*, 61 Congr., 1 sess., p. 3211; *JAAA*, XI (May 1911), 97-110 passim.

50. Ibid., 97-98, 101-110.

51. Ibid., XIV (February 1914), 9; *Yearbook of the Japan Society* (New York, 1913), n.p.; Howard Mansfield, "American Appreciation of Japanese Art," in Lindsay Russell, ed., *America to Japan* (New York, 1915), pp. 239, 244-246; on the Japan Society of San Francisco, see Sidney Gulick to American Board, September 22, 1915, ABCFM: 16.4.1, Vol. 38, number 478.

52. Gulick to Barton, April 16, 1914, ABCFM: 16.4.1, Vol. 38, number 463.

53. *JAAA*, XIII (September 1913), 239-242; ibid., (May 1913), 97-98; ibid., (October 1913), 273; *Literary Digest*, XLVI (April 19, 1913), 878; Caldwell to Secretary of State, January 27, 1915, NA 881.52/37; Straight to J.O.P. Bland, February 24, 1912, Straight papers.

54. Vevier, *United States and China*, passim, especially pp. 28-30, 41-53, 65-68, 75-76, 100-101, 130-131, 137, 151; see Warren I. Cohen, *America's Response to China: An Interpretative History of Sino-American Relations* (New York, 1971), pp. 76-82; Richard W. Van Alstyne, *The United States and East Asia* (New York, 1973), pp. 92-97, 100-101; and Charles E. Neu, *The Troubled Encounter: The United States and Japan* (New York, 1975), pp. 45-46, 69-71; Herbert Croly, *Willard Straight* (New York, 1924), pp. 460-461.

55. Straight to Bland, February 24, 1912, Straight papers.

56. Straight to Bonar, March 13, 1912; Straight to McKnight, January 21, 1913; Straight to McKnight, March 14, 1913; all in Straight papers.

57. *New York Times,* March 10, 1914, p. 15, and March 13, 1914, p. 13; ibid., April 26, 1913, p. 2; Croly, *Willard Straight,* p. 466.

58. Straight to Reinsch, June 30, 1914, Straight papers.

59. [Straight], "Tsingtau and After," *New Republic,* 2 (February 6, 1915), 20–21; Straight to *New Republic* (cable), March 1915, Straight papers; Straight to Thomas, April 9, 1915, ibid.; see Helen Dodson Kahn, "The Great Game of Empire: Willard D. Straight and American Far Eastern Policy" (PhD dissertation, Cornell Unversity, 1968), pp. 449–452.

CHAPTER THREE: *THE MIND OF THE FOREIGN-POLICY PUBLIC*

1. Ernest R. May, *American Imperialism: A Speculative Essay* (New York, 1968), entire work.

2. Thomas F. Millard, "The Need of a Distinctive American Policy in China," in George H. Blakeslee, ed., *China and the Far East* (New York, 1910), pp. 92–94.

3. See Robert E. Osgood, *Ideals and Self-Interest in America's Foreign Relations: the Great Transformation of the Twentieth Century* (Chicago, 1953), pp. 121–125; *New Republic,* 1 (November 21, 1914), 18–19; ibid., 2 (February 27, 1915), 88.

4. Ibid., pp. 88–89; ibid. (May 1, 1915), p. 318.

5. Osgood, *Ideals and Self-Interest,* pp. 99–100, 125; Hunt, *Frontier Defense,* pp. 235–236.

6. Lewis Einstein, "Japan at Tsingtau and American Policy," *JAAA,* XIV (January 1915), 362, 361; see Hunt, *Special Relationship,* pp. 135–136.

7. Ibid., pp. 362, 360, 361.

8. Ibid., pp. 361, 362.

9. *Yearbook of the Japan Society* (1913), n.p.; *New York Times,* December 7, 1918, p. 18; ibid., July 25, 1919, p. 2.

10. Lindsay Russell, "America's Real Interest in the Orient," in Russell, ed., *America to Japan,* pp. 282–293.

11. Ibid., pp. 291–293; see "The Open Door," *Bulletin of the Japan Society* (New York), March 22, 1915, n.p.

12. See David Starr Jordan to Charles W. Eliot, August 10, 1912, Eliot papers.

13. Osgood, *Ideals and Self-Interest,* p. 243; ibid., pp. 86–107 passim; *New York Times,* April 27, 1913, pt. 2, p. 1; S. Okuma, "The Chinese Revolution and the World's Peace," *Independent,* 73 (July 25, 1912), 179–181; *JAAA,* XII (November 1912), 312–313; see Warren F. Kuehl, *Hamilton Holt* (Gainesville, 1960).

14. *Independent,* 76 (November 6, 1913), 236–237; ibid., 80 (November 9, 1914), 188–189.

15. Ibid.; ibid., 82 (May 17, 1915), 268.
16. Osgood, *Ideals and Self-Interest,* pp. 97, 135–140; Brown, *Lyman Abbott,* p. 186; Roosevelt to Baron Kaneko, November 23, 1914, Papers of Theodore Roosevelt, Library of Congress; Brown, *Lyman Abbott,* p. 239; May, *American Innocence,* p. 77; *Literary Digest,* XLVI (May 31, 1913), 1215; Hamilton W. Mabie, "Americans and the Far East," *Outlook,* 104 (August 2, 1913), 754–757.
17. Ibid., 110 (May 19, 1915), 121–123; ibid., 109 (February 24, 1915), 410.
18. Ibid., 104 (August 2, 1913), 739–740; ibid., 110 (May 19, 1915), 121–123; ibid., 108 (December 23, 1914), 904–905.
19. Ibid., 109 (February 24, 1915), 410; ibid., 105 (November 1, 1913), 464–465.
20. See May, *American Imperialism,* pp. 86–94.
21. Ibid., pp. 17–43 passim; see Robert H. Wiebe, *The Search for Order, 1877–1920* (New York, 1967), p. 237.
22. *Memoirs of Robert Dollar,* pp. 155–200 passim.
23. *JAAA,* XIII (June 1913), 140.
24. See May, *American Imperialism,* p. 49; Henry James, *Charles W. Eliot,* II (Boston, 1930), 215–219; E. B. Drew, "Memo—China," October 1911, Eliot papers.
25. David Starr Jordan to Eliot, August 10, 1912, ibid; Frederick P. Fish (President, Commercial Club of Boston) to Eliot, August 26, 1912, ibid.; *New York Times,* April 30, 1913, p. 10; Charles W. Eliot, *Some Roads Towards Peace* (Washington, D.C., 1913), pp. 36–38; North to Eliot, December 1, 1913, Eliot papers; Goodnow to Eliot, March 22, 1913, ibid.
26. See May, *American Imperialism,* pp. 65, 86–87.
27. Ibid., entire work.
28. *JAAA,* XIII (June 1913), 140–142; George Bronson Rhea to Lansing, October 11, 1919, NA 793.94/1029; *JAAA,* XIII (May 1913), 98; compare the *JAAA* list with that of Warren I. Cohen, *The Chinese Connection: Roger S. Greene, Thomas W. Lamont, George E. Sokolsky and American-East Asian Relations* (New York, 1978), pp. 293–303.
29. *San Francisco Examiner,* April 27, 1913, p. 77; *Private Diary of Robert Dollar,* p. 198.
30. See Herbert Croly to Willard Straight, March 2, 1916, Straight papers.
31. W. Cameron Forbes to Lodge, July 31, 1919, Papers of Henry Cabot Lodge, Massachusetts Historical Society; May, *American Innocence,* pp. 38, 58–60; W. T. Councilman, "William Sturgis Bigelow," in M. A. DeWolfe Howe, ed., *Later Years of the Saturday Club* (Boston, 1927), pp.

265–269; Wendell to Lodge, April 5, 1912, Lodge papers; Lodge to Wendell, April 8, 1912, ibid.

32. Straight to Henry P. Fletcher, May 28, 1913, Straight papers; Straight to Rhea, June 18, 1914, ibid.

33. *JAAA*, XIII (June 1913), 133.

34. See Varg, *Making of a Myth*, pp. 117–121.

35. Isaacs, *Images of Asia*, p. 48.

36. On the early history of Sinology in America, see John K. Fairbank, "Assignment for the 1970's: The Study of American-East Asian Relations," *American Historical Review*, LXXIV (February 1969), 864–866; *JAAA*, XIII (June 1913), 140–142; Hornbeck to Reinsch, November 30, 1914, Reinsch papers; K. Asakawa, "The Origin of Feudal Land Tenure in Japan," *American Historical Review*, XX (October 1914), 1–23; *Annals of the American Academy of Political and Social Science*, XXXIX (January 1912), entire number.

37. *JAAA*, XIII (June 1913), 140.

38. See Sidney L. Gulick, *Anti-Japanese War Scare Stories* (New York, 1917), passim; *Literary Digest*, XLIV (April 30, 1912), 796–797.

39. Frederick Moore, Peking, to Eliot, April 16, 1915, Eliot papers: *Literary Digest*, XLIV (January 13, 1912), 57–58; ibid., XLVI (May 17, 1913), 1107–1109; ibid., XLIX (September 5, 1914), 402–403; ibid., L (March 6, 1915), 464.

40. *Boston Transcript*, November 5, 1913; ibid., January 12, 1914; *Chicago Tribune*, November 5, 1913, p. 8; ibid., January 12, 1914, p. 5; ibid., February 11, 1913, p. 5; ibid., February 12, 1913, p. 2.

41. *New York Times*, November 5, 1913, p. 8; ibid., January 12, 1914, p. 3; ibid., February 6, 1913, p. 4; ibid., February 11, 1913, p. 7; ibid., February 12, 1913, p. 7; *JAAA*, XIII (October 1913).

42. *New Republic*, 1 (November 14, 1914), 1.

43. See A. Kinnosuke, "Anglo-American Arbitration and the Far East," *Review of Reviews*, 44 (November 1911), 602–604; "Anglo-Japanese Treaty," *Independent*, 71 (July 20, 1911), 120–121; "New Anglo-Japanese Treaty," *Outlook*, 98 (July 29, 1911), 699; "Japanese Treaty, 1911," *Independent*, 70 (March 2, 1911), 475–476; "New Japanese Treaty," *Outlook*, 97 (March 11, 1911), 522–523; F. E. Hinckley, "Extraterritoriality in China," *Annals of the American Academy of Political and Social Science*, XXXIX (January 1912), 97–108; and W. T. Ellis, "Cities under Eight Flags," *Harper's Weekly*, 55 (November 25, 1911), 21; and see, for example, *JAAA*, XIV (June 1914), 129–130, 148–152.

44. John W. Foster, *American Diplomacy in the Orient* (Boston, 1903); Burton F. Beers, *Vain Endeavor: Robert Lansing's Attempts to End*

the American-Japanese Rivalry (Durham, 1962), pp. 5–8; Iriye, *Pacific Estrangement*, pp. 185–187, 197–199, 225–226; *JAAA*, XI (January 1912), 354; see ibid., X (August 1910), 193–194; Paul S. Reinsch, *Intellectual and Political Currents in the Far East* (Boston, 1911); Sidney L. Gulick, *The American Japanese Problem* (New York, 1914); see, for example, Hosea Ballou Morse, *The Trade and Administration of the Chinese Empire* (London, 1908); contract for work to be entitled *The Open Door Policy in Its Relation to World Peace*, 1913, in Reinsch papers; Hornbeck to Reinsch, November 30, 1914, ibid.; see Stanley K. Hornbeck, *Contemporary Politics in the Far East* (New York, 1916).

45. *New York Times*, March 16, 1912, p. 10; ibid., February 8, 1912, p. 6; see Blakeslee, ed., *China and the Far East* (New York, 1910), *Japan and Japanese-American Relations* (New York, 1912), and *Recent Developments in China* (New York, 1913); Frederick McCormick to Lodge, June 11, 1915, Lodge papers; John Gardner Coolidge to Rockhill, November 10, 1914, Papers of W. W. Rockhill, Houghton Library, Harvard University; *JAAA*, XIII (June 1913), 139–142.

46. See the *Missionary Review of the World*, any issue; compare Hunt, *Special Relationship*, pp. 20–21, 101–108.

47. Charles S. Macfarland, "Christian Internationalism," pp. 212–213; for an international perspective on this entire matter, see William R. Hutchison et al., "Evangelization and Civilization: Protestant Missionary Motivation in the Imperialist Era," *International Bulletin of Missionary Research*, 5 (April 1982), 50–65; for some examples of missionary lobbying, see my "American Foreign Policy, the Politics of Missions and Josiah Strong, 1890–1900," *Church History*, 41 (June 1972), 230–245.

48. Iriye, *Pacific Estrangement*, entire work; Roger Daniels, *The Politics of Prejudice: the Anti-Japanese Movement in California and the Struggle for Japanese Exclusion* (Berkeley, 1962), pp. 42–64, 70–78; William R. Braisted, *The United States Navy in the Pacific, 1909–1922* (Austin, 1971), 30–35; Eliot to Butler, April 27, 1914, Eliot papers.

49. J. Smith to State, January 30, 1914, NA 811.52/37; John Hillman, Los Angeles, to War Department, October 7, 1915, NA 711.94/217; Clifford Elliot, Hamilton, Ohio, to State, September 27, 1914, NA 711.94/197.

50. Higham, *Strangers in the Land*, pp. 165–166, 171–173, 204; compare Michael Hunt's brilliant account of Chinese Exclusion in *Special Relationship*, pp. 47–50, 54–61, 145–160.

51. *Congressional Record*, 63 Cong., 2 sess., 2781, 2783.

52. *Independent*, 74 (May 8, 1913), 1011.

53. Isaacs, *Images of Asia*, p. 37.

54. See Varg, *Making of a Myth*, pp. 1–4, 16–19, 105–121, 173; compare Hunt, *Special Relationship*, pp. 113–116.

55. On the Protestant composition of the upper crust, see E. Digby Baltzell,

The Protestant Establishment: Aristocracy & Caste in America (New York, 1964); and Jerold S. Auerbach, *Unequal Justice: Lawyers and Social Change in Modern America* (New York, 1976); Isaacs, *Images of Asia*, pp. 24, 50–51, 86.

56. *Chicago Tribune*, December 29, 1911, p. 6; Pugach, "Progress, Prosperity and the Open Door," pp. 96–97; Rabe, "Evangelical Logistics," pp. 65–67; Trustees of Canton Christian College to William Howard Taft, Taft papers; *Private Diary of Robert Dollar*, pp. 60–61; *Memoirs of Robert Dollar*, p. 201.

57. See Handy, *A Christian America*, pp. 117–154; and Osgood, *Ideals and Self-Interest*, pp. 86–88, 91–95, 98, 103–105, 225–226, 238–242, 256–259, 429–431; the thesis advanced here is perfectly consistent with the interpretative framework of Michael Hunt's brilliant synthesis, *The Making of a Special Relationship*. Hunt's point that the Open Door policy was a function of "the open door constituency" is unexceptionable, and Hunt is surely correct that the balance of power among the various interest groups shifted over time. The present work estimates the size and influence of the various constituencies during a particularly telling moment in the evolution of American policy. The relationship between public opinion and foreign policy receives treatment, and relations with Japan— yet another special relationship—are not neglected. Hunt's excellent work will long remain the standard treatment of U.S.–China relations to 1914.

58. Benjamin R. C. Low, *Seth Low* (New York, 1925), pp. 58, 75; *World Missionary Conference, 1910*, IX, 12; *New York Times*, February 4, 1914, p. 8; *World Missionary Conference*, IX, 51, 62; ibid., 278–279.

59. F. W. Williams, "A Sketch of the Relations between the United States and China," in Blakeslee, ed., *China and the Far East*, p. 82.

60. Williams to Foster, April 22, 1911, Papers of John Watson Foster, Library of Congress; Foster, *Diplomacy in the Orient*, pp. 437–438; on the cultural dimensions of foreign policy generally, see the pioneering essay by Akira Iriye, "Culture and Power: International Relations as Intercultural Relations," *Diplomatic History*, 3 (Spring 1979), 115–128.

CHAPTER FOUR: RECOGNITION

1. My understanding of the Revolution, its origins and consequences, derives largely from Wright, ed., *China in Revolution;* Jordan to Sir Claude McDonald, December 30, 1911, FO 350/7/125.

2. Calhoun to State, May 21, 1912, NA 893.00/1338; see Hunt's fine synthesis of Chinese and American policy in *Special Relationship*, pp. 138–141.

3. See Wright, "Introduction: the Rising Tide of Change," pp. 4–19.

4. Ibid., pp. 30–33, 40–42; ibid., pp. 4–19.

5. See John G. Reid, *The Manchu Abdication and the Powers, 1908-1912: An Episode in Pre-War Diplomacy* (Berkeley, 1935).

6. Wright, "Introduction," pp. 49-50.

7. Ibid., pp. 49-50, 52-54.

8. Ibid., pp. 54-58.

9. Ibid.; Reid, *Manchu Abdication*, pp. 312-313; Peter Lowe, *Great Britain and Japan 1911-1915* (New York, 1969), pp. 68-71, 85-86; Jordan to Fraser, November 11, 1911, FO 350/7/110.

10. Reid, *Manchu Abdication*, pp. 245-248; William R. Braisted, *United States Navy*, pp. 97-99, 101-111, 114-115, 118-119; Ransford Miller to Bryan (memo), May 13, 1913, NA 893.00/1653; Iriye, *Pacific Estrangement*, p. 64; Wright, "Introduction," p. 54; Jordan to Admiral Sir Alfred Winsloe, November 14, 1911, FO 350/7/102.

11. See Braisted, *United States Navy*, pp. 94-119.

12. Reid, *Manchu Abdication*, p. 312; Lowe, *Britain and Japan*, pp. 85-88; Jordan to Sir Francis Campbell, December 20, 1911, FO 350/7/119.

13. Williams to State (cable), September 3, 1911, NA 893.00/593; Huntington Wilson to Williams (cable), September 7, 1911, NA 893.00/541; Secretary of the Navy to Secretary of State, September 9, 1911, NA 893.00/545.

14. Williams to State (cable), October 11, 1911, NA 893.00/557-558; Williams to State (cable), October 12, 1911, NA 893.00/560; Wilder to State (cable), October 13, 1911, NA 893.00/562.

15. See Paige Elliott Mulhollan, "Philander C. Knox and Dollar Diplomacy," (PhD dissertation, University of Texas, 1966), pp. 34-47; Henry F. Pringle, *The Life and Times of William Howard Taft*, 2 vols. (New York, 1939), II, 756-759; also see Hunt, *Frontier Defense*, pp. 182-183.

16. Miller to Knox (memo), October 14, 1911, Knox Papers.

17. Knox to Taft (telegram), October 17, 1911, NA 893.000/582A; Knox to Taft (telegram), Ocotber 27, 1911, NA 893.00/610A; Hilles to Knox (telegram), October 28, 1911, NA 893.00/611; Knox to Calhoun (cable), November 23, 1911, NA 893.00/679.

18. Calhoun to State (cable), December 6, 1911, NA 893.00/745; Knox to Calhoun (cable), December 7, 1911, NA 893.51/680; Japanese Ambassador to State, December 18, 1911, NA 893.00/785; Knox to Am-legation Tokyo (cable), December 21, 1911, ibid.; Jordan to Campbell, December 4, 1911, FO 350/7/112; Knox Circular to the Powers (cable), December 12, 1911, NA 893.51/692a-b; Knox to Calhoun (cable), December 16, 1911, NA 893.51/703A; Calhoun to Knox (cable), December 18, 1911, NA 893.00/784.

19. Braisted, *United States Navy*, pp. 109-110; Knox to Navy Secretary Meyer, January 22, 1912, NA 893.00/975.

20. Murdock to Navy (cable), January 26, 1912, enclosed in Secretary of Navy to Secretary of State, January 26, 1912, NA 893.00/1002; Murdock, Nanking, to Navy, February 12, 1912, enclosed in Secretary of Navy to Secretary of State, March 14, 1912, NA 893.00/1181.

21. Tenney, Nanking, to Calhoun (cable), February 11, 1912, enclosed in Calhoun to State, February 26, 1912, NA 893.00/1213.

22. Meribeth E. Cameron, "American Recognition Policy Toward the Republic of China, 1912–1913," *Pacific Historical Review*, II (June 1933), 215–218.

23. Calhoun to State (cable), March 2, 1912, NA 893.00/1135; *New York Times*, March 23, 1912, p. 1; see Young, "Yuan Shih-k'ai's Rise," pp. 419–420, 433–442.

24. See Mulhollan, "Philander C. Knox," pp. 231–240; Memorandum to the Japanese Ambassador, February 27, 1912, NA 893.00/1105; Wright, "Introduction," pp. 55–57; Fairbank, *East Asia*, pp. 646–648.

25. See Nemai Sadhan Bose, *American Attitudes and Policy to the Nationalist Movement in China, 1911–1921* (Bombay, 1970), pp. 11–33 passim.

26. Tenney, Nanking, to Calhoun, June 12, 1912, NA 893.00/1374; Tenney, Nanking, to Calhoun, February 10, 1913, NA 893.00/1555.

27. Calhoun, Peking, to State, May 21, 1912, NA 893.00/1338.

28. See Walter V. Scholes and Marie V. Scholes, *The Foreign Policies of the Taft Administration* (Columbia, Missouri, 1970), pp. 227–246.

29. May, *American Innocence*, p. 15.

30. *Wall Street Journal*, as quoted in *Literary Digest*, XLIII (October 28, 1911), 721–722; *JAAA*, XI (December 1911), 321–322.

31. *JAAA*, XI (November 1911), 289–290; ibid., XI (December 1911), 321–322.

32. Ibid., XI (January 1912), 353; San Francisco Chamber of Commerce to State, April 12, 1912, NA 893.00/634.

33. Straight to Frank McKnight, December 22, 1911, Straight papers.

34. Quoted in *JAAA*, XIII (June 1913), 140–142.

35. Ibid., XII (June 1912), 130, 132–136; Rockhill to Morrison, June 2, 1912, Rockhill papers; Rockhill to J. V. A. MacMurray, April 11, 1913, ibid.

36. See the excellent article by Michael V. Metallo, "American Missionaries, Sun Yat-sen, and the Chinese Revolution," *Pacific Historical Review*, XLVII (May 1978), 261–282; Garrett, *Social Reformers*, pp. 106–107, 118, 128–129; Howard S. Galt, "Report of the North China Union College, 1911–1912," T'ung Chou, February 8, 1912, typescript in ABCFM: 16.3.12, Vol. 31, number 116; see Hunt, *Special Relationship*, p. 186.

37. Ibid.; Lyman Peet, "Report of Foochow College for 1911," n.d. [1912], ABCFM: 16.3.5, Vol. 15, number 280; see Metallo, "American Missionaries," 264–268.

38. *New York Times,* January 23, 1912, p. 3; Wilder to Calhoun, January 25, 1912, enclosed in Calhoun to State, February 25, 1912, NA 893.00/ 1212; see *JAAA,* XII (April 1912), 71–72.

39. *Chinese Recorder* (Shanghai), XLII (November 1911), 611–612; ibid., XLIII (January 1912), 1–5; John Ross, "The Chinese Revolution and Missions," *MRW,* XXV (January 1912), 42–43; another episode in the relations between Protestant missions and incipient Chinese nationalism can be found in my "Partisans of China, 1919–1922: North American Protestant Missionaries and the May Fourth Movement," paper presented at annual meeting of the Canadian Historical Association, Toronto, June 1974.

40. Brown to State, October 24, 1911, NA 893.00/605; Stuntz to Taft, January 1912, NA 893.00/1057.

41. Quoted in *Literary Digest,* XLIV (February 17, 1912), 337; *MRW,* XXIV (December 1911), 881–882; ibid., XXVI (September 1913), 643–644; *Missionary Herald* (Boston), CLVIII (January 1912), 5; see Metallo, "American Missionaries," 266–267, 271–273, 277–281.

42. *Memoirs of Robert Dollar,* p. 237.

43. *San Francisco Examiner,* November 16, 1911, p. 1; *Chicago Tribune, Boston Transcript,* and *New York Times* for the period.

44. *Walla Walla Union,* October 13–November 18, 1911; ibid., October 15, 1911, p. 1; ibid., September 28, 1912, p. 1.

45. *Literary Digest,* XLIII (October 28, 1911), 721–722; ibid., XLIII (November 11, 1911), 837–838; ibid., XLIV (January 13, 1912), 57–58.

46. Ibid., XLIV (February 24, 1912), 360–361; ibid., XLIV (January 13, 1912), 57–58; *New York Times,* February 13, 1912, p. 10.

47. Ibid., December 31, 1911, pt. 5, pp. 1–2.

48. *Catholic World* for the period, especially XCIV (December 1911), 421–425; ibid., XCIV (March 1912), 858; ibid., XCV (May 1912), 276–279; the *Pilot* for the period; ibid., January 6, 1912, p. 3; ibid., January 27, 1912, p. 4; ibid., March 16, 1912, p. 4.

49. *Jewish Advocate* (Boston), for the period; ibid., November 24, 1911, p. 1; ibid., January 5, 1912; ibid., February 16, 1912.

50. *San Francisco Examiner,* October 15, 1911, p. 1; ibid., November 6, 1911, p. 2; Chinese National Association, San Francisco, to State (telegram), October 16, 1911, NA 893.00/578; Y. S. Tsao, "China's Revolution Spells Progress," *MRW,* XXIV (December 1911), 919–924; *New York Times,* March 2, 1912, p. 3; ibid., February 18, 1912, pt. 3, p. 5; see Hunt, *Special Relationship,* pp. 160–164.

51. A good deal of the Department's mail on the recognition issue, and all the items mentioned here, can be found in NA 893.000/634; *JAAA,* XII (November 1912), 289–290.

52. All the communications, again, repose in NA 893.00/634; see especially the letters from the Laymen's Missionary Movement (April 21, 1913), Presbyterians of Newark (March 4, 1913), Rotary Club of Harrisburg (November 23, 1912), Cleveland Y.M.C.A. (March 3, 1913), Foreign Christian Missionary Society of Cincinnati (December 5, 1911), Christian Woman's Board of Missions of Indianapolis (November 23, 1911), San Antonio Rotary Club (November 16, 1912), Pueblo Rotary Club (November 9, 1912), Helena Commercial Club (October 17, 1912), Pacific Grove Chautauqua Assembly (August 6, 1912), Anna M. Baldwin (November 4, 1912); Lafferty to State (with enclosure), February 21, 1912, NA 893.00/1097.

53. Willard Straight, as quoted in *JAAA,* XIII (July 1913), 168; also see *Literary Digest,* XLV (August 24, 1912), 293–294.

54. From among these items, all of them lodged in NA 893.00/634, see Arthur Judson Brown (August 12, 1912), Massachusetts Women's Christian Temperance Union (March 28, 1913), Lord's Day League of New England (October 12, 1912), San Francisco Labor Council (January 24, 1913); Jordan to Woodrow Wilson, January 30, 1913, ibid.; J. N. Butler to State, March 6, 1913, ibid.

55. Lamont to Eliot, October 22, 1912, Eliot papers; Straight to Eliot, November 27, 1912, ibid.; Straight to Arthur Judson Brown, February 18, 1913, NA 893.00/1787.

56. *New York Times,* November 16, 1912, p. 11; *JAAA,* XII (December 1912), 321–322; J. O. P. Bland, "The Opium Abolition Question," in George H. Blakeslee, ed., *Recent Developments in China* (New York, 1913), p. 235; Straight to Henry P. Fletcher, November 21, 1912, Straight papers.

57. Entries for November 13–14, 1912, MS Diary of J. O. P. Bland, Bland papers, Thomas Fisher Rare Book Library, University of Toronto.

58. On the links between Protestant culture and the Republican Party in the Middle West, see Paul Kleppner, *The Cross of Culture: A Social Analysis of Midwestern Politics, 1850–1900* (New York, 1970); and Richard Jensen, *The Winning of the Midwest: Social and Political Conflict, 1888–1896* (Chicago, 1971).

59. See Pringle, *William Howard Taft,* II, 815–819, 825–829, 832–837.

60. *New York Times,* January 4, 1912, p. 1; *Congressional Record,* 62 Cong., 2 sess., p. 634.

61. *JAAA,* XI (January 1912), 354; *Congressional Record,* 62 Cong., 2 sess., pp. 2645, 2652, 4702–4704, 4868.

62. Huntington Wilson to Taft, February 26, 1912, NA 893.000/1105.
63. Reid, *Manchu Abdication,* pp. 283–290; Knox to German Ambassador, February 3, 1912, NA 893.00/1029.
64. Memorandum in hand of Huntington Wilson [February 3, 1912], ibid.; Huntington Wilson to Taft, February 21, 1912, NA 893.00/1078; *San Francisco Examiner,* February 8, 1912, p. 1; *Literary Digest,* XLIV (February 17, 1912), 322.
65. Far Eastern Division memo to Huntington Wilson, February 19, 1912, NA 893.00/1146a; see Hilles to Huntington Wilson, February 26, 1912, ibid.
66. Memorandum to the Japanese Ambassador, February 27, 1912, NA 893.00/1105; Huntington Wilson to Taft, February 26, 1912, ibid.
67. Miller to Knox, July 19, 1912, NA 893.00/1389; Huntington Wilson to Calhoun (cable), May 6, 1912, NA 893.51/873a; Calhoun to State (cable), May 7, 1912, NA 893.00/1304.
68. Miller to Knox, July 19, 1912, NA 893.00/1398; Arthur Judson Brown to Ransford Miller (telegram), July 31, 1912, NA 893.00/1402; entry for July 17, 1912, Bashford diary, Vol. 39, 55–56.
69. "Confidential Memorandum" to the American Embassies at Tokyo, London, Paris, Berlin, St. Petersburg, Rome, and Vienna (cable), July 20, 1912, NA 893.00/1383A–B; for the replies of the Powers see NA 893.00/1391, 1396–7, 1399, 1403, 1406–7, 1413–14, 1420; Knox to Reid (cable), August 1, 1912, NA 893.00/1406B.
70. Huntington Wilson to Calhoun (cable), September 26, 1912, NA 893.51/1070; U. S. Department of State, *Papers Relating to the Foreign Relations of the United States, 1912* (Washington, D.C., 1919), pp. xi–xii, xxi–xxii; Cameron, "American Recognition Policy," p. 223; Knox to Senator Shelby M. Cullom (Chairman, Committee on Foreign Relations), with enclosure, February 4, 1913, NA 893.00/1529A.
71. Li, *Wilson's China Policy,* pp. 15–89, offers the most thorough account of these policy moves.
72. The interpretation advanced in William Appleman Williams, *The Tragedy of American Diplomacy* (rev. ed., New York, 1962), pp. 67–78, is among the more deliberately provocative.
73. Arthur S. Link, *Woodrow Wilson and the Progressive Era, 1910–1917* (New York, 1954), pp. 107–144; Wilson to Bryan, January 16, 1913, Bryan papers; Wilson to Bryan, February 5, 1913, ibid; see Metallo, "American Missionaries," 274–275.
74. Ibid.; Wilson to Bryan, February 17, 1913, ibid.; Dodge to Wilson, March 8, 1913, Wilson papers; Dodge to Wilson (telegram), March 8, 1913, ibid.; Wilson to Jenkins (enclosing cable to Mott), March 17, 1913, ibid.; Wilson to Mott (cable), March 21, 1913, ibid.

75. *Daniels Cabinet Diaries,* ed. Cronon, p. 42.

76. *Literary Digest,* XLVI (April 5, 1913), 758-759; ibid. (April 19, 1913), 879; ibid. (March 29, 1913), 691-693; Straight to Bland, March 25, 1913, Straight papers; J. J. Morony to Wilson, March 21, 1913, Wilson papers; Dodge to Wilson, April 1, 1913, ibid.

77. *JAAA,* XIII (April 1913), 65-66; *New York Herald,* quoted in *Literary Digest,* XLVI (March 29, 1913), 691-693; Jordan to Sir Walter Langley, March 24, 1913, FO 800/246/335; Straight to Bland, March 25, 1913, Straight papers.

78. W. T. Ellis, "China in Revolution," *Outlook,* 99 (October 28, 1911), 454.

79. J. E. Cone to Taft, October 15, 1912, NA 893.00/634.

80. On Bland, see Hugh Trevor-Roper, *Hermit of Peking: The Hidden Life of Sir Edmund Backhouse* (New York, 1977) passim.

81. Entry for January 14, 1913, Bland diary.

82. *New York Times,* December 8, 1912, pt. 5, p. 4; ibid, November 18, 1912, p. 4.

83. Entry for January 1, 1913, Bland diary.

CHAPTER FIVE: NONRECOGNITION

1. Max Weber, "Politics as a Vocation," in *From Max Weber: Essays in Sociology,* ed. and trans. H. H. Gerth and C. Wright Mills (New York, 1947), pp. 77-128.

2. Memorandum from the Chinese Minister, n.d. [Feb. 19, 1915], U.S. Department of State, *Papers Relating to the Foreign Relations of the United States, 1915* (Washington, D.C., 1924), pp. 93-95.

3. Ibid., p. 94; see Marius B. Jansen, "Yawata, Hanyehping, and the Twenty-one Demands," *Pacific Historical Review,* XXIII (February 1954), 31-48; Remer, *Foreign Investments,* pp. 439-440.

4. *FRUS, 1915,* p. 94.

5. Ibid., pp. 94-95; Bryan to Wilson, March 22, 1915, Bryan papers; Lowe, *Britain and Japan,* pp. 239-240; Braisted, *United States Navy,* pp. 263-285.

6. *JAAA,* XV (April 1915), 65-66; ibid., XV (June 1915), 129-130. The only business groups that in fact expressed concern were the Cotton Goods Export Association (New York), which had an old axe to grind; and the 16-member American Association of North China, known at the Department to be under the influence of Mr. Thomas Millard, the anti-Japanese journalist. See Williams to Bryan (memo) February 26, 1915, NA 793.94/240; Reinsch to State, March 6, 1915, NA 793.94/291; Sammons, Shanghai, to Reinsch, April 14, 1915, NA 793.94/365.

7. See Jordan to Langley, March 5, 1915, FO 350/13/6.

8. For the perspective of a prominent Japanese, see Count Okuma, "Japan's Purpose toward China," *Independent,* 82 (April 12, 1915), p. 55.

9. For some account of the American attitude toward the spheres, see Raymond A. Esthus, "The Changing Concept of the Open Door, 1899–1910," *Mississippi Valley Historical Review,* 46 (December 1959), 435–454 passim.

10. *FRUS, 1915,* p. 95.

11. For the best rendition of the Open Door episode and related happenings, see Marilyn Young, *The Rhetoric of Empire: American China Policy, 1895–1901* (Cambridge, Mass., 1968), entire work.

12. Ibid., passim; *New Republic,* 2 (February 27, 1915), 87–89.

13. Jordan to Langley, January 26, 1915, FO 350/13/17; Jordan to Langley, March 5, 1915, FO 350/13/5.

14. Ibid.; Remer, *Foreign Investments,* 361.

15. Beilby Alston to Jordan (private), March 19, 1915, FO 350/14/15–16; Robert J. Gowen, "Great Britain and the Twenty-one Demands: Co-operation versus Effacement," *Journal of Modern History,* 63 (March 1971), 76–106.

16. See Howard Ayers (President, Cotton Goods Export Association) to Secretary of Commerce William C. Redfield, April 16, 1915, NA 711.94/213.

17. This sketch, like those that follow, is my own. It, like the others, is based primarily upon state papers and the relevant private materials. Though secondary works of course have been consulted, the reader should be aware that I have not always adopted the judgments advanced by these authorities. In the case of Reinsch, the most useful works are the excellent thesis by Noel Pugach, "Progress, Prosperity and the Open Door," and Reinsch's autobiography, *An American Diplomat in China* (Garden City, 1922); Jordan to Langley, November 24, 1914, FO 350/12/109.

18. See Pugach, "Making the Open Door Work," pp. 157–175.

19. Reinsch to State (cable), January 23, 1915, NA 793.94/209. A blow-by-blow account of American policy toward the Twenty-one Demands can be found in my PhD dissertation, "The Missionary Mind and American Far Eastern Policy, 1911–1915" (Harvard University, 1976), Chapter 5.

20. Reinsch, *American Diplomat,* pp. 129–149 passim; see Pugach, "Progress, Prosperity and the Open Door," p. 202; Hunt's account of these doings in *Special Relationship,* pp. 142–143, is derivative.

21. Reinsch to State (cable), January 24, 1915, NA 793.94/210.

22. Williams wrote of Sidney Gulick, "Dr. Gulick is a good man, but in his efforts to secure what he considers just treatment for the Japanese he is

sometimes unjust to his own government." Gulick's stand on the immigration issue, Williams observed, "only tends to inflame the Japanese. . . . He is thus promoting hostility rather than good feeling between the two countries." Williams memo, October 17, 1914, NA 811.52/33.

23. Williams to Bryan (memo), January 25, 1915, NA 793.94/498.
24. Quite possibly the best full-length account of Bryan as public servant is Paolo Coletta, *William Jennings Bryan: Progressive Politician and Moral Statesman* (Lincoln, Nebraska, 1969).
25. Chinda to Bryan, May 9, 1913, NA 811.52/164; Chinda to Bryan, June 4, 1913, NA 811.52/165; Chinda to Bryan, August 26, 1913, NA 811.52/ 190; Coletta, *William Jennings Bryan,* pp. 214–222, 236–237; Bryan to Wilson, February 27, 1915, Bryan papers.
26. Bryan to Wilson, January 23, 1915, Correspondence between William Jennings Bryan and Woodrow Wilson, State Department Archives. Cited as Bryan-Wilson Correspondence.
27. On the President's European preoccupation during the Twenty-one Demands period, see Ernest R. May, *The World War and American Isolation, 1914–1917* (Cambridge, Mass., 1959), pp. 137–159.
28. Li, *Wilson's China Policy,* pp. 14–15.
29. Wilson to Bryan, January 27, 1915, Bryan-Wilson Correspondence.
30. Beers, *Vain Endeavor,* is a well-known work, which the reader should consult. My own understanding of Lansing and the Twenty-one Demands is substantially different.
31. MS Desk Diary of Robert Lansing, Lansing papers; Lansing to Bryan (enclosing legal memo by E. T. Williams), January 28, 1915, NA 793.94/ 209.
32. Darwin F. Pickard, Watertown, N.Y., to Lansing, December 18, 1914, Lansing papers; see Beers, *Vain Endeavor,* pp. 7, 11; [Robert Lansing], *War Memoirs of Robert Lansing* (Indianapolis, 1935), pp. 282–284.
33. Reinsch to State (cable), January 29, 1915, NA 793.94/215; Wilson to Bryan, January 29, 1915, NA 793.94/498.
34. Williams to Bryan, "Memorandum: The Crisis in China," January 27, 1915, NA 793.94/210; Reinsch to State (cable), February 1, 1915, NA 793.94/219; Roy Watson Curry, *Woodrow Wilson and Far Eastern Policy, 1913–1921* (New York, 1957), p. 113.
35. Wilson to Reinsch, February 8, 1915, Wilson papers.
36. Bryan to Page (cable), February 2, 1915, NA 793.94/220A; Lowe, *Britain and Japan,* pp. 229–230; Page to Bryan (cable), February 13, 1915, NA 793.94/230; entry for February 11, 1915, Lansing diary, Lansing papers.
37. *FRUS, 1915,* pp. 83–85.
38. Ibid., pp. 84–85.

39. Guthrie to Bryan (cable), February 21, 1915, NA 793.94/237; *FRUS, 1915*, p. 97; see Bryan memo, February 16, 1915, NA 793.94/461; Williams to Bryan (memo), February 15, 1915, NA 793.94/225.

40. Pugach, "Progress, Prosperity and the Open Door," p. 202; *New York Times*, February 13, 1915, p. 1; *Congressional Record*, 63 Cong., 3 sess., pp. 4046–4054; Representative Richmond P. Hobson to Bryan, February 18, 1915, NA 793.94/233; *Literary Digest*, L (March 6, 1915), p. 464.

41. *New York Times*, February 20, 1915, p. 1; Reinsch to State (cable), February 15, 1915, NA 793.94/231; Williams to Bryan (memo), February 15, 1915, NA 793.94/240.

42. A very different interpretation of this episode can be found in Beers, *Vain Endeavor*, pp. 36–51.

43. Entries for February 22–23, 1915, Lansing diary, Lansing papers; Williams to Bryan (memo), February 26, 1915, NA 793.94/240.

44. Entries for February 26–27 and March 1, Lansing diary, Lansing papers; Lansing to Bryan, March 1, 1915, NA 793.94/240.

45. For a less sympathetic account of Bryan's role, see the very thorough chapter on the East Asian crisis of 1915 in Arthur S. Link, *Wilson: The Struggle for Neutrality* (Princeton, 1960).

46. Bryan to Wilson, February 22, 1915, NA 793.94/240.

47. Bryan to Wilson, March 8, 1915, Bryan papers.

48. Wilson to Bryan, March 8, 1915, Bryan-Wilson Correspondence; Wilson to Bryan, March 4, 1915, Bryan papers.

49. The March 13 note went through a large number of revisions; for the details of its making, see the successive drafts collected in NA 793.94/240; entries for March 11–12, Lansing diary, Lansing papers; Wilson to Bryan, March 12, 1915, NA 793.94/240.

50. Note of the Secretary of State to the Japanese Ambassador, March 13, 1915, *FRUS, 1915*, pp. 105–111.

51. Ibid.

52. Ibid.

53. Ibid.

54. Ibid; on the South Manchuria freight-rate issue, see Beers, *Vain Endeavor*, pp. 29–35.

55. *FRUS, 1915*, pp. 110–111; the Root-Takahira agreement, for example, referred to "the independence and integrity of China" but did not employ the exact terminology used in the March 13 note (see *FRUS, 1908*, pp. 510–511).

56. *FRUS, 1915*, p. 111.

57. Madeleine Chi, *China Diplomacy, 1914–1918* (Cambridge, Mass., 1970), p. 46.

58. Bryan to Wilson, April 6, 1915, NA 793.94/285A; Bryan to Wilson, March 25, 1915, NA 793.94/266A.

59. Guthrie to State (cable), March 17, 1915, NA 793.94/251; Guthrie to State (cable), March 21, 1915, NA 793.94/258; Bryan to Wilson, March 22, 1915, Bryan papers.

60. Ibid.

61. Bryan to Wilson, March 22, 1915, NA 793.94/258A.

62. Bryan to Wilson, March 25, 1915, NA 793.94/266A; see Wilson to Bryan, March 24, 1915, NA 793.94/264 1/2; and Wilson to Bryan, March 25, 1915, NA 793.94/283 1/2.

63. Entry for March 26, 1915, Lansing diary, Lansing papers; see Bryan to Guthrie (cable), March 26, 1915, NA 793.94/258.

64. Bryan to Reinsch (cable), March 18, 1915, NA 793.94/252; Reinsch to State (cable), April 12, 1915, NA 793.94/293; Reinsch to State (cable), March 30, 1915, NA 793.94/275.

65. Wilson to Bryan, March 31, 1915, Bryan papers.

66. Chi, *China Diplomacy*, p. 47.

67. Ernest R. May, "The Nature of Foreign Policy: The Calculated Versus the Axiomatic," *Daedalus*, 91 (Fall 1962), 653–667; for background on Wilson's East Asia axioms, see Eugene P. Trani, "Woodrow Wilson, China, and the Missionaries, 1913–1921," *Journal of Presbyterian History*, XLIX (1971), 328–351.

68. Address by Sidney Gulick in New York, April 19, 1915, as quoted in the *Boston Transcript*, April 20, 1915, p. 4; *Outlook*, 110 (May 12, 1915), 83; Straight to J. A. Thomas, April 9, 1915, Straight papers; Petition and Memorial of Peking Missionaries to the President of the United States, April 8, 1915, NA 793.94/471; see Sammons, Shanghai, to State, July 25, 1915, NA 793.94/446; *JAAA*, XV (June 1915), 129–130; *MRW*, XXVIII (April 1915), 242–243; *New York Times*, May 2, 1915, pt. V, p. 4; *Literary Digest*, (April 2, 1915), p. 737; Eleanor Tupper and George E. McReynolds, *Japan in American Public Opinion* (New York, 1937), p. 114; *Walla Walla Union*, May 5, 1915, pp. 1, 5; Wilson to Lane (with enclosures), April 12, 1915, Wilson papers.

69. Reinsch to State (cable), March 31, 1915, NA 793.94/276; Reinsch to State (cable), April 2, 1915, NA 793.94/280; Reinsch to State (cable), April 8, 1915, NA 793.94/287; see Chow Tse-tsung, *The May Fourth Movement: Intellectual Revolution in Modern China* (Stanford, 1967), pp. 19–25.

70. Reinsch to State (cable), April 14, 1915, NA 793.94/294; see Jordan to Langley, April 16, 1915, FO 350/13/46.

71. Wilson to Bryan, April 14, 1915, NA 793.94/294 1/2.

72. Wilson to Bryan, April 16, 1915, NA 793.94/292.

73. Chi, *China Diplomacy,* pp. 52–61; Langley to Jordan, March 31, 1915, FO 350/14/20.

74. *San Francisco Examiner,* May 6, 1915, p. 1; *Chicago Tribune,* May 2, 1915, p. 1; *New York Times,* May 6, 1915, p. 1; *Walla Walla Union,* May 7, 1915, p. 1; Lowe, *Britain and Japan,* pp. 240–249; Chi, *China Diplomacy,* pp. 60–61.

75. Wilson to Bryan, April 27, 1915, NA 793.94/317 1/2; see Wilson to Bryan, April 28, 1915, Bryan papers.

76. Reinsch to State (cable), April 27, 1915, NA 793.94/317; see *FRUS, 1915,* pp. 128–130; entry for April 30, 1915, Lansing diary, Lansing papers; Bryan to Wilson, May 3, 1915, Bryan papers.

77. Press release in Bryan to Reinsch (cable), May 6, 1915, NA 793.94/ 338A; Bryan to Chinda, May 5, 1915, Bryan papers; Bryan to Wilson, May 5, 1915, Wilson papers.

78. Bryan to Reinsch (cable), May 6, 1915, NA 793.94/400a; Bryan to Guthrie (cable), May 6, 1915, NA 793.94/402a; Bryan to Guthrie (cable), May 6, 1915, NA 793.94/405a.

79. See Reinsch to State, April 24, 1915, NA 793.94/300; on the refusals of the Powers, see NA 793.94/340–343; Langley to Jordan, May 12, 1915, FO 350/14/30; Sir Cunningham Greene, Tokyo, to Langley, May 10, 1915, FO 800/247/219; Langley to Jordan, June 15, 1915, FO 350/ 14/34.

80. Lansing to Bryan, May 7, 1915, NA 793.94/339 1/2; *San Francisco Examiner,* May 4, 1915, p. 3.

81. Bryan to Wilson, May 7, 1915, Bryan papers; see Bryan to Wilson, May 8, 1915, NA 793.94/342 1/2.

82. Reinsch to State (cable), May 9, 1915, NA 793.94/341; Wilson to Bryan, May 10, 1915, NA 793.94/342 1/2.

83. Address before Presbytery of the Potomac, April 21, 1915, as quoted in the *Chicago Tribune,* April 22, 1915, p. 3.

84. Lansing to David Lander, May 3, 1915, Lansing papers.

85. Bryan to Guthrie, May 11, 1915, NA 793.94/351a.

Bibliography

PRIMARY SOURCES

Manuscripts

Archives of the American Board of Commissioners for Foreign Missions. Houghton Library, Harvard University.

Archives of the British Foreign Office. Public Record Office, London.

Archives of the Department of State. National Archives.

Diary of James W. Bashford. Missionary Research Library, Union Theological Seminary, New York.

Papers of J.O.P. Bland. Thomas Fisher Rare Book Library, University of Toronto.

Papers of William Jennings Bryan. Library of Congress.

Papers of Charles W. Eliot. Pusey Library, Harvard University.

Papers of John Watson Foster. Library of Congress.

Papers of Philander C. Knox. Library of Congress.

Papers of Robert Lansing. Library of Congress.

Papers of Henry Cabot Lodge. Massachusetts Historical Society, Boston.

Papers of Paul S. Reinsch. State Historical Society of Wisconsin, Madison.

Papers of W. W. Rockhill. Houghton Library, Harvard University.

Papers of Theodore Roosevelt. Library of Congress.

Papers of Willard Straight. Olin Library, Cornell University.

Papers of William Howard Taft. Library of Congress.

Archives of the United Church of Canada. Victoria University in the University of Toronto.

Papers of Woodrow Wilson. Library of Congress.

Newspapers, Magazines, and Other Periodicals

American Historical Review, Washington, 1911–1915.

Annals of the American Academy of Political and Social Science, Philadelphia, 1911–1915.

Boston Evening Transcript. 1911–1915.

Bulletin of the Japan Society. New York, 1913–1915.

Catholic World. New York, 1911–1915.

Chicago Tribune. 1911–1915.

China Mission Year Book. Shanghai, 1915.

Chinese Recorder. Shanghai, 1911–1915.

Christian Advocate. Chicago, 1912.

Christian Movement in Japan. Yokohama, 1913.

Independent. New York, 1911–1915.

Japan Weekly Mail. Yokohama, 1911–1912.

Jewish Advocate. Boston, 1911–1915.

Journal of the American Asiatic Association. New York, 1910–1915.

Literary Digest. New York, 1910–1915.

Missionary Herald. Boston, 1890–1900, 1910–1922.

Missionary Review of the World. New York, 1910–1915.

New Republic. New York, 1914–1915.

New York Times. 1911–1915.

North-China Herald and Supreme Court and Consular Gazette. Shanghai, 1919.

Outlook. New York, 1911–1915.

Pilot. Boston, 1911–1915.

San Francisco Examiner. 1911–1915.

Walla Walla Union. 1911–1915.

Books and Articles

Asakawa, K. "The Origin of Feudal Land Tenure in Japan," *American Historical Review,* XX (October 1914), 1–23.

Barton, James L. "The Modern Missionary," *Harvard Theological Review,* VIII (January 1915), 1–17.

Beach, Harlan P. *Dawn on the Hills of T'ang.* New York, Student Volunteer Movement for Foreign Missions, 1898.

——. ed. *Geography and Atlas of Protestant Missions.* 2 vols. New York, Student Volunteer Movement, 1906.

——. "The Present Status of Missions in Japan," *Missionary Review of the World,* XXIV (September 1911), 690–694.

——, and Burton St. John, eds. *World Statistics of Christian Missions.* New York, Student Volunteer Movement, 1916.

Blakeslee, George, H., ed. *China and the Far East.* New York, Crowell, 1910.

——, ed. *Japan and Japanese-American Relations.* New York, G. E. Stechert, 1912.

——, ed. *Recent Developments in China.* New York, G. E. Stechert, 1913.

Bland, J. O. P. *Recent Events and Present Policies in China.* Philadelphia, J.B. Lippincott, 1912.

——. "The Opium Abolition Question," in *Recent Developments in China,* ed., George H. Blakeslee. New York, G. E. Stechert, 1913.

Brown, Arthur Judson, *The Chinese Revolution.* New York, Student Volunteer Movement, 1912.

Bryan, W. J. "World Missionary Movement," *Outlook,* 95 (August 13, 1910).

Crow, Carl. "The Business of Christianizing the World," *World's Work,* 26 (October 1913), 632–652.

The Cabinet Diaries of Josephus Daniels, 1913–1921, ed. E. David Cronon. Lincoln, University of Nebraska Press, 1963.

Dennett, Tyler. "The Business Side of Foreign Missions," *Asia,* 19 (July 1919), 690–691.

Dennis, James S. et al., eds. *World Atlas of Christian Missions,* New York, Student Volunteer Movement, 1911.

Memoirs of Robert Dollar. San Francisco, W. S. Van Cott, 1917.

Private Diary of Robert Dollar on His Recent Visits to China. San Francisco, W. S. Van Cott, 1912.

Eddy, Sherwood. "In the Wake of the Boxer Massacres in China," *Missionary Review of the World,* XXIV (November 1911), 834–837.

——. *The New Era in Asia.* New York, Missionary Education Movement, 1913.

Einstein, Lewis. "Japan at Tsingtau and American Policy," *Journal of the American Asiatic Association,* XIV (January 1915), 359–362.

Eliot, Charles W. *Some Roads Towards Peace.* Washington, Carnegie Endowment for International Peace, 1913.

Ellis, W. T. "China in Revolution," *Outlook,* 99 (October 28, 1911), 454.

——. "Cities Under Eight Flags," *Harper's Weekly,* 55 (November 25, 1911), 21.

Foster, John W. *American Diplomacy in the Orient.* Boston, Houghton Mifflin, 1903.

Franklin, James H. "Results of a Tour of Asia," *Missionary Review of the World,* XXVII (January 1914), 7–16.

Freeman, L. R. "American Trade with China: Possibilities and Limitations," *Review of Reviews,* 49 (February 1914), 227–229.

Gleason, A. H. "Christian Statesman," *Harper's Weekly* (March 21, 1914), pp. 10–11.

Griffis, W. E. "Christian Missions in Japan," *Century,* 82 (September 1911), 749–750.

Gulick, Sidney L. *The American Japanese Problem.* New York, Scribner's, 1914.

———. *Anti-Japanese War Scare Stories.* New York, Fleming H. Revell, 1917.

Hinckley, R. E. "Extraterritoriality in China," *Annals of the American Academy of Political and Social Science,* XXXIX (January 1912), 97–108.

Hornbeck, Stanley K. *Contemporary Politics in the Far East.* New York, Appleton, 1916.

Horwill, H. W. "The New Missionary Outlook," *Atlantic Monthly,* 107 (April 1911), 441–451.

Huntington Wilson, Francis M. *Memoirs of an Ex-Diplomat.* Boston, B. Humphries, 1945.

Ichinomiya, R. "The Foreign Trade of Japan," in *Japan and Japanese-American Relations,* ed. George H. Blakeslee. New York, G. E. Stechert, 1912.

James, Henry. *The American Scene.* New York, Harper, 1907.

Kinnosuke, A. "Anglo-American Arbitration and the Far East," *Review of Reviews,* 44 (November 1911), 602–604.

War Memoirs of Robert Lansing. Indianapolis, Bobbs-Merrill, 1935.

Lewis, Robert E. "The Vintage of the Colleges for the Foreign Field," *Missionary Review of the World,* XXIV (November 1911), 838–839.

Lobinger, C. S. "America's Torch-bearing in Asia," *Review of Reviews,* 59 (December 1914), 714–717.

Loomis, Henry. "The Present State of Christianity in Japan," *Missionary Review of the World,* XXIV (September 1911), 665.

Mabie, Hamilton Wright. "Americans and the Far East," *Outlook,* 104 (August 2, 1913), 754–757.

———. *Japan Today and Tomorrow.* New York, Macmillan, 1914.

Macfarland, Charles S. "Christian Internationalism," in *America to Japan,* ed. Lindsay Russell. New York, Putnam, 1915.

Mansfield, Howard, "American Appreciation of Japanese Art," in *America to Japan,* ed. Lindsay Russell. New York, 1915.

Meyers, H. W. "Christ in the Slums of Japan," *Missionary Review of the World,* XXVI (April 1913), 287–289.

Millard, Thomas F. "The Need of a Distinctive American Policy in China," in *China and the Far East,* ed. George H. Blakeslee. New York, Crowell, 1910.

Morse, Hosea Ballou. *The Trade and Administration of the Chinese Empire.* London, Longmans, 1908.

Mott, John R., *The Evangelization of the World in This Generation.* New York, Student Volunteer Movement, New York, 1900.

Okuma, S. "The Chinese Revolution and the World's Peace," *Independent,* 73 (July 25, 1912), 179–181.

———. "Japan's Purpose toward China," *Independent,* 82 (April 12, 1915), 55.

Redfield, William C. "The Progress of Japanese Industry," in *Japan and*

Japanese-American Relations, ed. George H. Blakeslee. New York, Stechert, 1912.

Reinsch, Paul S. *Intellectual and Political Currents in the Far East.* Boston, Houghton Mifflin, 1911.

———. *An American Diplomat in China.* Garden City, Doubleday, 1922.

Ross, E. A. "Christianity in China," *Century,* 81 (March 1911), 754–764.

Ross, John. "The Chinese Revolution and Missions," *Missionary Review of the World,* XXV (January 1912), 42–43.

Russell, Lindsay. "America's Real Interest in the Orient," in *America to Japan,* ed. Lindsay Russell. New York, Putnam, 1915.

Sammons, Thomas. "Record Year in Japanese Trade," *Journal of the American Asiatic Association,* XIII (July 1913), 172–176.

Smith, Arthur H. *Chinese Characteristics.* New York, Fleming H. Revell, 1894.

———. *China and America To-day.* New York, Fleming H. Revell, 1907.

———. *The Uplift of China.* New York, Young People's Missionary Movement, 1908.

———. "A Year of the Republic of China," *Missionary Review of the World,* XXVI (January 1913), 3–4.

Speer, Robert E. *Christianity and the Nations.* New York, Fleming H. Revell, 1910.

Stauffer, Milton T. ed. *The Christian Occupation of China.* Shanghai, China Continuation Committee, 1922.

Straight, Willard. "The Politics of Chinese Finance: Address at the Dinner of the East Asiatic Society of Boston." Boston, 1913.

———. "Tsingtau and After," *New Republic,* 2 (February 6, 1915), 20–21.

Strong, Josiah. *Our Country,* ed. Jurgen Herbst. Rev. ed. Cambridge, Harvard University Press, 1963.

Strong, William E. *Story of the American Board.* Boston, American Board of Commissioners for Foreign Missions, 1910.

Takamine, Jokichi. "The Japanese in America," in *Japan and Japanese-American Relations,* ed. George H. Blakeslee. New York, Stechert, 1912.

Tsao, Y. S. "China's Revolution Spells Progress," *Missionary Review of the World,* XXIV (December 1911), 919–924.

Williams, F. W. "A Sketch of the Relations between the United States and China," in *China and the Far East,* ed. George H. Blakeslee. New York, Crowell, 1910.

Williams, Talcott. "The Missionary as He Looks to the Man in the Pew," *Missionary Herald,* 108 (July 1912), 305–306.

"The World in Chicago," *Survey,* 39 (July 19, 1913), 529–532.

World Missionary Conference, 1910. 9 vols. Edinburgh, Oliphant, Anderson & Ferrier, 1910.

Yearbook of the Japan Society. New York, Japan Society, 1913.

State Papers and Other Public Documents

Congressional Record. 1911–1915.

U.S. Bureau of the Census. *Historical Statistics of the United States: Colonial Times to 1957.* Washington, 1960.

U.S. Department of Commerce, Bureau of the Census. *Religious Bodies, 1916.* 2 vols. Washington, 1919.

——. Bureau of Foreign and Domestic Commerce, *Statistical Abstract of the United States, 1915.* Washington, 1916.

U.S. Department of State. *Papers Relating to the Foreign Relations of the United States, 1911–1915.* 6 vols. Washington, 1918–1924.

——. *Papers Relating to the Foreign Relations of the United States: the Lansing Papers, 1914–1920.* 2 vols. Washington, 1939.

SECONDARY SOURCES

Adler, Cyrus. *Jacob H. Schiff: His Life and Letters.* 2 vols. New York, Doubleday, 1928.

Adler, Selig. *The Isolationist Impulse: Its Twentieth Century Reaction.* New York, Free Press, 1962.

Ahlstrom, Sidney E. *A Religious History of the American People.* New Haven, Yale University Press, 1972.

Auerbach, Jerold S. *Unequal Justice: Lawyers and Social Change in Modern America.* New York, Oxford University Press, 1976.

Baltzell, E. Digby. *The Protestant Establishment: Aristocracy & Caste in America.* New York, Random House, 1964.

Beers, Burton F. *Vain Endeavor: Robert Lansing's Attempts to End the American-Japanese Rivalry.* Durham, Duke University Press, 1962.

Bose, Nemai Sadhan. *American Attitudes and Policy to the Nationalist Movement in China (1911–1921).* Bombay, Orient Longmans, 1970.

Braisted, William R. *The United States Navy in the Pacific, 1909–1922.* Austin, University of Texas Press, 1971.

Brown, Ira V. *Lyman Abbott.* Cambridge, Harvard University Press, 1953.

Cameron, Meribeth E. "American Recognition Policy Toward the Republic of China, 1912–1913," *Pacific Historical Review,* II (June 1933), 214–230.

Chao, Kang. *The Development of Cotton Textile Production in China.* Cambridge, Council on East Asian Studies, 1977.

Chi, Madeleine. *China Diplomacy, 1914–1918.* Cambridge, East Asian Research Center, Harvard University, 1970.

Chow, Tse-tsung. *The May Fourth Movement: Intellectual Revolution in Modern China.* Stanford, Stanford University Press, 1967.

Cochran, Sherman. *Big Business in China: Sino-Foreign Rivalry in the Cigarette Industry, 1890–1930.* Cambridge, Harvard University Press, 1980.

Cohen, Warren I. *America's Response to China: An Interpretative History of Sino-American Relations.* New York, Wiley, 1971.

——. *The Chinese Connection: Roger S. Greene, Thomas W. Lamont, George E. Sokolsky and American-East Asian Relations.* New York, Columbia University Press, 1978.

Coletta, Paolo E., "'The Most Thankless Task': Bryan and the California Alien Land Legislation," *Pacific Historical Review,* XXXVI (February 1967), 163–187.

——. *William Jennings Bryan: Progressive Politician and Moral Statesman.* Lincoln, University of Nebraska Press, 1969.

Councilman, W. T. "William Sturgis Bigelow," in *Later Years of the Saturday Club.,* ed. M. A. DeWolfe Howe. Boston, Houghton Mifflin, 1927.

Croly, Herbert. *Willard Straight.* New York, Macmillan, 1924.

Curry, Roy Watson. *Woodrow Wilson and Far Eastern Policy, 1913–1921.* New York, Bookman Associates, 1957.

Curti, Merle E. *Bryan and World Peace.* Smith College Studies in History, XVI. Northampton, 1931.

Daniels, Roger. *The Politics of Prejudice: the Anti-Japanese Movement in California and the Struggle for Japanese Exclusion.* Berkeley, University of California Press, 1962.

Davis, Clarence B. "Limits of Effacement: Britain and the Problem of American Cooperation and Competition in China, 1915–1917," *Pacific Historical Review,* XLVII (February 1979), 47–63.

Esthus, Raymond A. "The Changing Concept of the Open Door, 1899–1910," *Mississippi Valley Historical Review,* 46 (December 1959), 435–454.

Fairbank, John K., "Assignment for the 1970's: The Study of American-East Asian Relations," *American Historical Review,* LXXIV (February 1969), 861–879.

——, et al. *East Asia: The Modern Transformation.* Boston, Houghton Mifflin, 1965.

——, ed., *The Missionary Enterprise in China and America.* Cambridge, Harvard University Press, 1974.

Feuerwerker, Albert. *The Foreign Establishment in China in the Early Twentieth Century.* Ann Arbor, Center for Chinese Studies, University of Michigan, 1976.

Field, James A., Jr. "Near East Notes and Far East Queries," in *Missionary Enterprise in China and America,* ed. John K. Fairbank. Cambridge, Harvard University Press, 1974.

Forsythe, Sidney A. *An American Missionary Community in China, 1895–1905*. Cambridge, East Asian Research Center, Harvard University, 1971.

Garrett, Shirley S. *Social Reformers in Urban China: the Chinese Y.M.C.A., 1895–1926*. Cambridge, Harvard University Press, 1970.

Gowen, Robert J. "Great Britain and the Twenty-one Demands: Cooperation versus Effacement," *Journal of Modern History*, 63 (March 1971), 76–106.

Graebner, Norman A. "The 'New' China: A Missionary View, 1900–1910." Paper presented at the 1972 Conference on Protestant Missionaries in China and America, Cuernavaca, Mexico.

Graham, Edward Dewey, "American Ideas of a Special Relationship with China, 1784–1900." PhD dissertation, Harvard University, 1969.

Griswold, A. Whitney. *The Far Eastern Policy of the United States*. New York, Harcourt, Brace, 1938.

Gusfield, Joseph R. *Symbolic Crusade: Status Politics and the American Temperance Movement*. Urbana, University of Illinois Press, 1963.

Handy, Robert T. *A Christian America: Protestant Hopes and Historical Realities*. New York, Oxford University Press, 1971.

Hidy, Ralph W., and Muriel E. Hidy. *Pioneering in Big Business, 1882–1911*. New York, Harper, 1955.

Hirschmeier, Johannes, and Tsunehiko Yui. *The Development of Japanese Business, 1600–1973*. Cambridge, Harvard University Press, 1975.

Hou, Chi-ming. *Foreign Investment and Economic Development in China, 1840–1937*. Cambridge, Harvard University Press, 1965.

Hunt, Michael H. *Frontier Defense and the Open Door: Manchuria in Chinese-American Relations, 1895–1911*. New Haven, Yale University Press, 1973.

——. *The Making of a Special Relationship: The United States and China to 1914*. New York, Columbia University Press, 1983.

Hutchison, William R. "Cultural Strain and Protestant Liberalism," *American Historical Review*, LXXVI (April 1971), 386–411.

——. "Modernism and Missions: the Liberal Search for an Exportable Christianity, 1875–1935," in *The Missionary Enterprise in China and America*, ed. John K. Fairbank. Cambridge, Harvard University Press, 1974.

——. *The Modernist Impulse in American Protestantism*. Cambridge, Harvard University Press, 1976.

——. "A Moral Equivalent for Imperialism: Americans and the Promotion of 'Christian Civilization,' 1880–1910." Paper presented at 1981 Durham (England) Conference on Missionary Ideologies in the Imperialist Era, 1880–1920.

——, et al, "Evangelization and Civilization: Protestant Missionary Motivation in the Imperialist Era," *International Bulletin of Missionary Research*, 6 (April 1982), 50–65.

Hyatt, Irwin T., Jr. *Our Ordered Lives Confess: Three Nineteenth-Century American Missionaries in East Shantung.* Cambridge, Harvard University Press, 1976.

Iriye, Akira. *Across the Pacific: An Inner History of American-East Asian Relations.* New York, Harcourt, Brace & World, 1967.

——. *Pacific Estrangement: Japanese and American Expansion, 1897–1911.* Cambridge, Harvard University Press, 1972.

——. "Japan as a Competitor, 1895–1917," in *Mutual Images: Essays in American-Japanese Relations,* ed. Akira Iriye. Cambridge, Harvard University Press, 1975.

——. "Culture and Power: International Relations as Intercultural Relations," *Diplomatic History,* 3 (Spring 1979), 115–128.

Isaacs, Harold R. *Images of Asia: American Views of China and India.* New York, Harper and Row, 1972. Originally published as *Scratches on Our Minds.* New York, Day, 1958.

Israel, Jerry. *Progressivism and the Open Door: America and China, 1905–1921.* Pittsburgh, University of Pittsburgh Press, 1971.

James, Henry. *Charles W. Eliot.* 2 vols. Boston, Houghton Mifflin, 1930.

Jansen, Marius B. "Yawata, Hanyehping, and the Twenty-one Demands," *Pacific Historical Review,* XIII (February 1954), 31–48.

Jensen, Richard. *The Winning of the Midwest: Social and Political Conflict, 1888–1896.* Chicago, University of Chicago Press, 1971.

Kahn, Helen Dodson. "The Great Game of Empire: Willard D. Straight and American Far Eastern Policy." PhD dissertation, Cornell University, 1968.

Kennan, George F. *American Diplomacy, 1900–1950.* Chicago, University of Chicago Press, 1951.

Kleppner, Paul. *The Cross of Culture: A Social Analysis of Midwestern Politics, 1850–1900.* New York, Free Press, 1970.

Kuehl, Warren F. *Hamilton Holt.* Gainesville, University of Florida Press, 1960.

Lamont, Thomas W. *Henry P. Davison: The Record of a Useful Life.* New York, Harper, 1933.

Latourette, Kenneth Scott. *A History of Christian Missions in China.* New York, Macmillan, 1929.

——. *A History of the Expansion of Christianity.* 7 vols. New York, Harper, 1937–1945.

Li, Lillian M. *China's Silk Trade: Traditional Industry in the Modern World, 1842–1937.* Cambridge, Council on East Asian Studies, 1981.

Li, Tien-yi. *Woodrow Wilson's China Policy, 1913–1917.* New York, Twayne Publishers, 1952.

Link, Arthur S. *Wilson: The Road to the White House.* Princeton University Press, 1947.

——. *Woodrow Wilson and the Progressive Era, 1910-1917.* New York Harper, 1954.

——. *Wilson: The New Freedom.* Princeton University Press, 1956.

——. *Wilson: The Struggle for Neutrality.* Princeton University Press, 1960.

Liu, K. C. *Americans and Chinese: A Historical Essay and a Bibliography.* Cambridge, Harvard University Press, 1963.

——, ed. *American Missionaries in China,* Cambridge, East Asian Research Center, Harvard University, 1966.

Low, Benjamin R. C. *Seth Low.* New York, Putnam, 1925.

Lowe, Peter. *Great Britain and Japan 1911-1915: A Study of British Far Eastern Policy.* New York, St. Martin's, 1969.

Lutz, Jesse G. *China and the Christian Colleges.* Ithaca, Cornell University Press, 1971.

Marchand, C. Roland. *The American Peace Movement and Social Reform, 1898-1918.* Princeton University Press, 1972.

Marty, Martin E. *Righteous Empire: The Protestant Experience in America.* New York, Dial Press, 1970.

Mathews, Basil. *John R. Mott: World Citizen.* New York, Harper, 1934.

May, Ernest R. "American Policy and Japan's Entrance into World War I," *Mississippi Valley Historical Review,* XL (September 1953), 279-290.

——. *The World War and American Isolation, 1914-1917.* Cambridge, Harvard University Press, 1959.

——. "The Nature of Foreign Policy: The Calculated Versus the Axiomatic," *Daedalus,* 91 (Fall 1962), 653-667.

——. *American Imperialism: A Speculative Essay.* New York, Atheneum, 1968.

May, Henry F. *The End of American Innocence: A Study of the First Years of Our Own Time, 1912-1917.* New York, Alfred Knopf, 1959.

McClellan, Robert F. *The Heathen Chinee: A Study of American Attitudes toward China, 1890-1905.* Columbus, Ohio State University Press, 1970.

Metallo, Michael V. "American Missionaries, Sun Yat-sen, and the Chinese Revolution," *Pacific Historical Review,* XLVII (May 1978), 261-282.

Miller, Jessie Ashworth. "China in American Policy and Opinion, 1906-1909." PhD dissertation, Clark University, 1940.

Miller, Stuart Creighton. "Ends and Means: The American Missionary's Justification of Force in Nineteenth Century China," in *The Missionary Enterprise in China and America,* ed. John K. Fairbank. Cambridge, Harvard University Press, 1974.

Mulhollan, Paige Elliott, "Philander C. Knox and Dollar Diplomacy." PhD dissertation, University of Texas, 1966.

Najita, Tetsuo. *Hara Kei in the Politics of Compromise, 1905-1915.* Cambridge, Harvard University Press, 1967.

Neu, Charles E. *An Uncertain Friendship: Theodore Roosevelt and Japan, 1906-1909.* Cambridge, Harvard University Press, 1967.

———. *The Troubled Encounter: the United States and Japan.* New York, Wiley, 1975.

Neumann, William L. "Ambiguity and Ambivalence in Ideas of National Interest in Asia," in *Isolation and Security,* ed. Alexander DeConde. Durham, Duke University Press, 1957.

Nish, Ian H. *Alliance in Decline: A Study in Anglo-Japanese Relations, 1908-1923.* London, Athlone Press, 1972.

Osgood, Robert E. *Ideals and Self-Interest in America's Foreign Relations: the Great Transformation of the Twentieth Century.* Chicago, University of Chicago Press, 1953.

Phillips, Clifton J. *Protestant America and the Pagan World.* Cambridge, East Asian Research Center, 1969.

———. "The Student Volunteer Movement and Its Role in China Missions, 1886-1920," in *The Missionary Enterprise in China and America,* ed. John K. Fairbank. Cambridge, Harvard University Press, 1974.

Pringle, Henry F. *The Life and Times of William Howard Taft.* 2 vols. New York, Farrar & Rinehart, 1939.

Pugach, Noel. "Progress, Prosperity and the Open Door: the Ideas and Career of Paul S. Reinsch." PhD dissertation, University of Wisconsin, 1967.

———. "Making the Open Door Work: Paul S. Reinsch in China, 1913-1919," *Pacific Historical Review,* 38 (May 1969), 157-175.

———. *Paul S. Reinsch: Open Door Diplomat in Action,* Millwood, New York, KTO Press, 1979.

Rabe, Valentin H. "The American Protestant Foreign Mission Movement, 1880-1920." PhD dissertation, Harvard University, 1964.

———. "Evangelical Logistics: Mission Support and Resources to 1920," in *The Missionary Enterprise in China and America,* ed. John K. Fairbank. Cambridge, Harvard University Press, 1974.

———. *The Home Base of American China Missions, 1880-1920.* Cambridge, Council on East Asian Studies, Harvard University, 1978.

Reed, James. "American Foreign Policy, The Politics of Missions and Josiah Strong, 1890-1900," *Church History,* 41 (June 1972), 230-245.

———. "Partisans of China, 1919-1922: North American Protestant Missionaries and the May Fourth Movement." Paper presented at annual meeting of Canadian Historical Association, Toronto, June 1974.

———. "The Missionary Mind and American Far Eastern Policy, 1911-1915." PhD dissertation, Harvard University, 1976.

———. "Last Chance at the United Nations: The United States and the Issue of Chinese Representation in 1965–66." Paper presented at annual meeting of American Historical Association, San Francisco, December 1978.

Reid, John G. *The Manchu Abdication and the Powers, 1908–1912: An Episode in Pre-War Diplomacy.* Berkeley, University of California Press, 1935.

Remer, C. F. *Foreign Investments in China.* New York, Macmillan, 1933.

Rosenstone, Robert A. "Learning from Those 'Imitative' Japanese: Another Side of the American Experience in the Mikado's Empire," *American Historical Review,* LXXXV (June 1980), 572–595.

Scholes, Walter V., and Marie V. Scholes. *The Foreign Policies of the Taft Administration.* Columbia, University of Missouri Press, 1970.

Stanley, Peter W. *A Nation in the Making: The Philippines and the United States, 1899–1921.* Cambridge, Harvard University Press, 1974.

Steele, A. T. *The American People and China.* New York, McGraw-Hill, 1966.

Thomson, James C. *While China Faced West: American Reformers in Nationalist China, 1928–1937.* Cambridge, Harvard University Press, 1969.

——, et al. *Sentimental Imperialists: The American Experience in East Asia.* New York, Harper & Row, 1981.

Trani, Eugene P. "Woodrow Wilson, China, and the Missionaries, 1913–1921," *Journal of Presbyterian History,* XLIX (1971), 328–351.

Trevor-Roper, Hugh. *Hermit of Peking: The Hidden Life of Sir Edmund Backhouse.* New York, Alfred Knopf, 1977.

Tupper, Eleanor, and George E. McReynolds. *Japan in American Public Opinion.* New York, Macmillan, 1937.

Van Alstyne, Richard W. *The United States and East Asia.* New York, Thames and Hudson, 1973.

Varg, Paul A. *Open Door Diplomat: The Life of W. W. Rockhill.* Urbana, University of Illinois Press, 1952.

——. *Missionaries, Chinese, and Diplomats.* Princeton University Press, 1958.

——. *The Making of a Myth: The United States and China.* East Lansing, Michigan State University Press, 1968.

Vevier, Charles. *The United States and China, 1906–1913: A Study of Finance and Diplomacy.* New Brunswick, Rutgers University Press, 1955.

Weber, Max. *From Max Weber: Essays in Sociology,* ed. and trans. H. H. Gerth and C. Wright Mills. New York, Oxford University Press, 1947.

Wiebe, Robert H. *Businessmen and Reform: A Study of the Progressive Movement.* Cambridge, Harvard University Press, 1962.

——. *The Search for Order, 1877–1920.* New York, Hill and Wang, 1967.

Wilkins, Mira. *The Emergence of Multinational Enterprise: American Business Abroad from the Colonial Era to 1914.* Cambridge, Harvard University Press, 1970.

———. *The Maturing of Multinational Enterprise: American Business Abroad from 1914 to 1970.* Cambridge, Harvard University Press, 1974.

Williams, William Appleman. *The Tragedy of American Diplomacy.* Rev. ed., New York, Dell, 1962.

Winkler, Max. "America, the World's Banker," *Foreign Policy Association Information Service,* III (special supplement number 3, June 1927).

Wright, Mary C. "Introduction: The Rising Tide of Change," in *China in Revolution: The First Phase, 1900–1913,* ed. Mary C. Wright. New Haven, Yale University Press, 1968.

Young Ernest P. "Yuan Shih-k'ai's Rise to the Presidency," in *China in Revolution,* ed. Mary C. Wright. New Haven, Yale University Press, 1968.

———. *The Presidency of Yuan Shih-k'ai: Liberalism and Dictatorship in Early Republican China.* Ann Arbor, University of Michigan Press, 1977.

Young, Marilyn. *The Rhetoric of Empire: American China Policy, 1895–1901.* Cambridge, Harvard University Press, 1968.

Index

Abbot, Lyman, 32, 78
Academics (American): as Methodist laymen, 34; their treatment of East Asia, 88-89, 92; early conferences, 93; and the Missionary Mind, 104; and the Chinese Revolution, 134-135, 146; their role in American East Asia policy, 163
Adee, Alvey, 139
Advance, 37
America and the Far Eastern Question (1909), 70
American Asiatic Association, 83, 97; membership and activities, 57, 58, 59; annual dinner (1911), 63-64; and immigration issue, 65; Willard Straight as President of, 67; and the Chinese Revolution, 131; and China recognition, 137, 144; and the Twenty-one Demands, 154, 188
American Association of China (Shanghai), 58, 61, 154
American Association of Japan (Yokohama), 58
American Board of Commissioners for Foreign Missions, 10, 12, 27, 28, 29, 32, 124
American Diplomacy in the Orient, 92, 104
American Group, 48-49, 66, 118, 132-134, 141
American Historical Review, 89
American Japanese Problem (1914), 92
American Manufacturers' Export Association, 58, 60

American Trading Company, 58
Anglo-Japanese Alliance, 79, 92, 99, 180
Annals of the American Academy of Political and Social Science, 89
Anti-Japanese legislation: in California, 32; crises arising from, 36, 90, 167; juxtaposed with prayer for China, 38; savaged by *Independent,* 76; its politics, 97-99; and the Lansing "bargain," 175-177. *See also* Immigration laws (American); Racial equality issue; Racism (American)
Asiatic Fleet, 115
Asiatic Institute, 93
Associated Press, 36
Atlantic Monthly, 16, 91

Backhouse, Sir Edmund, 148
Bacon, Senator Augustus, 140
Bankers' Magazine, 57
Baptist Church, North, 20, 32
Baptist Church, South, 20
Barton, James L., 10
Bashford, Bishop James W., 23-24, 25, 27, 29, 125, 127, 140
Beers, Burton, 231n30
Belmont, August, 65
Beloit College, 9
Bemis, W. E., 50, 54, 55
Berkeley, California, 38
Bethlehem Steel Company, 153, 182, 185
Bigelow, William Sturgis, 86
Blakeslee, George H., 93, 104
Bland, J. O. P., 134-135, 147-148
Boston, 15, 188; its business community,

Harvard East Asian Monographs

21. Kwang-Ching Liu, ed., *American Missionaries in China: Papers from Harvard Seminars*

22. George Moseley, *A Sino-Soviet Cultural Frontier: The Ili Kazakh Autonomous Chou*

23. Carl F. Nathan, *Plague Prevention and Politics in Manchuria, 1910–1931*

24. Adrian Arthur Bennett, *John Fryer: The Introduction of Western Science and Technology into Nineteenth-Century China*

25. Donald J. Friedman, *The Road from Isolation: The Campaign of the American Committee for Non-Participation in Japanese Aggression, 1938–1941*

26. Edward Le Fevour, *Western Enterprise in Late Ch'ing China: A Selective Survey of Jardine, Matheson and Company's Operations, 1842–1895*

27. Charles Neuhauser, *Third World Politics: China and the Afro-Asian People's Solidarity Organization, 1957–1967*

28. Kungtu C. Sun, assisted by Ralph W. Huenemann, *The Economic Development of Manchuria in the First Half of the Twentieth Century*

29. Shahid Javed Burki, *A Study of Chinese Communes, 1965*

30. John Carter Vincent, *The Extraterritorial System in China: Final Phase*

31. Madeleine Chi, *China Diplomacy, 1914–1918*

32. Clifton Jackson Phillips, *Protestant America and the Pagan World: The First Half Century of the American Board of Commissioners for Foreign Missions, 1810–1860*

33. James Pusey, *Wu Han: Attacking the Present through the Past*

34. Ying-wan Cheng, *Postal Communication in China and Its Modernization, 1860–1896*

35. Tuvia Blumenthal, *Saving in Postwar Japan*

36. Peter Frost, *The Bakumatsu Currency Crisis*

37. Stephen C. Lockwood, *Augustine Heard and Company, 1858–1862*

38. Robert R. Campbell, *James Duncan Campbell: A Memoir by His Son*

39. Jerome Alan Cohen, ed., *The Dynamics of China's Foreign Relations*

40. V. V. Vishnyakova-Akimova, *Two Years in Revolutionary China, 1925–1927*, tr. Steven I. Levine

41. Meron Medzini, *French Policy in Japan during the Closing Years of the Tokugawa Regime*

42. *The Cultural Revolution in the Provinces*

43. Sidney A. Forsythe, *An American Missionary Community in China, 1895–1905*

44. Benjamin I. Schwartz, ed., *Reflections on the May Fourth Movement: A Symposium*

45. Ching Young Choe, *The Rule of the Taewŏn'gun, 1864–1873: Restoration in Yi Korea*

69. Eric Widmer, *The Russian Ecclesiastical Mission in Peking during the Eighteenth Century*

70. Charlton M. Lewis, *Prologue to the Chinese Revolution: The Transformation of Ideas and Institutions in Hunan Province, 1891–1907*

71. Preston Torbert, *The Ch'ing Imperial Household Department: A Study of its Organization and Principal Functions, 1662–1796*

72. Paul A. Cohen and John E. Schrecker, eds., *Reform in Nineteenth-Century China*

73. Jon Sigurdson, *Rural Industrialization in China*

74. Kang Chao, *The Development of Cotton Textile Production in China*

75. Valentin Rabe, *The Home Base of American China Missions, 1880–1920*

76. Sarasin Viraphol, *Tribute and Profit: Sino-Siamese Trade, 1652–1853*

77. Ch'i-ch'ing Hsiao, *The Military Establishment of the Yuan Dynasty*

78. Meishi Tsai, *Contemporary Chinese Novels and Short Stories, 1949–1974: An Annotated Bibliography*

79. Wellington K. K. Chan, *Merchants, Mandarins, and Modern Enterprise in Late Ch'ing China*

80. Endymion Wilkinson, *Landlord and Labor in Late Imperial China: Case Studies from Shandong by Jing Su and Luo Lun*

81. Barry Keenan, *The Dewey Experiment in China: Educational Reform and Political Power in the Early Republic*

82. George A. Hayden, *Crime and Punishment in Medieval Chinese Drama: Three Judge Pao Plays*

83. Sang-Chul Suh, *Growth and Structural Changes in the Korean Economy, 1910–1940*

84. J. W. Dower, *Empire and Aftermath: Yoshida Shigeru and the Japanese Experience, 1878–1954*

85. Martin Collcutt, *Five Mountains: The Rinzai Zen Monastic Institution in Medieval Japan*

STUDIES IN THE MODERNIZATION OF THE REPUBLIC OF KOREA: 1945–1975

86. Kwang Suk Kim and Michael Roemer, *Growth and Structural Transformation*

87. Anne O. Krueger, *The Developmental Role of the Foreign Sector and Aid*

88. Edwin S. Mills and Byung-Nak Song, *Urbanization and Urban Problems*

89. Sung Hwan Ban, Pal Yong Moon, and Dwight H. Perkins, *Rural Development*

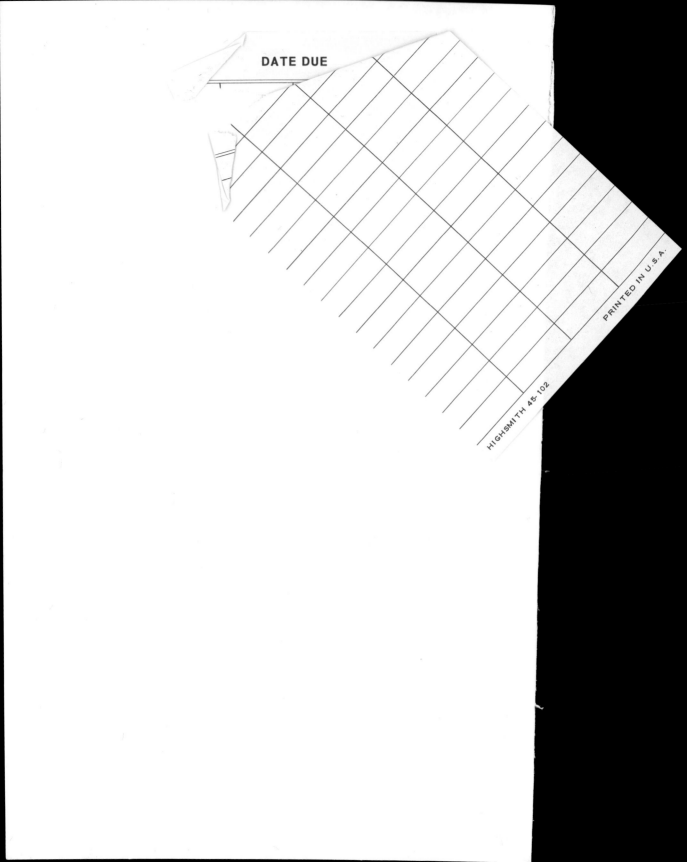

DATE DUE

HIGHSMITH 45-102

PRINTED IN U.S.A.